# SACRED PLACES OF THE ANCIENT WORLD

Philip Matyszak

# SACRED PLACES OF THE ANCIENT WORLD

T&H

# CONTENTS



*Previous pages* The propylon, a freestanding monumental gateway to the main temple at the sanctuary of Hecate in Lagina, Turkey.

*Following pages* The theatre at Epidaurus, Greece, was considered one of the best in the ancient world. Built into a hillside some 2,300 years ago it is still in use as thousands of tourists regularly attend dramatic performances there.

INTRODUCTION

# Gods with Many Faces

Tumbled stones on an arid Anatolian plateau, mysterious ruins deep in the Amazonian jungle and ancient sacrifices dredged from a Nordic bog all testify to the fact that human societies have everywhere and at all times worshipped, consulted or tried to placate powers greater than themselves. Such activities were concentrated at certain spots, and these numinous places are the focus of this book.

Worship of the divine – along with the tendency to live in social groups, create and enjoy music, and form strong familial bonds – is a universally defining feature of humanity. However, what is universal is nevertheless very different in particulars. While all societies may have some form of religion, the manner of expressing it can vary dramatically – from the Aztecs, who routinely performed multiple human sacrifices, to the Jains of India, some of whom will not eat a vegetable if harvesting it destroys the plant.

Just as different groups expressed their religiosity in radically different ways, the places where they worshipped encompass a huge variety, even within the Mediterranean cultures of antiquity. Some were entirely natural: forest groves, sacred pools or marshes, mountain tops and caves. Other places were very much human-made. Indeed, some of the greatest architectural creations of many ancient (and modern) societies were built as sacred sites.

To explore the sacred places of a particular people, therefore, tells us not only about their gods and how they were worshipped but also about those people themselves. Was their religion matriarchal or patriarchal? Were the priests or priestesses a separate, secluded class, or publicly elected politicians? Was religion strictly divided from the profane or deeply integrated into public life? Almost all we know of some of the very oldest human settlements on Earth comes from their sacred places, because these – unlike transient human dwellings – were built to endure through the generations.

**Across time and space**

Humans have lived in the Mediterranean basin and Middle East for a very long time. The period between the death of Cleopatra of Egypt in 30 BC and the latest generation of iPhones is less than half the time between Cleopatra's birth and the first shrines which appeared in the Nile valley around 4500 BC. And those Nile valley shrines are young compared to structures in Asia Minor dating to the tenth millennium BC, which may have been used for ritual purposes.

For well over ten thousand years humans around the Mediterranean have been worshipping their gods in a variety of places and in many different ways. Our intention here is not to document all these sacred sites but to demonstrate their variety through selected examples. The main focus is on Europe, North Africa, Anatolia and Mesopotamia. The time span begins in the mists of antiquity and, by and large, comes to a jarring halt at the surprisingly precise date of AD 391. That's when the Christian Roman emperor, Theodosius I (whose name means 'given by God'), decreed that pagan temples should be closed and that anyone going there to worship would be subject to massive fines.

It remains a vast scope – a time frame of many thousands of years of religious activity across an area of some 5 million square kilometres (almost 2 million square miles). There are many sites of huge religious and cultural importance – such as Egypt's Valley of the Kings, or Varanasi in India – that are already well known and widely published, and so they are not all repeated here. We have chosen to include some of the lesser known, such as the German temple to Hercules Magusanus – a fascinating example of cross-cultural religious fusion.

Not all ancient sacred sites are places of worship, for humanity also interacts with the divine in other ways. Graves and tombs, especially those where the occupants were launched into the next world with unique ceremony and style, or when the deceased was a particularly notable individual, may also be sacred. At other locations, the gods spoke directly to mortals through oracles, and humans even sought face to face contact with divinity through *katabasis* – a journey to the Realm of the Dead via gates to the Underworld known in Greek as *ploutonions*.

**The shadow of the Cross**

Perception of religion in the modern West and the Middle East has been profoundly influenced by the spread of the Abrahamic faiths. How people in these regions understand the divine has fundamentally changed over the past two thousand years. To take just one particular instance, today it is usually taken for granted that congregations worship within a sacred structure and that this structure allows some degree of public access at other times.

In some ancient Mediterranean cultures, such as the Greek and Roman, a temple was the earthly habitation of a particular god, and they would no more countenance people wandering around inside than modern societies would allow the general public to pop into the Oval Office or the Elysée Palace. Ancient ceremonies and sacrifices were usually conducted at altars outside temples, with only selected priests allowed within.

Likewise, belief in a universal, all-seeing deity has largely removed the ancient idea that there are certain places where a god might be more easily approached. This was not necessarily one of the great gods of a particular pantheon but a *genius loci* – the spirit of a grove or pool, who might help with everyday human concerns such as a sick child or an unsatisfactory relationship.

Ancient religion was transactional. No one expected their gods to grant benefits out of simple benevolence. (The legalistically minded Romans naturally had to codify this in what they called the *Pax deorum*.) Communities 'bought' divine favour through official rituals and sacrifices, while individuals sought to please the gods with votive offerings. Such sacrifices are of great interest to modern archaeologists, and at different times and places they have varied from crude clay figurines to (distressingly to modern minds) real children.

Today, practitioners of 'pagan' worship are well aware that they are regarded by the mainstream as eccentric at best and positively dangerous at worst. It is a far cry from the time when such religious practices were loud and proud, not only celebrated by the whole community but an essential and totally integrated part of it. Today we can find echoes of that vanished era in its sacred places – some remarkably intact, others evocative ruins – where such celebrations took place. In that way these sacred places of the ancient world continue to perform their original function as gateways to a mystical world beyond our own.

*Previous pages* Sakyamuni Buddha from Gandhara, second to fourth century AD. Gandharan art represents a fusion of ancient Greek art and Buddhism. In this case the Buddha is rendered in a Hellenistic style, including a light robe known as a *himation*.

PART ONE

# Sacred Places of Prehistory

## Lost gods, forgotten rituals

Thousands of years before the first Roman priests scanned the skies for auguries and long before the Greek gods had found a home on Mount Olympus, the peoples of the prehistoric Mediterranean world and Egypt were already shaping sacred geographies through caves, springs, megaliths and memorials to their ancestors. Further to the east in Anatolia and Mesopotamia, carven images tell of vanished gods and unknown rituals practised long before the first pantheons appear in the cuneiform record.

These sacred places, from western European megaliths to Mesopotamian shrines, were repositories of communal memory. The very earliest existed before the development of agriculture and perhaps served as focal points for regular tribal gatherings, a renewal of cultural roots through ritual and for trade and intermarriage. The survival in stone of the remnants of these sites creates an architecture of the invisible. We know that these people were there, but almost nothing of who they were and what gods they worshipped, or how.

The landscape was not just a backdrop to these activities but an active participant. Whether priests set the astronomical almanac upon mountain tops (or artificial mountains such as the ziggurats of Mesopotamia), or priestesses sat by pools deep in underground caverns, the sacred places of the natural world were liminal areas where the divine came closer to humans. It is believed that the gods who haunted these first religious sites were animistic: supernatural entities whom the peoples of the Classical era classified as wood nymphs or dryads, *genii loci* – the spirits of a particular place.

## Gods for a dangerous world

Cultural psychologists (yes, there are such people) argue that religion was a natural consequence of the prehistoric reality of those early peoples. Life was no pastoral idyll. Those first graveyards show that many died young and even more in infancy. Skeletons are deformed by disease, or by grotesque violence. Hunger was an ever-present reality, along with the constant danger from prey that violently objected to being eaten. (Early humans also fell into the 'prey' category, thanks to large European predators. Cave lion remains have been found as far north as Germany.)

Given the uncertainty of life in such times, it was natural for humans to try to assert at least an illusion of control by imagining deities capable of controlling the forces that threatened their existence and then influencing these deities through prayer. We also see humans not only asking their gods for favours but trading for them. Sacrifice – giving to the gods in order to receive yet more in return – is an established part of many religions and helped to create the quid pro quo that most people in the Mediterranean world came to expect from their gods. Sacrifice happened at all levels of society, from elaborately staged rituals marking important points in the religious calendar to crude votive offerings that individuals deposited for the gods in sacred places. (Fortunately for present-day researchers some of these places were caverns, lakes and bogs, which have held on to these treasures until the modern era.)

Yet these early places of worship suggest something more than a spiritual marketplace. The silence of the sacred groves, the stillness of the deep forest in winter, the sensory deprivation of a dark cavern – all these evoke even today a feeling of wonder, of being in the presence of something different from and greater than oneself. These places are undoubtedly sacred – the only issue being to whom or what.

Thus, long before the widespread adoption of writing or centralized, structured religion, the sacred places of the ancient world were shaping a communal identity for the peoples whom they served. Nor did these identities develop in isolation. For almost as long as there have been humans in Europe and the Middle East there have existed networks along which trade goods and ideas have flowed. Pharaonic tombs contain Baltic amber, lapis lazuli from Afghanistan and incense from the horn of Africa, while tin from Britain has been found in three-thousand-year-old shipwrecks in the eastern Mediterranean.

Seas and rivers were not barriers but highways that carried ideas and objects far from their places of origin, be those the headwaters of the Thames, the cataracts of the Nile or the waters of the Euphrates.

Certainly religions developed in different ways, each reflecting the spiritual needs of their communities. Nevertheless it is possible to detect a common thread in early bone figurines and votive offerings, which show how ideas were transmitted across the waves and reshaped by new generations.

*c.* 9000 BC – *c.* 7500 BC

# Göbekli Tepe

## The Oldest Monuments

*One of the first manifestations of human-made monumental architecture.*

**The United Nations Educational, Scientific and Cultural Organization (UNESCO)**

Six thousand years before Stonehenge, sixty-five centuries before the pyramids in Egypt and many generations before Babylon was even a small village, people in southeastern Anatolia were working on something never before seen on the Earth. They were quarrying huge stone monoliths from the hillside, dragging them back to be placed within circular enclosures and then carving on the raised stones bas-reliefs of animals, humans and everyday items of clothing.

## An ancient mystery

Why this enormous effort was expended is a great mystery. Nobody knows who laboured there, what gods those people worshipped or how numerous they were. Even the site's name has been lost for millennia. Today it is called Göbekli Tepe ('Pot-belly Hill'), which is the name given to it by Kurdish farmers who worked the land in the modern era. It is unsurprising that these farmers were unaware that they stood beside the earliest monumental structures yet known. Even after decades of careful excavation all that has been revealed of this most ancient of monuments is the stone monoliths and a few traces of humanity in the archaeological remains. Even these traces are scarce, because humans had not yet developed more than the most basic of tools and even pottery was unknown.

One thing we can say about these people at the dawn of civilization is that they appreciated a good view. They built their monumental complex at the edge of the Germus mountains on a

A reconstruction showing how Göbekli Tepe might have looked, with the distinctive T-shaped monoliths and large dry stone walls around the circular enclosures.

slope with the wide plain of Harran spreading out for miles below. Such a location with an outstanding view means that the site itself could be seen from a great distance, and this has lent weight to the arguments of those who believe that Göbekli Tepe was a ceremonial centre where tribes of hunter-gatherers and nomads regularly converged to trade goods, meet and marry, and perform sacred rites.

## Changing times

At this time – at the end of the last Ice Age, some nine thousand or more years ago – agriculture was still a nascent idea and the people of Anatolia lived off the land. This was relatively easy to do as prehistoric Anatolia was wetter and much more fertile than a changing climate has rendered it today. In those days Göbekli Tepe stood on a grassy slope where grains such as einkorn and barley grew wild for the taking. Mountain sheep and goats fed upon the grasslands and these animals in turn fed the people at Göbekli Tepe. Also it appears that the site lay across the migration route of the native species of gazelle. These were hunted in large numbers from midsummer to late autumn, which would, therefore, have been a logical time for large numbers of people to gather at the site. The first archaeological team to excavate the site argued that such gatherings would have included ceremonial and religious elements – indeed, that these may have been the primary reasons for such gatherings. Other theories have subsequently emerged (see below).

The main focus of Göbekli Tepe, then and now, was on the strange monoliths which make the site so distinctive. These are not trivial pieces of stone. The tallest stand 5.5 metres (18 feet) – about the height of a modern two-storey building – and they weigh up to 50 tonnes. So far archaeologists have found almost two hundred of them, all with a peculiar T-shaped top that seems unique to the area. There is no domestic, utilitarian or other practical reason for the creation of these monoliths, which supports the argument that they were created for religious purposes.

## The mysterious monoliths

It was originally believed that dragging the huge monoliths to their enclosures would have taken hundreds of people working together – a belief that tied in well with the 'large tribal gathering' thesis. Modern experiments upon the friction co-efficient of wet grass, however, have proven that the stones could have been moved by around seventy-five well-motivated individuals. Indeed the largest of the monoliths – a

An aerial view of the site in 2024. Some areas are covered for protection from the elements and much is still to be excavated.

stone some 7 metres (23 feet) long – has been discovered still lying in the quarry where it was carved. It is tempting to speculate that this massive stone remained unused because it was simply too ambitious for the people who actually had to shift the thing.

It has been speculated that the T shape is meant to suggest a human body, an idea reinforced by the fact that some columns have arms carved into the sides. If the monoliths represent deities, the animal carvings on them may be their totemic animals, and the untranslatable pictograms carved on to other stones could be sacred symbols. For example, the items of clothing might represent domestic deities. If all that were correct, the monoliths and structures at Göbekli Tepe would represent the world's oldest religious site, the 'first temple', as the original excavators suggested.

However, that initial characterization – as a sacred site for periodic large-scale ceremonial gatherings – has been challenged. Recent fieldwork has found evidence for domestic structures and hearths, which argues against the interpretation of Göbekli Tepe as a purely ritual site. It could have been the permanent home of a relatively small group of people, who were obsessed with monoliths for reasons that we do not now understand. Or did a caretaker priesthood live at the site and host large tribal gatherings? We

Scorpions, vultures and snakes are among the creatures carved on some pillars in sophisticated reliefs. Other pillars show abstract human forms.

simply do not know, and debate will continue. A century ago, no one knew that Göbekli Tepe or its mysterious builders existed. Even today the story of these people is only slowly beginning to be retold.

### Withdrawal

The evidence indicates that Göbekli Tepe was occupied for some 1,500 years. During this time a rainwater harvesting system was built, by which water was diverted to underground cisterns through channels cut in the rock. The circular enclosures which contained the first monoliths were gradually replaced by square structures with stone benches for seating. It is uncertain why Göbekli Tepe was eventually abandoned, though the growing aridity of the region may have made life there increasingly difficult.

It was originally believed that the last peoples at Göbekli Tepe carefully preserved the site by burying their monoliths under tonnes of earth and stone. 'Prioritizing the sense of return and protection after a thousand years of use' is how one description of the site reverently puts it. The reality may be more prosaic. The drying climate destabilized the slope upon which Göbekli Tepe was built. Some of the latest construction at the site included terrace walls built in an attempt to prevent landslips on the northern slope. Eventually it seems that the effort of preserving Göbekli Tepe became greater than the effort of relocating, and the site was left to slumber forgotten beneath the earth for over ten thousand years.

---

## Göbekli Tepe today

In 1963 a research team from the University of Chicago noted the peculiar features of the tell – the earthen mound which often indicates a buried settlement. This investigation began in earnest in the 1990s under the German archaeologist Klaus Schmidt, who until recently oversaw the excavation of what is now recognized as one of the most significant sites of the Neolithic era. UNESCO added Göbekli Tepe to its list of prospective World Heritage Sites in 2011.

Göbekli Tepe is now receiving a large influx of temporary visitors – not tribal gatherings but tourists from all over the globe. The Turkish government has worked hard to preserve the integrity of the site while still making it accessible to what is expected to be an ever-growing number of visitors. Today buses run regularly to Göbekli Tepe from Şanlıurfa Metropolitan Municipality, the largest nearby urban centre.

*c.* 2100 BC – 539 BC

# The Great Ziggurat of Ur

## An Awesome Edifice

*There is a solid tower in the middle of the sacred enclosure....A second tower rises from this and a third from that and so on until there are eight levels. Atop the last tower is a shrine.*

**Herodotus, *History* 1.178**

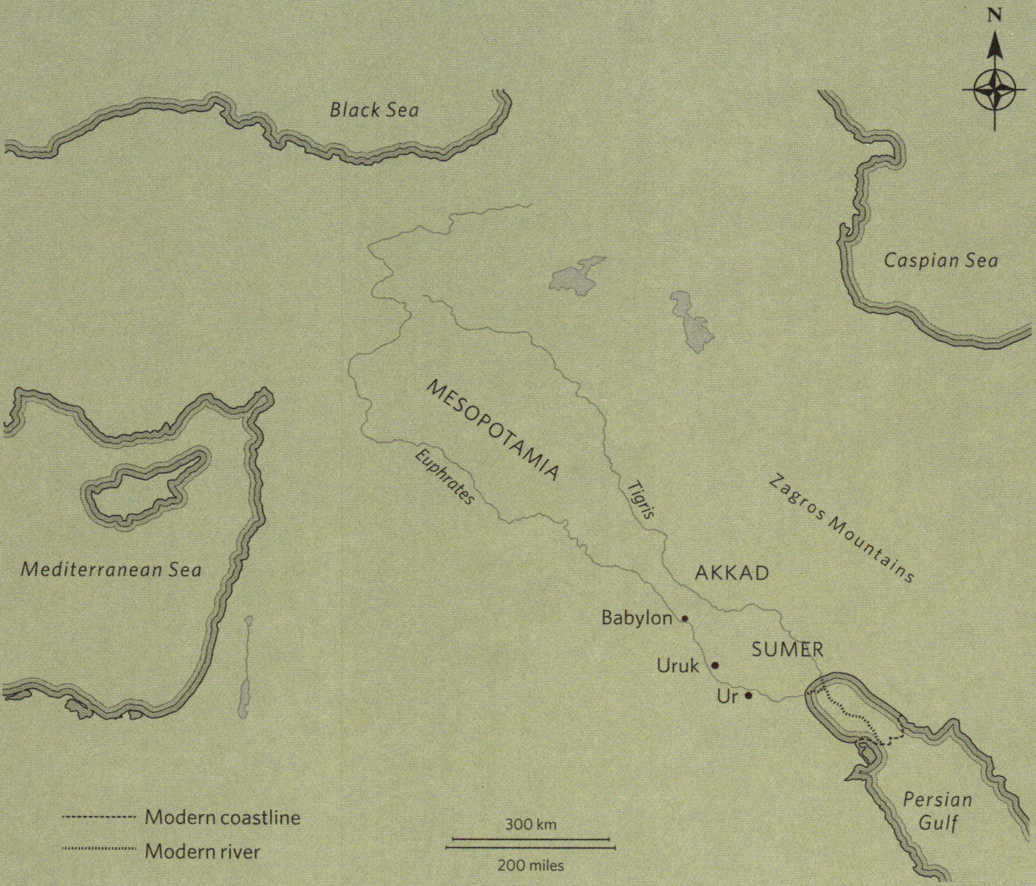

The gigantic structure described by the Greek historian Herodotus (which some believe to have been the biblical Tower of Babel) was already ancient when he saw it in the fifth century BC. By that time the Persian empire ruled the region (in present-day Iraq). While Herodotus described eight levels for the building, in fact it consisted of three major sections, the top two standing on a base of around 3,000 square metres (32,000 square feet). The height has been variously estimated but could have been more than 30 metres (98 feet) – enough to loom massively over the one- or two-storey houses of the ancient city of Ur.

## Nanna-Sin, lord of the cattle herds

When the Ziggurat was built in around 2100 BC the Neo-Sumerian empire of Mesopotamia was near the peak of its power and influence. The city of Ur, situated close to where the Euphrates river flowed into the Persian Gulf, was one of the crown jewels of that empire. It was here that King Ur-Nammu (r. 2112–2095 BC), fresh from a victory over the Gutian people, decided to build a great Ziggurat in honour of Nanna-Sin, lord of the cattle herds and personification of the Moon, the god under whose guidance and protection the land had flourished. He named it *E-temen-ana-ki* (roughly 'the awesome foundation of heaven and earth').

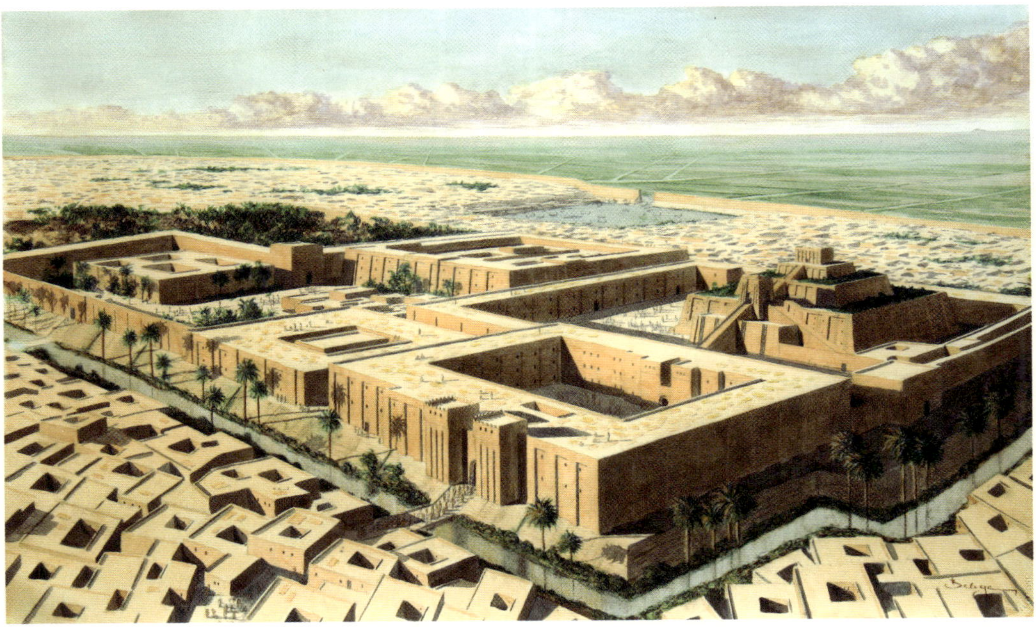

A reconstruction of the Ziggurat of Ur surrounded by royal palaces and the city, c. 2000 BC.

A collection of treasure from the Royal Cemetery of Ur, c. 2600 BC. From top to bottom: Gold amulet of conjoined antelopes; fish amulets, two gold and one lapis lazuli; two bracelets made of cylindrical lapis lazuli, gold and carnelian beads; a necklace with cylindrical beads and leaf pendants made of gold, carnelian and lapis lazuli.

The Ziggurat (the word is probably from the Akkadian word *zaqārū* meaning 'to build up') was one of many in ancient Mesopotamia, though King Ur-Nammu's edifice was larger than most. It was built entirely of brick – around three-quarters of a million of them, each brick being a block about 30 centimetres (12 inches) square, 7 centimetres (3 inches) deep and weighing 15 kilograms (33 pounds). The huge pyramidal structure was solid with no internal rooms. The core was made of sun-dried brick, with stronger kiln-baked bricks used on the lower levels to withstand the crushing weight.

King Ur-Nammu did not live to see his ziggurat completed. He died in battle, leaving the work to be finished by his son Shulgi, 'The Growling Lion of Utu', who in the course of his fifty-year reign used the power embodied in the massive structure to proclaim himself a god.

## The earthly home of a god

According to Herodotus the shrine at the summit was empty apart from a luxurious couch and a golden table. Here, on an auspicious night designated by the priests, a chosen woman (selected 'by the god', though the actual process is now unknown) would wait for Nanna-Sin to descend from the heavens to consummate his relationship with the Sumerian people.

The Great Ziggurat was thus not a temple in the modern sense. Being the home of a god when he descended to Earth, the Ziggurat was usually off-limits to all but a corps of designated priests. However, the wide staircases ascending the sides may have been used for sacred processions on particular feast-days.

The Ziggurat itself stood at the heart of a walled temple complex which included a kitchen and dining hall for the priests and scribes who were housed there along with imperial administrators. As well as providing living quarters for a god, the Ziggurat had a practical purpose as a secure treasure store, being about the only building in Ur which was safe from the devastating floods which regularly inundated the city. Also, of course, the raised platform of the Ziggurat was a splendid stage on which priests could perform sacred rites in view of a large audience.

## Babylonian priests

However, the main purpose of the Ziggurat was simply to demonstrate the power and permanence of the empire. Ur was situated on land so flat that anyone standing on a box could see clear across the

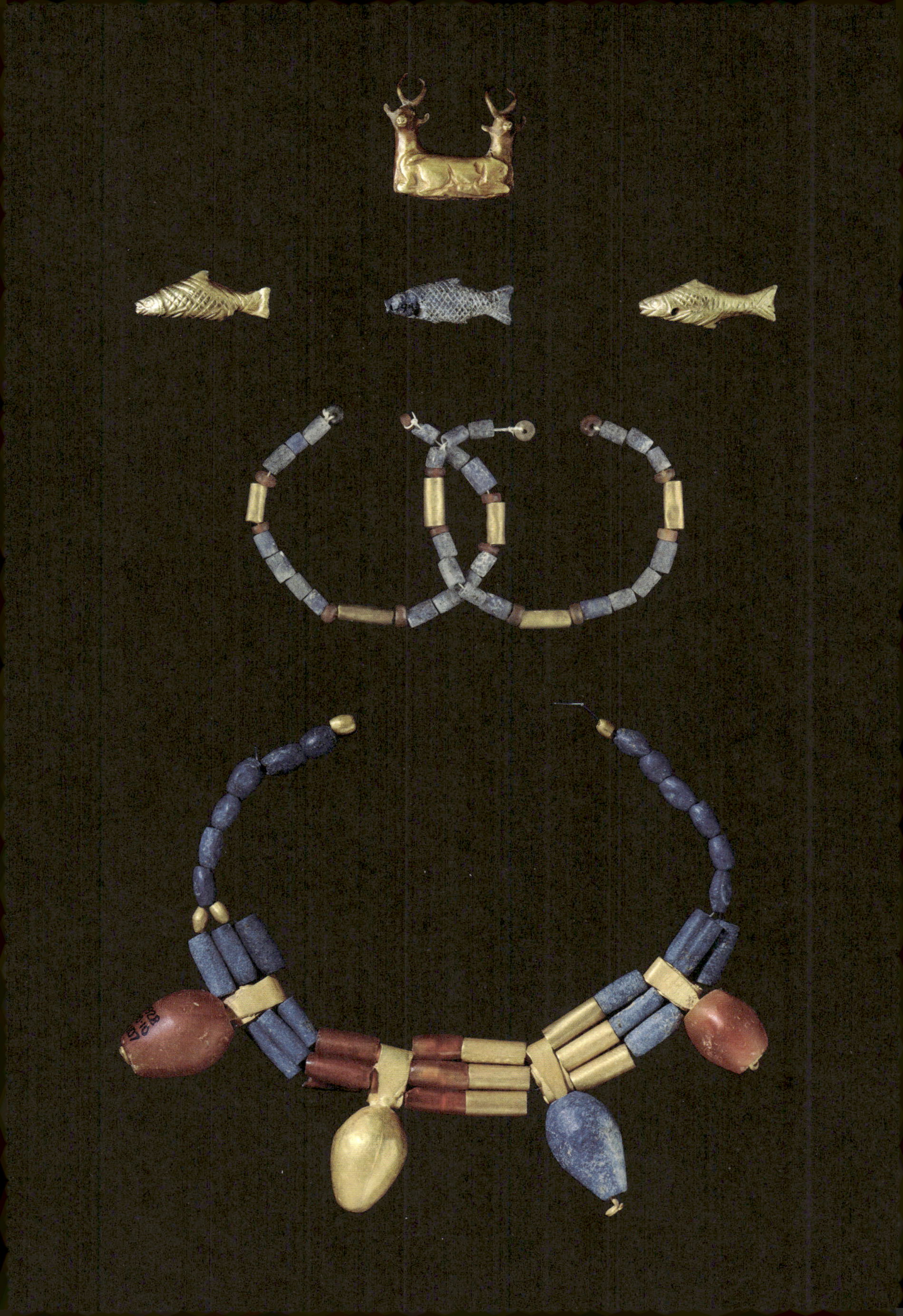

A *kudduru* (boundary stone) of Meli-Shipak II, the 33rd king of Babylon, r. 1186–1172 BC. The symbols shown above represent the goddess Ishtar (left), the god Nanna-Sin (centre) and the god Shamash (right).

Mesopotamian plain, so the immense bulk of the Ziggurat would have been visible not only from everywhere in the city, but for miles around.

In the sixth century BC Ur came under the control of the Babylonians, but the city was already in decline because the silting of the Euphrates river had cut it off from the trade routes which were its lifeblood. Nevertheless the last Babylonian king, Nabonidus (r. 556–539 BC), who was something of an amateur archaeologist, took an interest in the decaying Ziggurat and repaired and extensively remodelled the upper tiers.

According to the Roman-era historian Diodorus Siculus, 'Here the Chaldaeans [Babylonian priests] made their observations of the stars, because the height of the structure allowed their rising and setting to be accurately observed' (*History* 2.9).

Diodorus goes on to say that the entire building was ingeniously built from bitumen and brick (the bitumen serving as waterproofing and as mortar) and huge expense was once lavished upon it. Expanding on the account of Herodotus, Diodorus describes the table in the shrine of the moon god as laden with golden drinking cups and ewers, the table itself being immensely heavy as it was made from hammered gold. Its dimensions translate in modern measures to 12 by 4 metres (some 40 by 13 feet). However, the Ziggurat was in ruins by Diodorus' time, and the details may have been exaggerated over the centuries.

## The decline of the Ziggurat

The literal decline and (partial) fall of the Great Ziggurat, as with the dozens of other ziggurats of Mesopotamia, was directly due to the Persians who conquered the area in 539 BC (about a century before Herodotus). As worshippers of the fire god Ahura-Mazda, the Persians were not interested in maintaining the temples and allowed them to fall into decay. By the third century BC the city of Ur was completely abandoned, the land around desiccated by desertification and drought.

Over time the upper levels of the Ziggurat collapsed, creating a low scrub-covered hill over the base. The sacred temple remained in this sad state until the early twentieth century, when the archaeologist Sir Leonard Woolley (1880–1960) set about restoring and recovering what he could in a project jointly sponsored by the University of Pennsylvania and the British Museum.

At the end of the twentieth century the Ziggurat was further reconstructed and embellished by the Iraqi dictator Saddam Hussein, who was keen to showcase the ancient glories of his country. This did not stop Saddam from parking several of his fighter jets alongside the Ziggurat during the Gulf War of 1991. He believed, unwisely, that the Americans would not attack so close to a temple which had stood for millennia. The Americans' supposedly precision-guided weaponry destroyed the jets but also somewhat dented the Ziggurat, which was also left peppered with several hundred bullet holes.

Today the Ziggurat stands in lonely splendour on the dusty plain near the village of An-Nasiriyah. Guided tours to the Ziggurat can be organized from Baghdad, and even though only the base and elements of the second level remain, the bulk of the structure still awes tourists today as it did Herodotus twenty-five centuries ago.

*c.* 3500 – 3200 BC
# The Giant's Bed
## Mystical Megaliths

*Built by giants and dwarves.*
Writer and clergyman Johan Picardt (1600–1670)

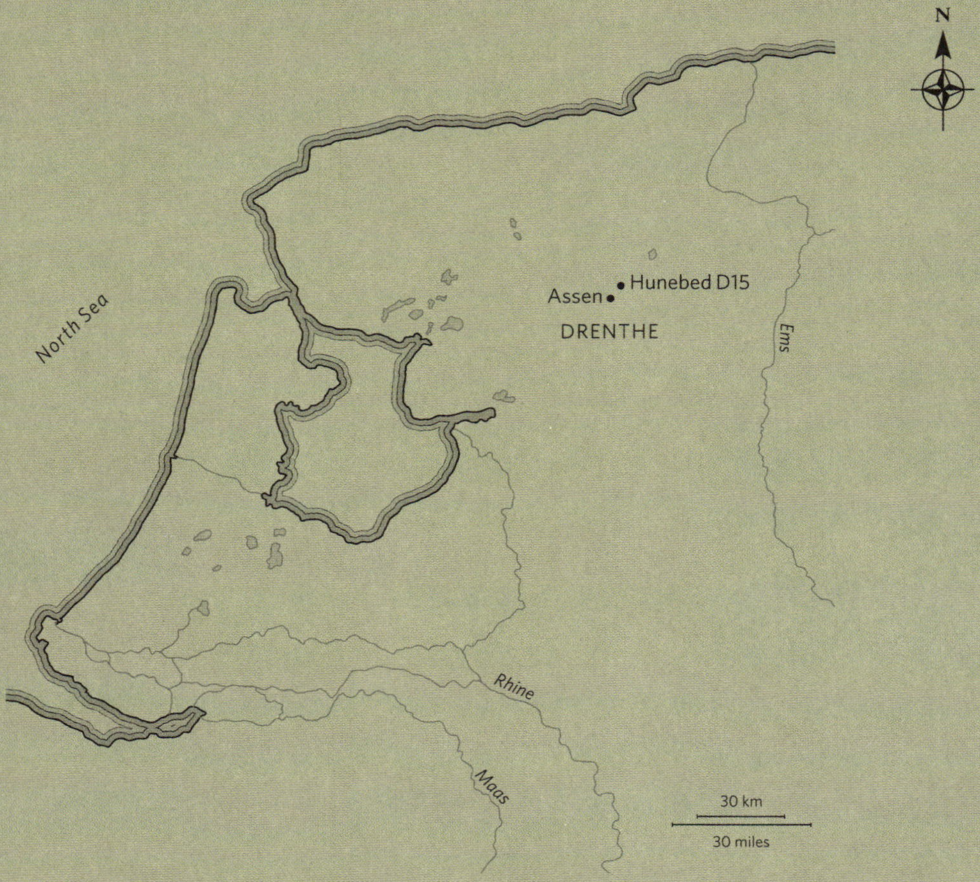

Few relics from the prehistoric era excite the imagination as do megaliths. From the giant edifice of Stonehenge to obscure circles in the Orkney Islands and passage graves, these ancient stones have always accumulated myths and legends. In the time of the Caesars the Roman historian and ethnographer Tacitus called the stone circles in Germany 'Pillars of Hercules', though he doubted whether the hero had actually erected them (*Germania* 34).

In the Netherlands megalithic graves, called *hunebeds*, were believed to have been built by a race of giants called *huynen*. They were inhabited by fairies, while dwarves carved out a network of tunnels underneath. A picture imagining the giants at work appears in *Certain Forgotten and Buried Antiquities of Drenthe*, a book published by one Johan Picardt in 1660.

A *hunebed* is a type of dolmen – a prehistoric megalithic tomb. A number of massive stones, or orthostats, support large horizontal capstones, creating a chamber in which it was once believed giants were buried.

Even today the megalithic monuments are afforded a certain reverence. Northern European tales, such as 'The Waking of Angantyr', and their modern retellings describe burial mounds opening and their inhabitants conversing with the living. There are folkloric claims that standing stones come alive or even dance at certain times of the year, such as the solstices. Writers Diana Gabaldon and Terry Pratchett have used stone circles as literary devices to transport their characters respectively through time and into another dimension.

Giants and dwarves collaborate on the construction of a *hunebed* in these illustrations from the book *Certain Forgotten and Buried Antiquities of Drenthe* (1660). Early antiquarians struggled to explain ancient monumental architecture without understanding the Neolithic period.

## The geology of the matter

The true story of the *hunebed* at Loon begins in the last Ice Age but one, or around 130,000 years ago. At this time Drenthe and the rest of what would later be the Netherlands lay under hundreds of metres of ice. Embedded in this ice were large slabs of stone – some weighing over 25 tonnes – transported by huge glaciers which scraped the rocks up in Scandinavia. When the ice melted the stones came to rest upon the ground.

The Netherlands are a tectonically quiet area where the land mainly consists of silt deposited by river systems over the millennia. Large slabs of rock are rare, so the glacial rocks were the building material of choice for the earliest of European monument builders. The same wet Dutch earth has not been kind to the human remains interred in these 'beds' but sufficient have been found to show that, regrettably, the builders were not giants but ordinary-sized peoples of the Neolithic (late Stone Age).

Archaeologists call these mysterious people of 5,500 years ago the 'Western Funnel Beaker Culture', a name derived from their most distinctive type of pottery. This was a bulbous vessel with a long funnel-shaped neck, sherds of which are found in abundance at most sites including the one at Loon (which ancient and evocative place archaeologists know by the uninspiring name of 'Site D15').

The Funnel Beaker people were enthusiastic megalith builders, and they constructed them by the tens of thousands across northwestern Europe. Therefore, although the megaliths that survive today represent only a small percentage of the original number, enough exist to demonstrate how the 'Giant's Bed' of Loon would have been made.

## Making the Giant's Bed

First the site was carefully chosen with regard to the surrounding landscape – here on a slightly raised point in a rolling meadow. Next the boundary was put in place, an oval ring of stones of around 16.5 by 10 metres (about 54 × 33 feet) maximum. This stone fence separated the sacred area around the burial place from the profane world beyond. This oval was carefully aligned on an east–west axis along the path of the sun and some stones were positioned to mark significant stages of the solar year.

Then within the sacred area the 9-metre-long (29½-foot) burial chamber was dug into the ground with the long narrow entranceway which gives such structures the name of 'passage graves'. (Those with a smaller entranceway and generally simpler structure are known as 'dolmens', though some academics consider passage graves to be a more refined form of dolmen.) Large slabs of stone made up the walls of the *hunebed*, with the gaps between them being filled with smaller stones. Five capstones were mounted above. Usually, as in the case of this Giant's Bed, the western capstone is the largest. The chamber was then covered with earth, leaving an oval mound with only the capstones visible at the top. Capstones were usually selected for their distinctive slightly reddish colour.

Clearly, such an effort could only be made for the burial of a person so important that the burial site thereafter became a focus for community rituals. The corpses themselves have rotted away – only a few bone fragments and some teeth have been found – but the grave goods deposited with the deceased have proven more durable. These include stone tools (the Funnel Beaker culture had not discovered bronze-working), beads, mostly amber, animal remains and lots of pottery.

## Time and change

At this time these early Europeans were making their first experiments with growing crops and domesticating animals rather than living as hunter-gatherers. Some researchers now believe that the construction of megaliths sped up the process of settlement

A beaker, *c.* 3000–2500 BC, of a type sometimes called 'Corded Ware' because of the impressions made by pressing a twisted cord into the wet clay to create a decorative pattern before it was fired.

and agriculture by providing a sacred focal point which anchored the community to a single location.

The *hunebed* at Loon remained a cult centre even after the Funnel Beaker people had passed away. Indeed with some *hunebeds* later peoples even added their own burials to the mounds. Bronze Age offerings were also made to the spirits at the site, and in the case of the Loon *hunebed* the tradition appears to have continued up to the early Middle Ages when an offering of a model boat was made. In fact the different strata of offerings at the sacred mound provide a fascinating map of the changing patterns of culture and settlement in the area.

## Rare and endangered

The early modern era was not kind to the megaliths of the Netherlands. The low-lying country required earthworks to keep water from flooding the fields. The first Dutch dikes were shored up with timber, but the national penchant for exploration introduced the shipworm to the country and these pests began feasting on the wooden dike supports. To prevent their dikes from breaking, local people replaced wood with inedible stone from the nearest resource – the megalithic graves. Many of these graves had already vanished, repurposed as church walls and road surfaces.

In 1734 the authorities put a stop to this by making the *hunebeds* protected sites – this being one of the first laws ever passed to protect prehistoric monuments. Fortunately the Loon *hunebed* survived this early round of pillaging, the only damage being the loss of the central capstone. This was apparently prised off by treasure-hunters, unaware that *hunebeds* contain items of interest only to archaeologists.

Today the Loon *hunebed* is seen by thousands of people every year. This is not because hordes of tourists make the trip from the nearby town of Assen (though a good many do) but because the field upon which the megalith stands is in plain view of a nearby railway track.

The megalith is now protected by law, but these laws do nothing to deter the lichen which have attached themselves to the now-exposed stone and are slowly eating it away. The obvious solution would be to scrape the lichen off the stone. But, as mentioned before, such slabs of stone are rare in Holland so the lichens are themselves rare and endangered – leaving the Dutch with something of a dilemma.

*c.* 3000 BC – AD 381

# Lerna

## Portal to the Underworld

*At the source of the Amymone grows a plane tree, beneath which, they say, the Hydra grew. I am ready to believe that this beast was superior in size to other water-snakes, and that its poison had something in it so deadly that Heracles treated the points of his arrows with its gall.*

**Pausanias, *Guide to Greece* 2.37.4**

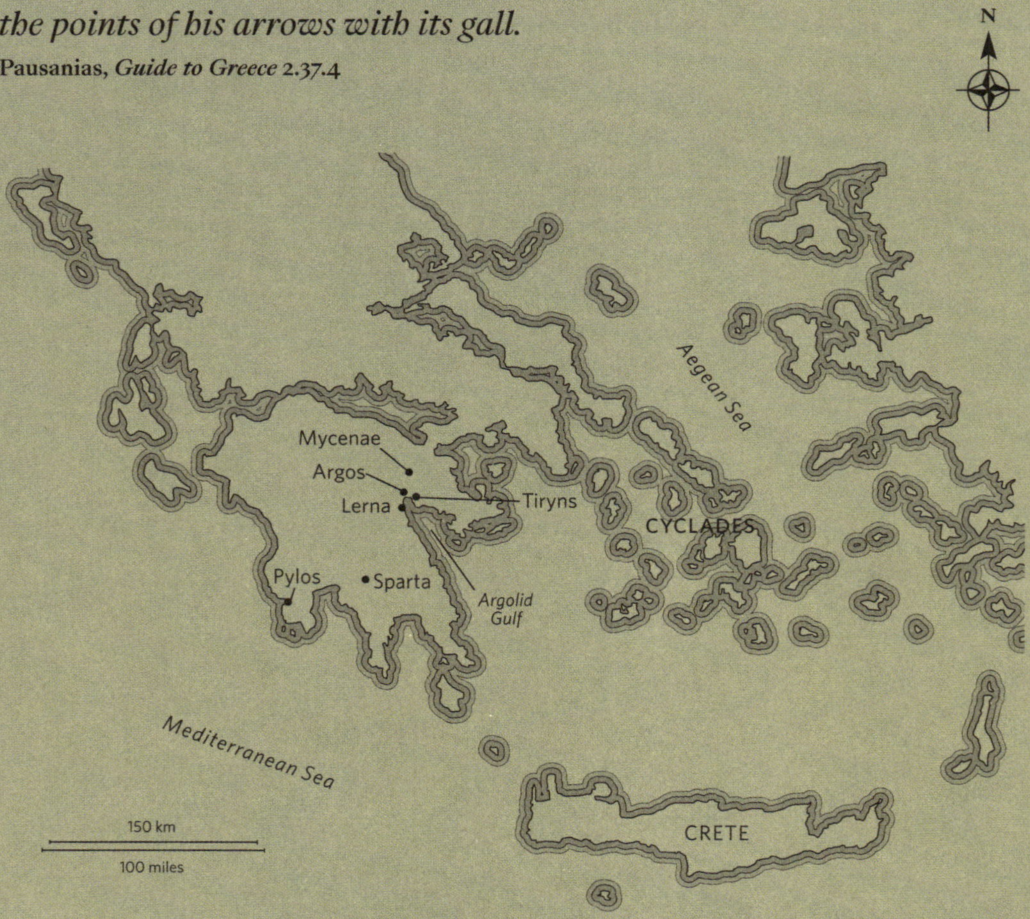

A stylized terracotta figure from Neolithic Greece of a type found across the peninsula. The wide hips have been have interpreted as literally embodying health and fertility.

In ancient times Lerna went from a lively maritime community to a cemetery and god-haunted marsh, a place stalked by monsters where cults performed secret rites to their gods. Located on the shores of the Gulf of Argos in central Greece, Lerna was inhabited from earliest times with the first traces of human activity dating back to almost ten thousand years ago.

The first settlers were Neolithic farmers attracted by fertile soil watered by a multiplicity of freshwater springs. In its prime, several centuries later, the settlement at Lerna turned to the sea. This was during what archaeologists call the Early Helladic Period, which began around 4,700 years ago. Being on the coast, Lerna was in a position to control maritime traffic along the shores of the Argolid Gulf – an ability which its people may have abused, because someone took the extreme measure of destroying the town and burning the principal buildings.

This happened some time in the early Bronze Age (about 4,200 years ago) and though a half-hearted attempt was made at resettlement Lerna was eventually abandoned. Human activity in the area had led to deforestation and this changed the environment. The freshwater lake outside Lerna expanded from a width of some 4.5 kilometres (3 miles) to include an indeterminate area beyond, creating a morass of bogs, wetland and malarial swamp. In time the place became so unhealthy that one ancient writer says that the expression 'a Lerna of ills' became proverbial (Strabo, *Geography* 8.6.8).

## Haunted waters

The Lernean population then considered the benefits of moving to the nearby up-and-coming town of Argos. This was located on Aspida Hill and the heights offered some relief from swamp bugs and illness. (Though the Greeks had not made the connection between mosquitoes and malaria, they thoroughly disliked both.) As a result Lerna was abandoned at about the same time as the famed Greek Bronze Age city of Mycenae was founded. The people of Argos thereafter used Lerna as a graveyard, adding to its already haunted reputation.

Lerna Lake – properly called the Alcyonean Lake – is sometimes referred to as the 'sacred' lake. Most did not venerate the lake, however, so much as give wary respect to the dark powers that haunted it. It was through the waters of this lake that Hades, Lord of the Underworld, returned to his domain with his captured wife Persephone, daughter of the goddess Demeter. As a consequence

A study for John Singer Sargent's *Danaïdes* painting, 1922–25, in the Museum of Fine Arts, Boston. The daughters of Danaus are shown drawing water as an allegory of the acquisition of knowledge.

of this, members of a secretive cult of the goddess dedicated certain rituals to Demeter Prosymna at Lerna – though, as this group is called a 'mystery cult' for good reason, we may never know the nature of these rites.

Later, though still in the era of myth, the fugitive king Danaus fled to Argos with his fifty daughters. He was pursued by Aegyptus (the king who allegedly gave his name to that land) who wanted the daughters to marry his equally abundant sons. Coerced into marriage, the daughters voluntarily became widows by killing their husbands on their wedding night. They then severed the heads of the deceased and either buried them at Lerna, or by an alternative tradition, tossed them into Lake Alcyonea.

Not all the daughters of Danaus killed their husbands. One, Amymone, did not and was consequently thrown out of the household by her father. She eventually fell into the hands of the (literally) rapacious sea-god Poseidon, who afterwards attempted to make amends by showing her the secret springs which fed the lake. Amymone thereafter gave birth to a son, who went on to found the eponymous nearby city of Nauplia – today Nafplio, a pleasant port with some twenty thousand inhabitants.

## Portal to the underworld

The next divine being to visit the area was Dionysus, the wine god. He was in search of his mortal mother Semele who had died before he was born. (It's a long story.) Dionysus was able to retrieve his mother and bring her back to the living world through the same portal that Hades had earlier used.

As a result of Semele's rescue a temple to Dionysus was placed alongside that to Demeter Prosymna, with both located near the appropriately named Amymone spring. At the temple of Dionysus certain esoteric rites were performed, 'though more than that' says our informant Pausanias primly, 'I am not permitted to tell'. This cult seems to have received a boost in the second century AD, because the emperor Hadrian conflated his drowned lover Antinous with the god Dionysus. A statue of a beautiful youth, very probably Antinous, was discovered in the area and is believed to have come from the temple. Both temples remained in use until 'Pagan' worship in the empire was ended by decree of the emperor Theodosius in AD 381.

## The dread Hydra

It was perhaps to prevent the entrance to the Realm of the Dead from being used as a revolving door that the dread Hydra was stationed by the portal. The creature's lair was apparently a cave

An Attic (Athenian) Greek amphora, *c.* 550–500 BC, depicting Hercules in combat with the Hydra. Stylistic details on the vase show the cultural influence of the Near Eastern trade routes which opened up in this period.

*Hercules and the Lernaean Hydra* by Gustave Moreau, 1875–76. This painting is typical of the French Symbolist movement, which prioritized subjective feeling, suggestion and mythological themes over realism.

near the plane tree from the roots of which gushed the waters of the Amymone spring. The Hydra was a monstrous snake, so venomous that even those standing downwind were in danger of being poisoned by its scent. The Hydra was multi-headed, and according to some sources, two-tailed also. The number of heads varies from story to story, perhaps because every time someone managed to sever a head, two grew in its place.

The lethality of the monster made it an ideal choice for Eurystheus, the king appointed to set the Labours for the legendary hero Hercules. For dynastic reasons too complex to go into here, Eurystheus desperately wanted Hercules dead. He had tried once by ordering Hercules to kill the supposedly invulnerable Nemean Lion. That plan failed, so the Hydra seemed an excellent candidate for a second shot.

To complete this, his Second Labour, Hercules travelled to Lerna and found the cave beside the sacred lake. He drew out the monster by shooting fire arrows into the cave and killed the beast by having his young relative Iolaus cauterize the stump of each head as it was amputated.

Later writers have speculated that the story may have a kernel of truth, insofar as sometime in the Bronze Age the marshes around Lerna were drained by a nameless individual. He accomplished this by blocking or diverting the multi-headed springs which fed the lake. Later myth had the habit of transferring all such feats to Hercules, who thus got the credit for someone else's work. However, monster-slaying was more entertaining than civil engineering, so in later tales the lake became its own eponymous monster, the Lernean Hydra. (Note that in Greek *hydor*, ὑδωρ, is the word for 'water'.)

Lake Alcyonea was reputed to be bottomless. In historical times the Roman emperor Nero tested the theory by lowering into the water lead-weighted ropes tied one to another. The experiment was abandoned after no bottom had been found and the ropes were getting dangerously heavy. The ancient Roman travel writer Pausanias, who tells us this anecdote, adds that though the lake's waters were generally smooth and placid, even strong swimmers attempting to cross the lake were pulled beneath the surface and drowned.

The draining of the lake itself took place in the nineteenth century and the area is now well-cultivated farmland. Amymone's spring still supplies water to Nafplio, the town founded by her son, while relics from prehistoric Lerna are on display in the nearby Archaeological Museum of Argos.

## *c.* 1300 BC – *c.* 390 BC

# Su Tempiesu
## The Sacred Spring

*An imaginative and innovative use of the materials and techniques available to a prehistoric island community.*

**Italian government submission to UNESCO, 2021**

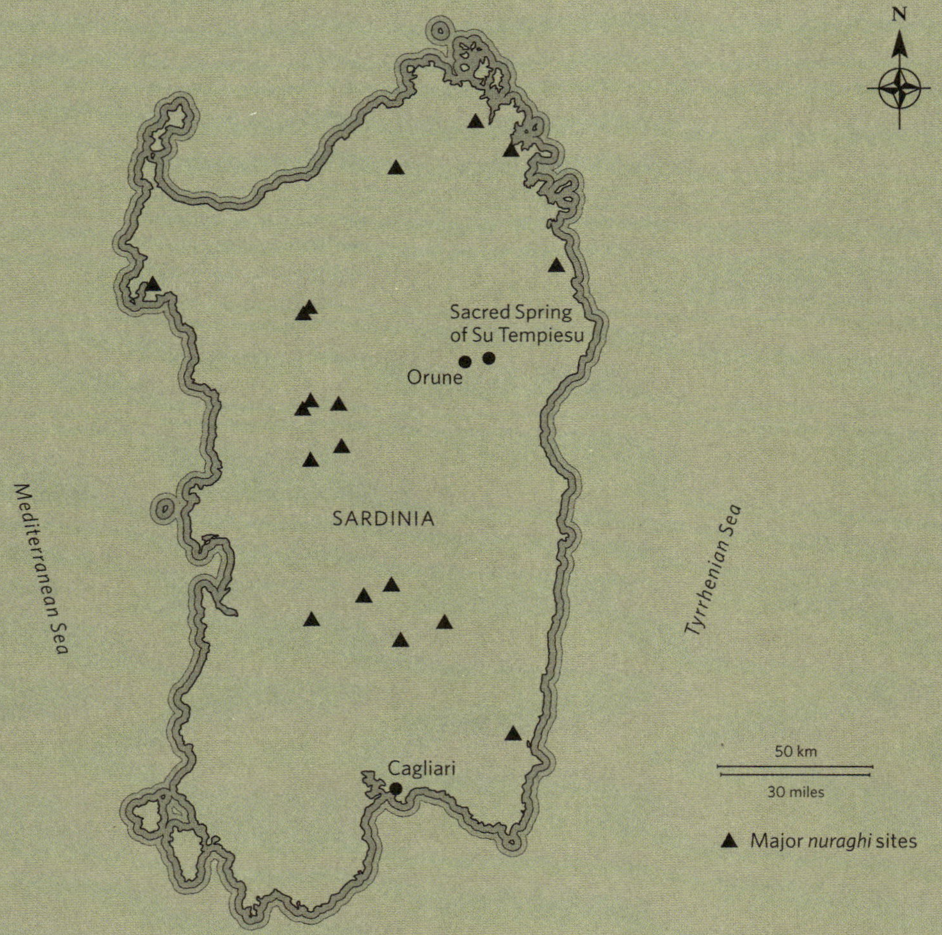

Before the Carthaginians and then the Romans came to Sardinia in the sixth and third centuries BC respectively, the island was home to a thriving civilization today called the Nuragic culture. We do not know what this people called themselves because they have left no written records of their own, and the Carthaginians and Romans between them effectively wiped out the indigenous culture.

The major relics of this vanished civilization are huge megaliths, carefully constructed stone towers called *nuraghi*, from which the culture gets its modern name. More or less contemporaneous with the better-known Mycenaeans of Greece, the *nuraghi*-builders spread across Sardinia during the Middle and Late Bronze Age. Why they built the stone towers – which are, even today, a common sight in Sardinia – is hotly debated by anthropologists and archaeologists.

However, there is more agreement as to why the people of the Nuragic culture built the other two types of structures for which they are known: firstly, the huge burial mounds that even archaeologists have taken to calling 'Tombs of the Giants'. These were sepulchres used for housing the (normal-sized) dead beneath earthen mounds in rooms up to 30 metres long and 3 metres high (98 × 10 feet). The second type are shrines or temples associated with water.

A stone staircase of weathered granite blocks leading down to the small, circular chamber (called a *tholos* chamber) that protects the sacred spring.

## The spirits of the springs

The Nuragic people revered the spirits who inhabited springs of fresh water, and the remains of places of worship at such locations have for centuries intrigued researchers. To get a proper grasp of the nature of Nuragic religion, what was really needed was an intact temple built over one such sacred spring, and in 1953 that is exactly what the researchers got.

The discovery was made purely by chance when workers repairing an aquifer came across what looked at first like a small pyramid of worked stone buried in the earth at Su Tempiesu near the Sardinian village of Orune. This discovery did not come as a complete shock, because the area around Orune is rich with relics of the vanished Nuragic culture. Nevertheless, as those excavating the site quickly realized, the Su Tempiesu site was unique. The workmen had come across a complete Nuragic water temple, still largely undamaged by the landslide that had buried it some time between 2,500 and 2,900 years ago.

The reason why so much of the temple had survived (only the upper portion was damaged) was because it was built of large blocks of volcanic rock. These had been carefully fitted together to make a stone structure of enduring solidity. It says a lot about how much the Nuragic people were invested in their sacred spring that this large building was constructed from stone that was not local, but had to be painfully imported some distance before being constructed against the wall of shale rock from which the sacred spring emanated. The roof, made of large blocks of solid stone in a pyramidal form, did not collapse even in the landslide which buried the temple. It was this pyramid shape that led to the building's rediscovery a few millennia later.

## Offerings to the gods

The water from the spring was channelled into a well deep within the building and here numerous offerings have been found. These include twenty bronze swords, apparently purpose-made as votive offerings to the spirit of the shrine, along with daggers and body decorations such as necklaces (only the beads remain), bracelets, rings and pendants. Also there are numerous small statuettes possibly depicting those who made the offerings. These include warriors, shepherds and other characters.

Most intriguing is a bronze statuette of a woman, presumably a priestess. She has a disc as headgear, which probably represents the sun or more likely the moon. It is believed that Nuragic people worshipped both, but ancient water goddesses have a strong

The extraordinary double-pitched roof and triangular tympanum of the main well structure are unique in having survived in this condition to the present day. They give a clear indication of how similar edifices might once have looked.

The figurines discovered at Su Tempiesu give an insight to the everyday life and culture of the Nuragic people.

connection with the moon, just as the moon has upon the tides and the female menstrual cycle. This particular priestess is shown with her arms stretched upwards, in greeting or in prayer. Apart from an apparent connection with the feminine and a stronger one with the flow of water we know little about the rites performed at the temple, nor about the deity or deities worshipped there.

Entry to the chamber where the sacred spring emptied into a well was guarded by another room, the so-called 'vestibule'. (In a Roman house the vestibule was where one changed in and out of outdoor clothing.) This is the tallest part of the 7-metre-high (23-foot) building. From the vestibule a small staircase leads down to the chamber of the well. Evidently the spring regularly produced more water than the well could absorb, for a channel in the floor diverted any overflow to a secondary well deeper in the building.

## Enduring mysteries

Much remains to be discovered about the culture and beliefs of the Nuragic culture, but the fact that they put so much effort into building a religious site over a sacred spring shows that they were linked to the Mediterranean-wide belief in the sanctity of pools, lakes and springs. (Indeed, before he was promoted to become god of the sea, Neptune was the god of springs and fountains for the early Latins, who at that time were a mountain people unfamiliar with salt water.)

As the only original evidence of a covered well structure, the water shrine at Su Tempiesu is a vital part of the puzzle about the beliefs of the peoples of the early Iron Age in the western Mediterranean. This matters because while the beliefs of some peoples – particularly Latins, Greeks, Hebrews and Egyptians – have been comprehensively studied, less well-known cultures such as the Nuragi, Iberian tribes, and African tribes such as the Garamantes also made a substantial contribution to the melange of ideas which formed the common culture of Mediterranean peoples.

Those wanting to see the site at Su Tempiesu for themselves will find it at the end of a rather pleasant walk along a scenic trail through the hills. There is a paved road for the first 4 kilometres (2½ miles) or so from Orune, but thereafter one must proceed on foot. Visitors to the site report that those working to uncover its secrets are happy to share their discoveries and to tell them how Su Tempiesu relates to the ancient civilization of their native Sardinia.

*c.* 1400 BC – *c.* AD 200

# The Colossi of Memnon

## Immortalized in Stone

*...I heard a noise in the first hour of the day. I really can't say if the noise came from the Colossus, or from the base or was made by those standing around it....I will believe any explanation other than that the stones actually spoke.*

Strabo, *Geography*, 17.1,46, *c.* AD 10

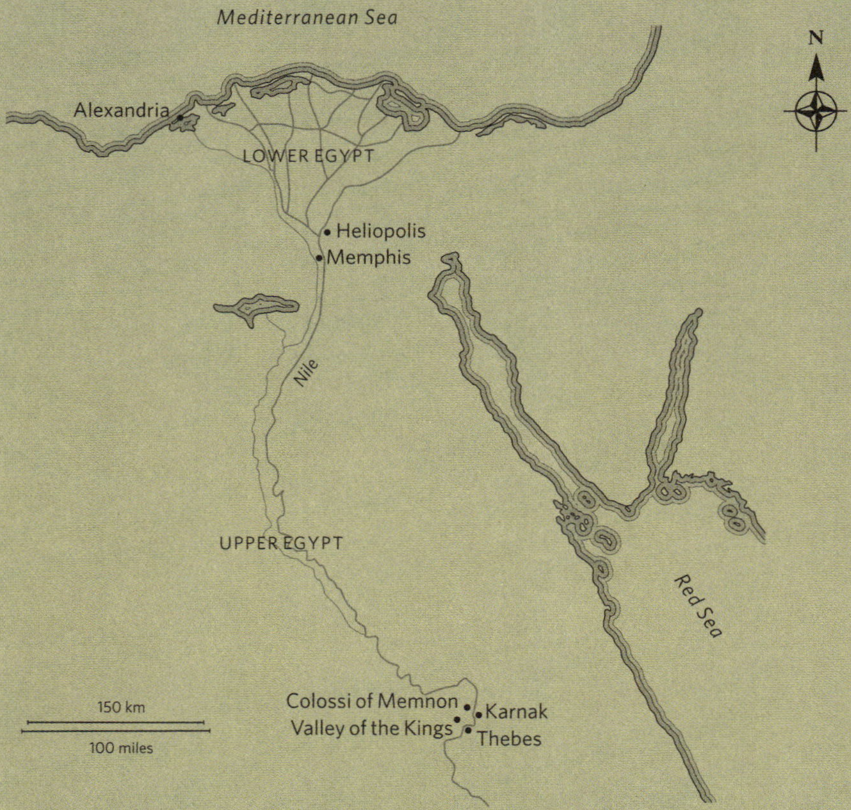

The sceptical Strabo was the exception among the many visitors to these gigantic statues, which were over a thousand years old even in his day. Most others flocked to the 'singing' statue in the belief that it uttered oracular pronouncements, or at the very least bestowed lifelong good luck upon those who heard the noise. Many of these ancient visitors left graffiti upon the stone, which the passing of two thousand years has transformed from vandalism to architectural treasures.

But who built these gigantic statues and why?

## Amenhotep, a king seeking immortality

The statues were not originally designed for pronouncements by supernatural beings, though they certainly had a connection with the afterlife. They were originally intended by the Egyptian pharaoh Amenhotep III (1390–1352 BC) to stand guard outside his massive funerary temple on the banks of the Nile. Not one for modesty, Amenhotep made each of the 18-metre (59-foot) high statues as a representation of his divine self. He did include depictions of his wife Tiye and one daughter, but their figures are tiny in comparison, their heads barely reaching his knees. The statues were each carved from a monolithic block of quartzite stone estimated at over 1,000 tons apiece.

The remains of a quartzite statue of Amenhotep III wearing the Blue Crown (called the khepresh), c. 1390–1352 BC. This type of crown was usually worn during ceremonies.

A funerary figure of the god Hapy, depicted with a baboon head, c. 1100–332 BC.

Panels on the sides of the seats of the Colossi identified Amenhotep with Hapy, the god of the Nile – appropriately enough, for Hapy is usually depicted with a pot belly (stressing the abundance and fertility his silt-laden floodwaters brought to Egypt) and examination of Amenhotep's mummified remains show that he was overweight. He also suffered badly from tooth decay.

The land in this region is so flat that visitors to the funeral complex would have seen the statues from far away, before the rest of the structure became visible. At the time that Amenhotep built this huge monument to himself Egypt was peaceful and prosperous. The pharaoh must have believed that he had succeeded in immortalizing himself in stone.

## Guardians of a vanished temple

Within two centuries, however, Amenhotep's massive funerary complex was in ruins. The structures were weakened because the Nile's annual floods had reached the buildings (perhaps Hapy didn't like the comparisons with Amenhotep). Then around the year 1200 BC the gods finished off the funerary complex with a massive earthquake. To add insult to injury much of the masonry was then removed and repurposed by later pharaohs who fancied the stone for their own building projects. Today there is nothing but a plain of scrubby grass.

The Colossi remained, still guarding the gates of a complex that no longer existed. Sadly even these failed to keep alive the memory of the deceased pharaoh. Later generations came to identify the statues not with Amenhotep, who had been largely forgotten, but with Memnon. Memnon was a semi-divine hero-king in both Egyptian and Greek tradition. The son of the goddess of the dawn, he raised an Egyptian army to help the Trojans lift the siege of Troy. As legend records, this attempt was unsuccessful and Memnon was slain by the Greek hero Achilles. The statues of Amenhotep became a hero shrine to Memnon.

After further earthquake damage in 27 BC, one statue had begun to emit a whistling sound each dawn. Devotees believed that Memnon spoke from the afterlife to those who visited his memorial. Some thought that the sound made by the statue was that of the dawn goddess as she sobbed for her dead son. The Roman travel writer Pausanias described it thus:

> *Every day with the rising of the sun it makes a sound, probably best described as that made by a lyre or harp as the string breaks.*
> (*Guide to Greece* 1.62.3)

The *Colossi of Memnon in Egypt* by the artist Hubert Sattler, 1846. By this time the Colossi had ceased 'speaking' due to the repair work requested by Emperor Septimius Severus.

## Tourist attraction

Romans and Greeks were among the many tourists who came to listen to this sound in ancient times and interpret it in their own manner. A typical inscription carved upon the foot of one statue reads: 'Trebulla was here. When I heard the sacred voice of the Memnon I thought of you, my mother, and I prayed that you might hear him also.'

Among other recorded visitors was one Camillus, probably the Roman governor of Egypt at the time, and also the peripatetic Roman emperor Hadrian (r. AD 117–38). The emperor came to the Memnon Colossi with his court, among whom was a companion of the empress called Julia Balbilla. She also recorded her impressions: 'When the rock spoke, I Julia Balbilla heard the voice of the Divine Memnon...I came here with the Empress Sabina when the Sun was in its first hour, on the 24th day of the month of Hathor, in the fifteenth year of Hadrian's reign [AD 130]'.

Around the end of the second century AD an attempt was made to repair the statue – by some reports, this was done on the orders of the Roman emperor Septimius Severus (r. AD 193–211), who wanted to gain the favour of the oracle. However, as Amenhotep had already discovered, the gods could be fickle. After the repairs the statue never spoke again.

There has been considerable speculation, both in modern times and ancient, as to what caused the statue to 'speak'. Perhaps the best guess is that cracks in the stone formed a natural amplifier and the sound was caused by the rock expanding as the morning sun warmed the surface.

## A magnet for graffiti

The Colossi continued to attract visitors even after they went mute and lost their sacred status. The graffiti from the early modern era include the words of French soldiers from Napoleon's expedition to Egypt in the late eighteenth century. Modern visitors are strongly discouraged from adding their own contributions to the stone. In any case, few could match the superb Latin of the otherwise unknown female poet who inscribed these words:

> *Caecilia Trebulla* [wrote this] *when for the second time*
> *Memnon spoke*
> *Before was only his voice, but today*
> *He greeted us as friends and close companions.*
> *Oh Nature, maker of all,*
> *Was Memnon, son of Eros and Tithon,*
> *Given perception and voice in stone?*

*Left* One side of the Colossi features a relief of the god Hapy. He is shown with a prominent belly and large drooping breasts, representing the fertility of the Nile.

*Right* Two millennia of graffiti can be found on the legs and feet of the Colossi; over 107 inscriptions feature in Greek and Latin.

*c.* 814 BC – 146 BC

# The Tophet of Carthage

## Unearthing Child Sacrifice

*The people of Judah have done evil in my eyes, declares the Lord. They have set up their detestable idols in the house that bears my name and they have defiled it. They have built the high places of Tophet in the Valley of Ben Hinnom there to burn their sons and daughters in the fire....*

Book of Jeremiah 7.30–31

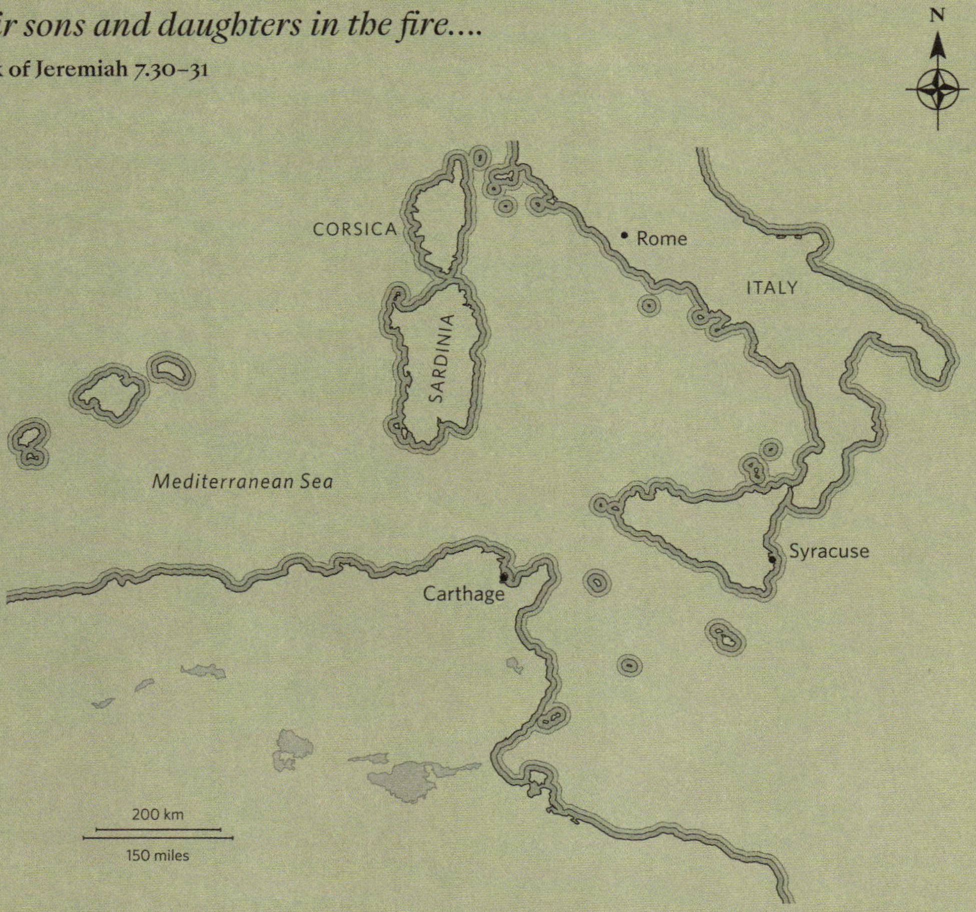

Many sacred sites are also a source of controversy and this is certainly true of the Tophet of Carthage – indeed even the name is controversial. The biblical Book of Jeremiah refers to Baal-worshippers in sixth-century BC Judea. 'Tophet' is the name given thereafter to the places where child sacrifice happened, and the Tophet in Carthage was perhaps the original and largest of them all.

The Tophet was an area of Carthage sacred to the gods Tanit and Baal-Hammon. Here, according to a number of ancient sources, the Carthaginians sacrificed noble-born children to their gods. Whether this did actually happen is a source of heated debate in the modern era.

## The sacred swamp

What is certain is that there did exist in ancient Carthage an area sacred to the divine duo, and that it includes a necropolis that contains a higher than expected proportion of children's graves. That the site should be a graveyard as well as a shrine is not particularly surprising. The sacred area was in the south of Carthage near the docks, in a low-lying marshy part of the city that would have been very unhealthy for the living. (As well as being unsuitable for any other purpose, marshes – being neither water nor land – were seen by many ancient peoples as liminal places where the mundane and sacred co-existed.)

Almost from the foundation of Carthage (traditionally in 814 BC, though archaeological evidence for this early date is lacking), the

This underground burial chamber in Carthage is typical of Punic funerary architecture. The disordered state of the chamber might be due to the Roman sack of Carthage in 146 BC or the work of later looters.

This dramatic illustration showing an infant sacrifice to Moloch is typical of sensational images from books in the Enlightenment period.

site was used for interring the dead. The occupants of the city followed the tradition of their Phoenician forebears by incinerating the deceased, and then placing the burned remains in urns which they buried within the sacred precinct. Since this area is only some 6,000 square metres (64,600 square feet) it filled up rapidly over the centuries, whereupon the Carthaginians appear to have covered the site with a fresh layer of earth and started again. Modern archaeologists working their way down through the different strata have unearthed tens of thousands of these funerary urns.

## Cremated children

Disturbingly, the remains of cremated children are common at the Tophet even though the Carthaginians usually only burned deceased adults. (Dead children were usually interred.) Burned animal remains have been found with some of these corpses, which again suggests that the remains were collected after sacrifices. The Roman author Diodorus Siculus gives a horrifying account of how some of these children may have ended up in the necropolis. In 309 BC Carthage was under attack by the army of Agathocles of Syracuse and the people of the city sought an explanation as to how things had come to so dire a pass, and what they could do to save themselves:

> *They also claimed that Cronus* [Baal-Hammon] *had abandoned them. In the past they had been traditionally sacrificed sons of the high nobility to this god. Recently they had taken to sacrificing children secretly purchased for this purpose – and indeed an investigation revealed that some of the children sacrificed had been substitutions.*
>
> *Now with the enemy encamped before their walls, the thought of this sacrilege filled them with superstitious dread, for they believed that they had abandoned the honour that their ancestors had given to their gods....* [Accordingly a large number of children were selected for a propitiatory sacrifice]...*There was in Carthage a bronze statue of Cronus. This had its arms extended with the palms up but sloping downward, so that each child placed on the arms rolled down into a large pit filled with fire.*
>
> (*History* 20.14)

But did this happen? Diodorus' description is explicit, and backed up by other writers such as Plutarch who claimed that the sacrifices were accompanied by the sound of drums and flutes intended to drown out the wails of bereaved mothers.

Yet Diodorus was writing almost a century after the Romans had destroyed Carthage, and Plutarch a century after that. The Romans had razed Carthage in 146 BC after an unprovoked war caused only by their fear that their long-time foe might again become powerful. They had, therefore, every reason to excuse their warmongering

A terracotta statuette of Baal-Hammon dating to the Punic or Neo-Punic period (fourth to first century BC), reflecting the god's status as the chief deity of Carthage and king of the gods.

with the claim that their actions had removed from the Earth a blot upon humanity. They certainly made sure that when they destroyed the city no records survived to give the Carthaginian side of the story.

## Did they or didn't they?

Significantly there is no mention of child sacrifice at the Tophet by Polybius, a Greek historian who recorded the fall of Carthage and may well have been there to witness it in person as a companion of the Roman general in charge.

Those defending the Carthaginians against the charge of child sacrifice point out that children were not regularly sacrificed to Baal by other Phoenician peoples. Yet this defence is weakened by the fact that 'Baal' is a generic name for any god, meaning something like 'Lord', and Baal-Hammon was a deity specific to Carthage. Significantly the Romans associated him with Cronus – a proto-deity in Greek mythology who ate his children.

Tanit was the other deity to whom the site was sacred. Ironically, given the use to which her sacred site was supposedly put, she was a mother goddess – but yet a virgin. (Christianity has the same dichotomy in the Virgin Mary.) The Greeks and Romans variously identified Tanit with the goddesses Artemis, Athena and Juno – many female goddesses were connected with the moon. However, Tanit appears to have been a specifically home-grown deity closely identified with the Berber people who were there before the Carthaginians arrived. In fact even now, millennia after the Carthaginians vanished, Tanit is still venerated in local Berber tradition.

## Unearthing the secrets

Excavation of the site has been ongoing since the early nineteenth century, along with removal of items – some would say looting – by well-meaning archaeologists. As a result artefacts from the Tophet are scattered around numerous European museums, making it harder to create an organized picture of the site's history. Particularly egregious was the 1875 case of thousands of artefacts intended for the Louvre. The ship carrying these sank even before it left port and the wreck was subsequently dynamited because it was blocking the harbour mouth.

The infamous 'Stela of the Priest' has sparked controversy as to whether the priest carries the child in his arms towards sacrifice, or not.

Looters came across one particularly significant find from the Tophet which has survived. Called the 'Stela of the Priest', this engraved block of limestone shows a man in religious dress who carries a child in his arms. A lively debate continues as to whether this child is being borne toward sacrifice or interment. As there are no funeral arrangements visible that might be expected of a corpse already in a cemetery, those who believe that children were killed at the Tophet regard this stela as evidence of their more sinister interpretation.

The stela is one of several from the Tophet which are now in the Bardo Museum in Tunisia, which contains numerous other artefacts from the Tophet and the rest of the city. These include funerary urns and sarcophagi, jewelry, votive offerings and ritual tools.

Today efforts are under way to explore the site more systematically and to undo the damage done by the more chaotic excavations of the past. The Tophet is part of a UNESCO World Heritage Site but visitors will find the location still a work in progress when it comes to displaying the material discovered.

# *c.* 3000 BC – 2500 BC
# Stonehenge
## A Site of Ancient Legend

*For in these stones is a mystery...Giants of old carried them from the furthest ends of Africa and set them up.*

**The wizard Merlin, quoted in Geoffrey of Monmouth's *Historia regum Britanniae* 8.11**

According to the medieval chronicler Geoffrey of Monmouth (d. 1155), Stonehenge was not only built by giants, but originally stood in Ireland. The wizard Merlin used his magical powers to whisk the stones overnight from their former location. He then set them up on Salisbury Plain in Wiltshire as a monument to Arthur's warriors who had fallen in war against the Saxons.

Modern archaeologists beg to disagree. Perhaps they would disagree most vehemently with the idea that Stonehenge was built overnight. By most estimations the construction we see today was well over fifteen hundred years in the making, involved several major rebuilds and stood in its final form many centuries before storytellers first conceived the legend of Merlin.

The first construction at Stonehenge seems to have taken place some five hundred years before the pyramids at Giza, thus torpedoing the early modern theory that it was built by Western savages in imitation of the great stone structures of the civilizations of the eastern Mediterranean. (Though interestingly, DNA studies from burials at Stonehenge have shown that some of the ancestors of the megalith builders may indeed have originated from the eastern Mediterranean.)

Magician at work. This illustration, from a fourteenth-century manuscript in the British Library, shows Merlin moving the 'Ring of Giants' (Stonehenge) from Ireland.

Stonehenge at the winter solstice. The faint straight line in the snowy field is the ancient processional way that connected Stonehenge to the River Avon.

## The first Stonehenge

Stonehenge was not a single project conceived by a Druidic architect following a master plan. In fact, like Merlin, the Druids came long after Stonehenge had been conceived, built and abandoned. Modern research reckons there were three distinct phases in the construction of Stonehenge and there may have been different uses of the site as well, with different cultures using the stone circle for their own purposes.

Work began on the first Stonehenge (Stonehenge I) around five thousand years ago. For reasons which are now unclear, the people then inhabiting what is today Salisbury Plain started construction of a large circular ditch enclosing an area some 100 metres (328 feet) in diameter. Earth banks were built on each side of this ditch. Within these earth walls fifty-six pits were dug – the so-called 'Aubrey Holes', named after the antiquarian who first investigated them. There may have been some 150 people interred in these pits (only charred bone fragments remain), meaning that Stonehenge I was not only a cemetery but the largest cemetery yet found in Neolithic Britain.

## The bluestone controversy

This brings us to the mystery of the Stonehenge bluestones, which many researchers now believe were erected to stand above the bodies. There is currently a fierce debate as to where these stones came from and neither of the proposed answers has properly solved the mystery. It does not help that analysis of the bones shows that some of those buried here seem to have come from the same region as the Preseli Hills in Wales where it is suggested that the bluestone was quarried.

Although analysis of the stone has matched the bluestones to localized geology in the Preseli Hills and Brecon Beacons, the problem is that no ancient quarry in the Preseli Hills has been definitively identified as the source of the bluestone (which is not really blue, but archaeological shorthand for a mix composed of sandstone, dolerite, rhyolite and tuff). Also, there's the not-so-minor problem of how people of a culture which considered antler-horn tools as cutting-edge technology could move the stones, the largest of which weighs 3 tonnes, 225 kilometres (140 miles) across a rugged landscape – or why they would want to.

'Our Neolithic ancestors may have been heroic. But they were not stupid', argues one researcher (geomorphologist Dr B. John). He believes that the bluestones were brought to Salisbury Plain not by strenuous human effort but as what is known as 'glacial erratics', which is the technical term for stones picked up by glaciers and carried far from their native habitat. Thus when the glaciers melted at the end of the last Ice Age, the stones were already waiting on Salisbury Plain for the first Neolithic builders.

The problem here is that there is no bluestone on Salisbury Plain apart from that used in Stonehenge and at another, now-vanished, structure 1.5 kilometres (almost a mile) away – called 'Bluestonehenge' – where the stones appear to have been cannibalized and reused for later work at Stonehenge itself. Also sceptics have argued that glaciation did not extend far enough into Britain to have deposited the stones. As of 2025 the debate continues, but so far the Merlin hypothesis is looking as good as the alternatives.

Perhaps more puzzling is the so-called Altar Stone, which can be found near the centre of Stonehenge and weighs 6 tonnes. Evidence suggests that it was transported from even further afield in northeast Scotland.

## Stonehenge II and III

Between 2600 and 2400 BC the first of the great stones which make up the Stonehenge we know today were being raised. These stones were of sarsen stone, which is different from bluestone and had the advantage of being locally available. However, sarsen stone is a type of silicified sandstone and is a lot more difficult to work.

This was less of a challenge for the builders of the 'new' Stonehenge (Stonehenge II) because unlike their predecessors the builders had bronze tools to work with. This is because the rebuilding of Stonehenge came at a time of great change in prehistoric Britain. A new people had arrived from the continent and displaced much of the native population. Today the later arrivals are called the 'Beaker people' after their distinctive pottery. Skilled metalworkers (at least in comparison to their predecessors), the Beaker folk were also good builders. The huge stone lintels of the stones in the outer circle of Stonehenge have stayed atop their supporting stones for so long because they do not simply rest there but are held in place by mortice and tenon joints – basically pegs in the lower stones fitted into holes in the lintel stones.

At some point the bluestones over the graves at Stonehenge were moved and rearranged into a circle. This rearrangement – perhaps between *c.* 2300 and 2200 BC – may have marked the transition of Stonehenge from a cemetery to a solar observatory. There is a long history of such structures in Britain. The oldest yet

Stonehenge in summer. Protecting Stonehenge from crowds of sightseers has become more urgent in the modern era after activists for various causes have defaced the ancient monument.

discovered is the Mesolithic calendar monument at Warren Field in Aberdeenshire. It was built around 8000 BC, and correlated the phases of the moon with the solar cycle. Such calendars had the very pragmatic purpose of allowing hunter-gatherer peoples to prepare for the annual migration of the herds which were a major food source for them.

The final touches to Stonehenge (Stonehenge III) were added when Stonehenge was probably at the peak of its usage in around 1700 BC. These are mostly rearrangements of the bluestones into a horseshoe shape – apparently because of a greater interest in lunar cycles – rather than a complete redefinition of the ritual space as some archaeologists have suggested. Overall, however, the later Iron Age seems to have had less use for the great stone circle and the land gradually reverted to pastoralism with sheep grazing around the ancient stones.

Today Stonehenge is a national monument, and if it was not considered a sacred site in the times when it was used as a solar observatory, certainly it is today. The European Court of Human Rights has recognized Stonehenge as a place of worship for 'Earth-based religions'. Thus modern Neo-Druids now celebrate the dawn of the summer solstice at Stonehenge, just as the original Druids didn't do five thousand years ago.

# 4000 BC – present day
# **Croghan Bog and Hill**
# Beneath the Marshes

*There was the bog. A whole new life was there to be learned; complex, mysterious, dank, slippery, reedy, treacherous, but with its own beauty. It could grow on you, so that you could forget the firmer world and love only that which quaked and gurgled.*

**From the medieval narrative *The Boyhood of Fionn* 8**

Swamps are not marshes and marshes are not bogs. Swamps are not only more likely to occur in warmer climates but they often have trees and other vegetation that have adapted to a semi-aquatic environment. Marshes are reedy wetlands that have a constant supply of water with lots of nutriment-rich silt. Then there are bogs. These occur in places such as North America, Ireland, Russia and Scandinavia. In one way bogs are the opposite to marshes because the water there is very low in nutrients, and indeed there is often little free-standing water but instead a very high water table with the soil covered in peat and moss. Bog water is also very saline. Because they are neither water nor dry land, bogs mark the division between one state and another – something seen in past eras as also marking a point where the mundane and supernatural met and merged.

Croghan bog as a brooding environment. Researchers suspect that more ancient human remains lie undiscovered beneath its surface.

## Hill and bog

The Croghan bog is what is called a 'raised bog' – vegetation has been growing, dying and rotting there for centuries, leading to an accumulation of peat that can be up to 8 metres (26 feet) deep. Like many of the bogs in Ireland, the Croghan bog is in the country's midlands. In fact it is in County Offaly, which is almost exactly in the middle of the island. From the bog – which is called the Bog of Allen – Croghan Hill rises 230 metres (755 feet) to dominate the landscape. For millennia, and certainly since the Bronze Age, bog and mountain have been sacred to the local people, some of whom still hold these places in some awe today.

The nearby hill of Uisneach also has otherworldly qualities and the pair are linked by the fact that, in the winter, solstice watchers on Uisneach Hill see the sun rise directly over Croghan Hill. On Samhain – the Celtic festival which happens on the night of 31 October – the gates between the worlds open so that the denizens of each can pass through, and one of these portals is on Croghan Hill. Such encounters and travels between natural and supernatural realms form one of the major themes in the legend of Fionn mac Cumhaill, a young hero of Irish folklore.

Another indication of the length of time that bog and mountain have been considered sacred is that there is an unexcavated tumulus on Croghan Hill which is probably an ancient burial. We know more about the Bog of Allen because of the variety of objects which were deposited there over the centuries: valuable items, including coins, weapons from the Bronze and Iron Ages and jewelry including an amulet plated with gold foil that was deposited some time in the eighth century BC. As with Croghan Hill, humans were also ritually placed in the bog. We know considerably more about these bodies because much of each corpse has survived intact.

## Bog bodies

While most ancient burials leave nothing but bone, in bogs the opposite happens. The acidity of the water dissolves the calcium phosphate of bone but does an excellent job of preserving the skin and internal organs from bacteria, which are in any case inhibited by low temperature, scarce oxygen and high salinity. As a result, any body buried in a bog has a high chance of remaining intact.

Artefacts from Croghan bog reflect the sacred nature of such places in ancient Celtic culture. Some relics now extracted from the bog were worn on the bodies deposited there, but others were separate offerings.

In Ireland alone scores of bodies have been thus discovered. This has resulted in a degree of stress for those doing the discovering, because peat has been harvested from bogs for centuries for use as fuel. As a result those cutting the peat sometimes find that they have

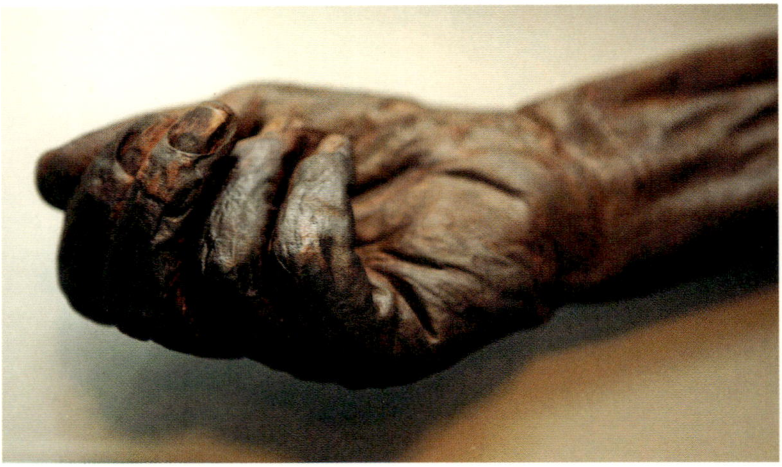

The arm of the body known as Old Croghan Man. The highly acidic and anaerobic nature of peat bogs has preserved organic material from decay and decomposition, so that modern researchers can even determine the last meal from a body's stomach contents.

included human body parts in their harvest. This also causes some distress for modern researchers who very much prefer to examine their ancient bodies undisturbed and *in situ*, while the circumstances mean that neither body nor site is likely to be in pristine condition.

## Old Croghan Man

This is certainly the case with Old Croghan Man, whose corpse was discovered at the foot of Croghan Hill in 2003. Almost all the Irish bog body remains that have been discovered consist of the torso and arms, though in this particular case that is hardly the fault of the peat-cutter. It appears that the body was deliberately cut in half and decapitated at the time of death. Fortunately for the victim it appears that he died beforehand from a stab wound to the chest. His last meal has been determined to have been of wheat and buttermilk, possibly the equivalent of the condemned man's last dinner.

Although nothing has been found apart from these enigmatic remains, much can still be ascertained from the body itself, from what is known of ancient Ireland and from other bog bodies from this era. For a start most of the Irish bog bodies were male, in their twenties and in good health apart from being dead. The men were well fed on a high-protein diet and in the case of Old Croghan Man the condition of his hands suggests that he did little manual labour. All the signs point to the fact that the bog bodies were high-status individuals and the ritualistic manner of their deaths suggests that they were killed for religious purposes.

Clonycavan Man, discovered in 2003 in Clonycavan, County Meath, is likewise missing his lower half, though it is uncertain if he suffered the same fate as Old Croghan Man or if his dismemberment was done by a modern peat-cutting machine. Like Old Croghan Man he was a high-status individual, as evidenced by his topknot which was layered with resin imported from overseas. His death also happened at around the same time – somewhere around the second or third century BC.

Why these men were sacrificed is not completely clear, but life for Irish nobility at this time was precarious. In a warrior culture there was a high risk of death in battle, and a further risk of death subsequently if the battle did not go well. Kings claimed to have a divine connection with the gods and so defeats, floods or a poor harvest could mean that the king or his religious advisers were doing a poor job. Therefore, they might be dispatched directly to the gods to explain their worshippers' plight in person.

## Later developments

Irish bogs are complex entities that have been shaped by interaction with humans for a very long time. It is even possible that at the time the bodies were deposited the Bog of Allen was not a bog at all but a lake. (Bodies of open water were also sacred to the Celts.) However, the silting of the lake and the accumulation of centuries of rotting reed mats created the bog as it is today and thus preserved the sacrificed corpses.

Today Old Croghan Man shares a residence in the National Museum of Ireland in Dublin with Clonycavan Man. Croghan Hill has retained its sacred status through the years. In Irish mythology the hill came to be called Bri Eile, haunted during Samhain by faeries who proved the undoing of several adventurers. Bodies were interred there in a medieval graveyard and church on the hill's eastern slope and the wells at the foot of the hill were also considered sacred places.

*c*. 2400 BC – *c*. AD 1378

# The Mystery of the Sphinx

## Eternal Protector

*Your head is that of Horus of the Duat,*
*O Imperishable One...You did not pass away,*
*your ka does not pass away.*

From the Pyramid Texts, Old Kingdom period, *c*. 2494–2345 BC

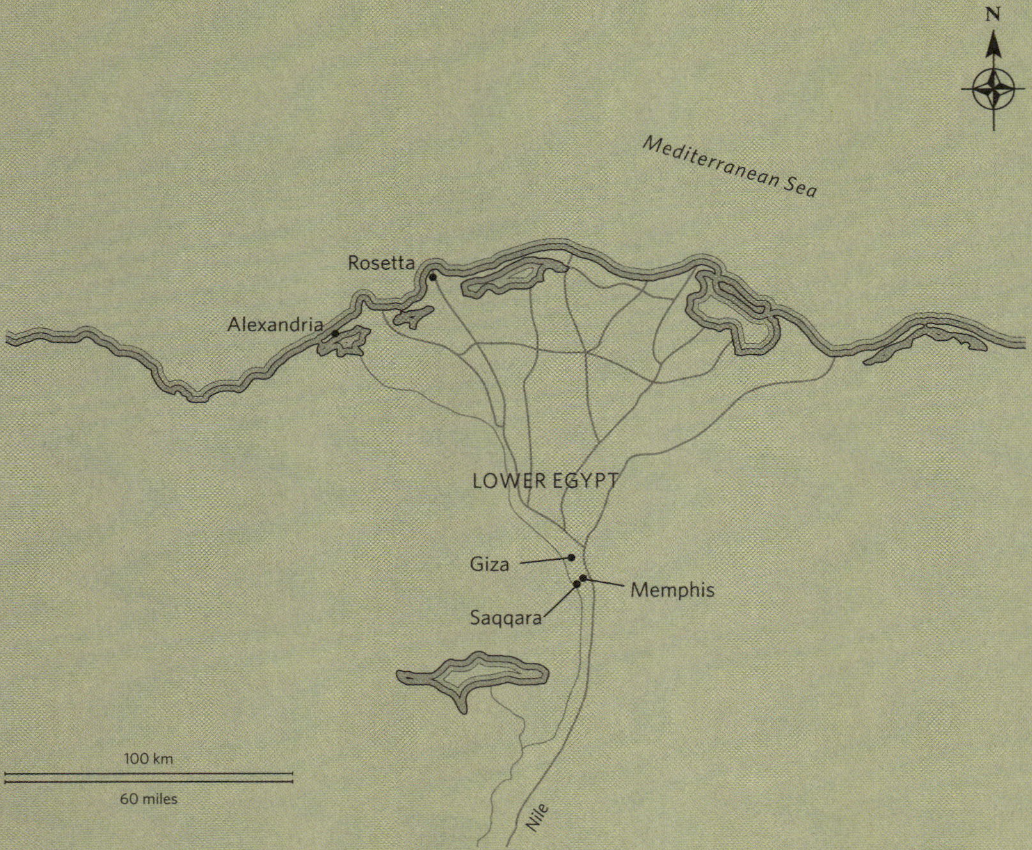

The so-called Pyramid Texts are inscribed within nine royal pyramids at Saqqara in Egypt. Together, they make up the oldest known body of sacred texts, dating to the Fifth Dynasty of the Old Kingdom (2494–2345 BC). The texts do not mention the Great Sphinx at nearby Giza by name, although the carved monolith was probably at least a century old when they were inscribed. It would take another half-millennium before the sculpture beside the Nile would come to be called 'the Sphinx'. Yet from the beginning this stone recreation of the mythical creature seems to have symbolized protection and strength, a brooding presence watching over the tombs of the pharaohs, and it is likely that passages such as that at the start of this chapter reference the monument.

## Ancient, but how ancient?

Exactly when the Great Sphinx at Giza was created, and how, has been a topic of considerable debate that goes back to at least the seventh century BC and shows no signs of slowing down.

The Sphinx on eternal sentry duty. This very ancient monolith was originally sculpted by nature and erosion to which humans added the final touches.

Egyptologists today generally place its construction no earlier than the Fourth Dynasty (2613–2494 BC), with renovations and reconstruction over the succeeding centuries, but much earlier dates have been claimed.

A modern geologist called Robert Schoch examined erosion patterns in the limestone body of the Sphinx and theorized that it must have been carved at the end of the Ice Age, around 10,000 BC (before the foundation of Egypt itself), because it did not rain enough in historical Egypt to account for the erosion. Other geologists point out that limestone weathers at different rates, and actually it rained rather a lot on Old Kingdom Egypt – certainly enough to erode the limestone massif of the Sphinx's body. The current drying out and desertification of the region is a relatively modern phenomenon.

Also, the Sphinx faces the rising sun. Considering the importance of the sun god Ra in Egyptian religion, it is probable that dawn ceremonies took place there at times of the year with ritual significance. Given that the Sphinx has the body of a lion, some have tried to establish an astronomical connection with the constellation of Leo. The 'Orion Correlation Theory' argues that the pyramids and Sphinx are massive representations in stone of the stars as they were aligned 10,000 to 12,000 years ago. Again, if true this would make the Sphinx by far the oldest monumental construction ever built.

It has also been theorized that the Sphinx was one of the first constructions of the people of lost Atlantis, when the melting glaciers inundated their homeland, and that the refugees first introduced civilization to Egypt (also around 10,000 years ago).

Most modern Egyptologists reject these hypotheses with indignation and exasperation. For example, the 'Orion Correlation' is an example of confirmation bias – i.e. starting with a fixed idea and then carefully selecting the evidence that supports it. Using modern New York as a template, you can also align the Empire State Building, the Brooklyn Bridge and the Statue of Liberty with any carefully selected constellation.

## The scientific case

So where did the Sphinx really come from? Basically it was always there. The lower part of the body is a natural outcrop on a plateau formed in the Eocene era around 50 million years ago. In fact, one suggested etymology for the name 'Sphinx' is from the Egyptian *sh's'p ankh*, which means '*living* statue' because it was formed from the living rock.

The pharaoh Khafre, builder (or modifier) of the Sphinx, is shown here carved in diorite, a hard dark stone imported from over a thousand kilometres away. Note the falcon, symbol of the god Horus, behind.

The most generally accepted hypothesis today is that the Sphinx was modelled by the pharaoh Khafre (r. 2558–2532 BC) in around 2500 BC. The natural formation had a yardang, a lump of harder stone which protects the softer rock below it while the rest is worn away by erosion. The result resembles – given the right shape of the harder stone, and plenty of imagination – a crude head on a neck.

Given that the rest of the massif was vaguely in the shape of a resting animal, it is speculated that Khafre had the body reshaped by carving away stone in some places and adding limestone blocks in others to represent a lion. The head was carved to resemble Khafre, thus conflating his semi-divine self with the eternal vigilance and protectiveness of the Sphinx. He may also have increased

Maintaining *ma'at* (cosmic order). The Pharaoh (right) presents offerings to Horus-Ra (left) and Hathor, the mother and consort of Horus.

the resemblance by attaching the massive stone beard (a royal attribute) which has been found nearby and probably dropped off the sculpture. Other structures in the area are definitely dated to the time of Khafre, and some appear to have required adjustment or rebuilding because of the Sphinx, which suggests that they were already there.

## Counter-counter argument

Opponents of this theory point out that Khafre could have reshaped an existing, earlier sculpture. Also the alleged resemblance of the face to representations of Khafre might itself be an example of confirmation bias. Before the Sphinx was linked to Khafre, early modern Europeans suggested that the face might be female, 'negroid' or both. Also, if Khafre were responsible for something as epic as the Sphinx, would he not have mentioned it somewhere?

(Though admittedly inscriptions from his reign are extremely scarce.) In short, it is much more likely that Khafre created the Sphinx than that its builders came from Atlantis, but the exact facts are hard to establish – much about the Sphinx remains a riddle.

## Reclaiming the Sphinx

Khafre was not the last Egyptian king to work on the Sphinx. It was definitely renovated some time in the fourteenth century BC. By then the temple complex at Giza had been abandoned and the encroaching desert had buried the Sphinx up to its neck. A pharaoh called Thutmose IV (r. 1400–1390 BC) felt inspired by the sun god Ra to restore the Sphinx, which he felt was related to 'Horus of the Horizon'. We know this because Thutmose left an inscription, the *Dream Stela*. This describes how his rescue of the Sphinx gave him the legitimacy to claim (in fact usurp) the throne.

By the time the rising civilizations of the Mediterranean became aware of Egypt the Sphinx had long been reinstated as one of the most revered objects in Giza. It is probable that other representations of the Sphinx, including its appearance in the Greek myth of Oedipus, are based on accounts from travellers who had seen the original at first hand. In Roman times the Giza Sphinx was a popular tourist destination. Notable visitors included the emperors Nero and Septimius Severus.

In the post-Roman era the Sphinx began once more submerging into the desert sand. Even then the Sphinx remained revered. By one account, in the fourteenth century a local Muslim ruler became incensed when he found that locals were making sacrifices to the Sphinx in the hope of better harvests. He had stonemasons chisel off the Sphinx's nose to show that the statue, and whatever power it represented, was impotent to prevent (nearly literal) defacement. The story may be apocryphal, but there is no doubt that the nose was at some point indeed deliberately chiselled off – and not removed by a cannonball in the Napoleonic wars as is sometimes claimed.

In fact Napoleon had a deep respect for all matters Egyptian and his scientists were the first to conduct a methodical study of the Sphinx. These investigations continue, still producing more questions than answers. Through it all, the Sphinx broods over the Nile as it has done for thousands of years, enigmatic and unknowable.

*c.* 4500 BC – *c.* 2500 BC

# The Hal Saflieni Hypogeum

## Ancient Tunnels

*One of the world's best preserved prehistoric sites*

***The Smithsonian Magazine***

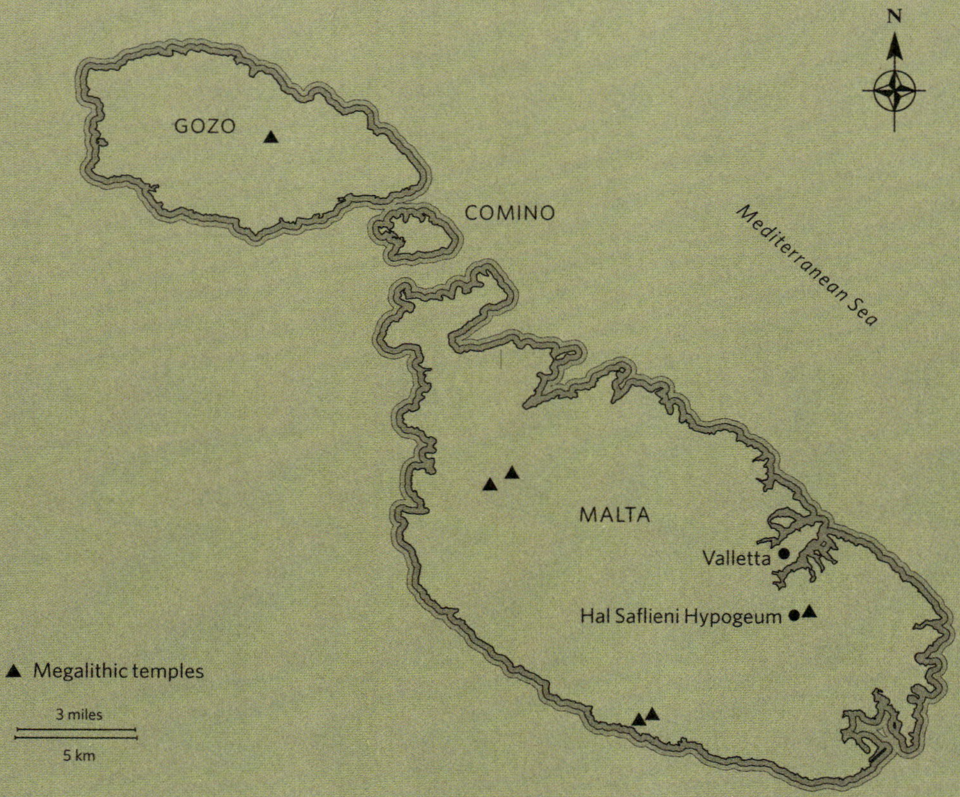

Not many people would want to live above a mass grave that contains over five thousand corpses. Nor, since these graves are thousands of years old and of immense archaeological value, is it likely that a developer would be allowed to build on the site in the first place. Therefore, it seems that when builders of a housing development at Hal Saflieni in Malta in 1902 accidentally broke through into an ancient underground burial site, they decided that their best course was to pretend that they had never discovered it.

Even in the early twentieth century such lax standards were unacceptable, and it was not long before word of the discovery got out. The authorities officially took possession of the site in 1903. By then all traces of the above-ground structures – which were vanishingly scarce in the first place – had been obliterated to make room for the modern houses.

To add to the destruction some of the first excavators cheerfully carted away ancient remains and skeletons as they dug down to get to the 'good stuff'. (Some of the more interesting skulls ended up in a nearby museum.) In short, a sacred ancient site which had got through the previous millennia relatively unscathed barely survived its first contact with the modern world.

## Ancient burials

Civilization on Malta was ancient long before the first scruffy farmers settled on the seven hills of Rome or the first temples

This ancient head with most of the features obscured by time is believed to depict either an ancient deity or one of the mysterious early inhabitants of Malta.

arose on the Acropolis of Athens. In fact, until the discovery of the megaliths at Göbekli Tepe, the ancient temples of Malta were considered the oldest free-standing human structures on Earth.

The Hypogeum at Hal Saflieni was built in three stages, which reflect the different phases of the millennia of civilization on the island. The first peoples arrived some 7,500 years ago, and immediately began clearing the conifer forests which originally covered the island. Several centuries later they started work on the Hypogeum. (*Hypogeum* is an old Greek word used to describe any underground temple or tomb.) The site was probably chosen because water had already eroded the soft limestone into natural caves that could be enlarged by crude tools of obsidian or antler horn.

There are five burial chambers, in which the earliest burials took place, and a large 'courtyard' where burial rites and processions either began or ended. For centuries thereafter the local people interred their dead in the Hypogeum, which accumulated corpses by the thousand, along with a mass of artefacts deposited as grave goods. The area that could be worked with Stone Age tools was very limited – about 500 square metres (5,380 square feet). So when the later inhabitants of the island wanted to enlarge the site the only way they could go was down. Fortunately they did not have to go very far, because some of the original chambers and tunnels were not much more than a metre from the surface.

## The chambers of the middle level

Thus, some 5,300 years ago, the most impressive features of the Hypogeum were constructed. These were painfully chiselled out of the rock by workers in the light of tallow lamps and rush torches until a series of cleverly constructed light wells brought in natural daylight from above. In fact one of the main chambers has the light well carefully situated so that at the winter solstice the sun would shine directly on to the main façade. This chamber is the so-called 'Holy of Holies', the only part of the Hypogeum where no human remains have been discovered.

Most spectacular is the Oracle Room – a chamber with the sides and ceiling designed to artfully distort and amplify sounds so that chants, songs and music would be projected powerfully through the entire underground structure. It also, as modern investigation has confirmed, lent an otherworldly resonance to priestly utterances.

The main circular chamber is several metres across with a number of entrances leading to the surface and to other rooms, with other, blind entrances apparently added just for the sake of symmetry.

The 'Sleeping Lady' of the Hypogeum has been variously interpreted as being dead, asleep or in a trance. She is almost certainly a mother goddess and if her pose indicates death, her form implies fertility and renewal.

One of the most fascinating artefacts found here is the enigmatic 'Sleeping Lady'. This is a terracotta figure of a woman with large hips lying on a pallet in a natural sleeping position. A wonderful work of art in its own right which can stand comparison with any modern sculpture, this figure has been at the centre of considerable academic debate. Does the 'sleep' represent a body awaiting restoration in the afterlife? Is it a fertility goddess, or other divinity? Or is it just a great work of decorative art?

Chequerboard patterns in black and white and spirals in red ochre decorate the walls – the only prehistoric paintings found on Malta. They have survived because the humidity of the enclosed space prevented the limestone from flaking and so destroying the paintings, as is assumed to have happened with the formerly painted remains of this ancient culture that are above ground. These surviving decorations are most prominent in the room alongside the Oracle Room where the sloping walls carry a rich array of geometric patterns.

## The third level

In later centuries the site was enlarged again. To get below the middle level the builders had to tunnel some 10 metres (33 feet) below the surface. It seems that the space here was intended to restore the Hypogeum to its original function as a burial place, even as the middle level continued to be used for religious purposes. One of the keenest wishes of modern Maltese anthropologists and archaeologists is to discover exactly what rites were performed in these ancient spaces and what gods were worshipped.

However, around 2350 BC this worship stopped. The population of the island changed again as new peoples arrived with new ideas and bronze tools. Some of these bronze tools were weapons vastly superior to anything the islanders could muster, and within a short time the megalithic culture of the earlier inhabitants had been replaced by the newcomers. Now abandoned, the Hal Saflieni Hypogeum began its long slumber through the centuries.

## Preserving the distant past

The twenty-first century is trying hard to undo some of the damage of the previous century, or at least to prevent any further deterioration. An international effort to preserve the site limits visitors to eighty per day, and a system of carefully installed ducts takes away the carbon dioxide from their exhalations. The same ducts also keep the humidity at the precise level needed to preserve the paintings. Visitors are firmly prevented from touching the walls, especially the paintings, as the oil on their skin would damage the fragile chemical composition of the surface. Even so, just the installation of artificial light to allow visitors to see their way around has encouraged the growth of fungi and micro-organisms which have to be controlled to prevent them from damaging the stonework.

Protecting the site from the modern era while still allowing visitors to marvel at the work of our ancient ancestors led to the Hypogeum being closed for almost a decade starting in 1991. Today many more people want to see the sacred remains than there is space to show them safely. Unless they have booked months in advance, most visitors will have to be content with the very comprehensive virtual tour which the authorities have arranged by way of compensation.

The ancient structure today combines the wonders of ancient architecture and the marvels of the modern technology required to preserve it.

PART TWO

# The Early Classical Era: Rationality and Belief

## New gods for a new era

As the Mediterranean world recovered from the anarchy that followed the disastrous end of the Bronze Age around 1200 BC, a new religious order slowly emerged from the chaos. In the east the Hebrews and Persians developed monotheistic religions based upon incorporeal deities, while the peoples of the west doubled down on polytheism, not only giving their gods physical form but depicting their bodies in (often beautiful) statuary.

Religion as it emerged from the Archaic period was both more codified and more deeply integrated into the formal civic life of the community. Because religion was very much a civic affair, the focus was on citizen participation in properly performed rituals (orthopraxy) rather than in belief in the formal strictures of a particular form of worship (orthodoxy). Religion was the focal point of civic identity. Almost every aspect of public life, from warfare to agriculture to politics, had a religious dimension that was not only unique to each particular community but a major factor in how that community defined itself. Indeed, some cities, such as Aphrodisias and Poseidonia, even named themselves after their patron deity. The best recorded example of how the rites were centred about the patron deity and deeply integrated into the civic life of the city is Athens, where the goddess' temple, the Parthenon, played a central role.

While some natural locations retained their sacred status, the new focus of religious life was the temple – a building that was considered the literal home of the god to whom it was dedicated. These temples were focal points of civic pride and massive resources were poured into making them as impressive and beautiful as their constructors could manage. This was done with huge success, as buildings such as the Parthenon of Athens and the Ephesian temple of Artemis demonstrate. Even further west, Greek cities from Sicily to Spain demonstrated their vast ambition by building impressive temples such as those dedicated to Hera at Paestum in central Italy.

## Intellectual inquiry

Yet in the midst of this religious flowering, for the first time in the human record, tension developed between myth-based religious belief and intellectual inquiry. Philosophers such as Pythagoras and Thales of Miletus began exploring exactly how the gods influenced the physical world, while Athenian playwrights such as Aeschylus and Euripides used religious themes which were in fact explorations of the human condition – explorations so perceptive and powerful that these plays are still regularly performed today. Nevertheless, even these early intellectual inquiries were embedded in a religious context. For example, the plays of Aeschylus and Euripides were performed at the Dionysia, an Athenian festival sacred to the wine-god Dionysus.

Religion in this period was far from a static, unchanging system of belief. Gods fought for their very existence. In Italy we see traditional gods such as Consus and Bellona gradually being replaced by the deities of the Classical pantheon – the gods of Olympus and the myriad minor divinities who accompanied them. Indeed, the ancient tales of the early wars of the Olympian gods against the Titans might be mythic reflections of the change in worship from gods such as Cronos to new divinities originating from abroad – such as Cretan Zeus.

As had happened in previous eras, religion was a shared human experience. Greek and Levantine religion was deeply influenced by the beliefs of the peoples of Egypt, Anatolia and Mesopotamia. In turn Greek and Phoenician traders carried their belief systems along with their merchandise to places as far afield as Iberia and Germany.

## Gods for a new era

Modern researchers are piecing together the details of worship in the Late Bronze Age even as they piece together the fragments of ceramic and copper upon which inscriptions were written. The Archaic Greek language called Linear B is now pretty much understood, even though its predecessor Linear A remains largely a mystery.

However, we know enough to see that at the start of the Classical era some gods were repurposed for a changed world. Poseidon, formerly a god of livestock, especially bulls and horses, became a god of the sea; Athena, formerly adviser to kings, became a more generalized goddess of wisdom, and in the process seems to have acquired her name from the city of which she was patron. The older form of the goddess, Menrva, survived in other cultures such as Rome, where she became Minerva. In Greece the Archaic god Paean changed his name to Apollo and took on additional duties such as becoming the god of prophecy at Delphi, where he seems to have replaced the snake-god Python (a hostile takeover reflected in contemporary Greek myth).

Where new gods were required, these were imported, most notably Dionysus, who muscled his way into becoming one of the twelve gods of the Olympian pantheon. With the new gods came new forms of worship. While some sacred places remained outdoor natural features, such as at the oracular grove at Dodona, or the sacred Hippocrene spring at Mount Helicon (home of the Muses), temples became central to worship. The size and grandeur of such temples became a matter of civic pride and competition between rival cities. Also, because temple design created very secure buildings, these structures quickly acquired the mundane task of storing valuables and often acted as the city treasury.

# *c.* 1000 BC – *c.* AD 325
# **Mount Helicon**
## Mountain of the Muses

*Let us begin our song on the great and holy Mount Helicon, where the Muses dance on their dainty feet beside the spring waters and the Altar of Zeus. And when they have bathed their tender bodies in the Permessus or the Hippocrene let their lovely dances be yet more vigorous on the highest reaches of Helicon.*
Hesiod, *Theogony* 1.1

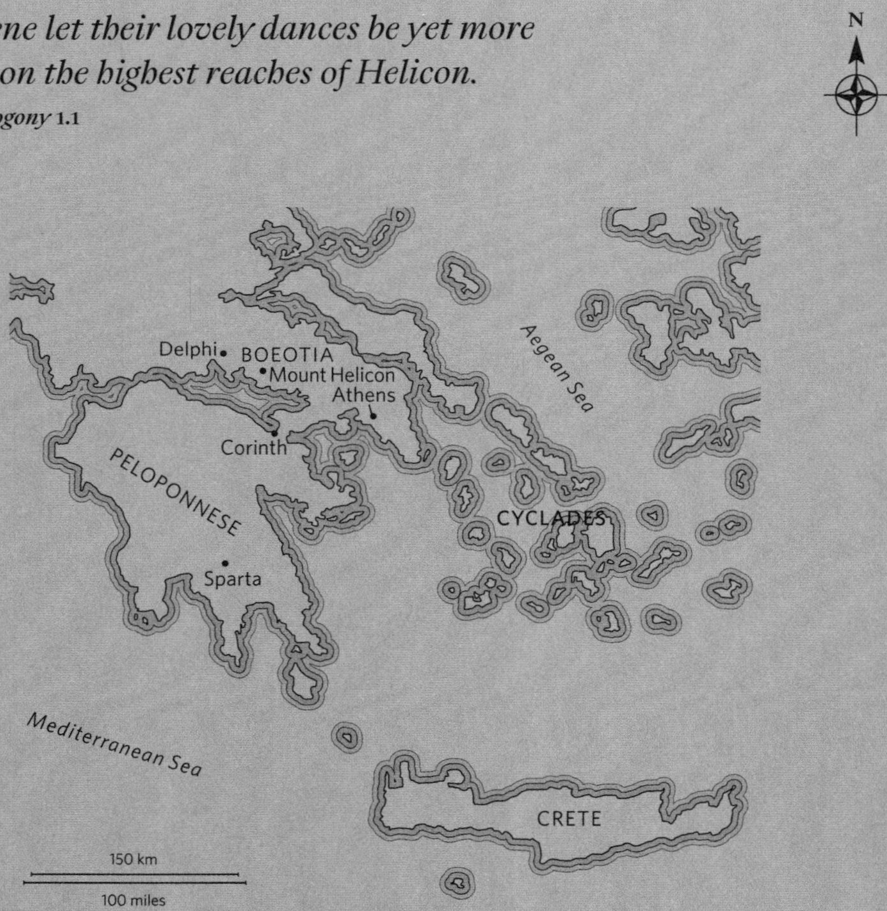

The *Theogony* of Hesiod (a poem describing the beginnings and family trees of the Greek gods) begins with an ode to the sacred mountain of Helicon. That is no surprise, for Hesiod, one of the first great Greek poets, lived at the foot of that mountain in the little town of Ascra. Hesiod, who wrote some time around 700 BC, seems to have disliked Ascra as much as he revered Helicon, referring to Ascra as 'horrible in winter, nasty in summer and never good' (*Works and Days*, 640). Hesiod toughed it out because, as well as being a poet, he was a farmer and the slopes of Mount Helicon were famously fertile.

## The sacred mountain

Mount Helicon is part of the Parnassus range and lies about 10 kilometres (6 miles) from the coast in Boeotia. Helicon is by no means the largest of the mountains in this range, but the wet winds blowing in from the Gulf of Corinth dump their moisture on its slopes. Indeed, 'of all the mountains in Greece none is more fertile than Helicon or produces a greater abundance of trees and bushes.

*Apollo and the Muses on Mount Helicon*, by the seventeenth-century artist Claude Lorrain, now in the Museum of Fine Arts, Boston.

Melpomene, the Muse of Tragedy. This is one of several very similar statues showing the Muse in a similar pose. She holds the mask of a tragic actor in one arm while in the other hand she carries the club of Hercules.

Several [of these plants] are useful in countering snakebite and none are themselves poisonous'. So remarks the Roman writer Pausanias in his *Guide to Greece* (9.28), a text written in the second century AD. By then (as Hesiod would have been pleased to know) Ascra had been wiped off the map, with only a single lonely tower to mark where the settlement once stood.

Hesiod himself was still commemorated, though. Pausanias notes that a statue of him stood on Helicon, not far from the banks of the Permessus, the little river of which the poet sang. The patron deity of the river was a god of the same name, though (somewhat confusingly) the river itself was sacred to Apollo. The site was once home to sweet-spoken Eupheme, the nymph from whose name is derived the modern host of 'euphemisms'.

## The Muses

Eupheme had the very important job of nursemaid to nine daughters of Zeus who were raised on Helicon. These daughters were Calliope, Clio, Euterpe, Erato, Melpomene, Polyhymnia, Terpsichore, Thalia and Urania. Collectively known as the Muses, the nine were the goddesses of the performing arts. Their mother was Mnemosyne, the personification of memory. This is appropriate, as it was through song, dance, poetry and history (originally read aloud to an audience) that the Greeks preserved their cultural memory. Today, of course, cultural memory is stored in temples to the Muses known as 'museums'.

The Muses lived mostly on the eastern slopes of Helicon and were often visited there by Apollo, who, as god of the civilized arts, had much in common with the nine. Very early in human history the Pierides, nine daughters of one of the first men, challenged the Muses to a contest in song. Their merely human efforts were made insignificant by the collective voices of the Muses. Indeed, so inspiring were the Muses that, according to the ancient writer Antoninus Liberalis, 'The stars stood still, the rivers ceased to flow and the stony mass of Mount Helicon itself began to rise to the heavens' (*Metamorphoses* 9).

What would have happened next to Mount Helicon is unknown, but probably nothing good as mountains are not naturally aerodynamic. Fortunately the god Poseidon noted the developing problem. As well as being lord of the sea, Poseidon was also a horse-god. As such he had command of the greatest of his equine subjects (and incidentally his child) the winged horse Pegasus. Pegasus flew (literally) to Helicon and brought the mountain down

to earth with a stamp of his hoof. So energetic was this stamp that a spring burst out from the imprint of his hoof – a spring thereafter known through the antique era as the Hippocrene. The Pierides, meanwhile, paid for their temerity in challenging the goddesses by being transformed into birds. Anyone who today hears the pigeon, the jay or the goldfinch can judge for themselves the quality of their song.

A sixteenth-century medallion showing Pegasus stamping down a surging Mount Helicon, creating the Hippocrene spring in the process.

### Prophets and thespians

Another denizen of Mount Helicon was Chariclo, a daughter of Apollo. She was a friend of the goddess Athena, who regularly visited the mountain. From one such visit, myth says that the legendary soothsayer Tiresias gained his power. Tiresias was the son of Chariclo and one day he accidentally came across his mother and Athena bathing in the Aganippe (another of the sacred springs on the mountain). To prevent him seeing her nakedness Athena clapped her hands over the eyes of Tiresias, and so inadvertently blinded him. It is a rule of mythology that the Greek gods cannot undo their actions. But they could mitigate them, and Athena did this by granting Tiresias the power of prophecy.

Given the proximity of Mount Helicon and the Muses, it is unsurprising that the nearby town of Thespis gave the world the invention of the theatre (which is why actors today are still sometimes referred to as 'thespians'). It was the original Thespians who eradicated Ascra, the home town of Hesiod, in some now-forgotten dispute. They partly made up for this by organizing the five-yearly Mouseia, a famed festival of the arts held on the slopes of Mount Helicon which began at least as early as the third century BC.

As Pausanias noted, Helicon was often visited in the Classical era, not least because the waters of its sacred springs were meant to bestow the gift of poetry. The area became crowded with statues – more than any other place in Boeotia, says Pausanias. At the end of the Classical period most of these statues were commandeered by the emperor Constantine the Great (r. AD 306–337) and carted away as ornaments for his new city of Constantinople (present-day Istanbul).

## Later Helicon

Some time in the tenth century AD Mount Helicon regained some of its sacred aura with the foundation of the monastery of Hosios

The monastery of Hosios Loukas. Situated on the slopes of Mount Helicon, the monastery has preserved the concept of the sacred mountain in a different context.

Loukas, which still stands today in a dramatically scenic setting. Meanwhile the legend of the Muses of the mountain lived on, with the Hippocrene often used as a metaphor for poetic inspiration. The nineteenth-century poet John Keats famously wrote in his 'Ode to a Nightingale' (stanza II): 'O for a beaker full of the warm South, / Full of the true, the blushful Hippocrene...'

Visitors to the mountain can sample a beaker for themselves, for the Hippocrene is generally believed to be still producing fine water under its modern name of the Makarioitissa spring. This and Mount Helicon can be reached by intrepid travellers today by taking a bus to the village of Aghia Anna and hiking uphill from there.

# *c.* 3500 BC – AD 393

# The Oracle at Dodona

## Voices in the Trees

*There is a land of the Hellenes with grasses and lush meadows abundant with flocks and shambling cattle....Zeus so loved it that he appointed there his oracle...and whosoever goes to that place bearing auspicious gifts may ask questions of the deathless god.*

**Hesiod, *Catalogue of Women* Fr. 97**

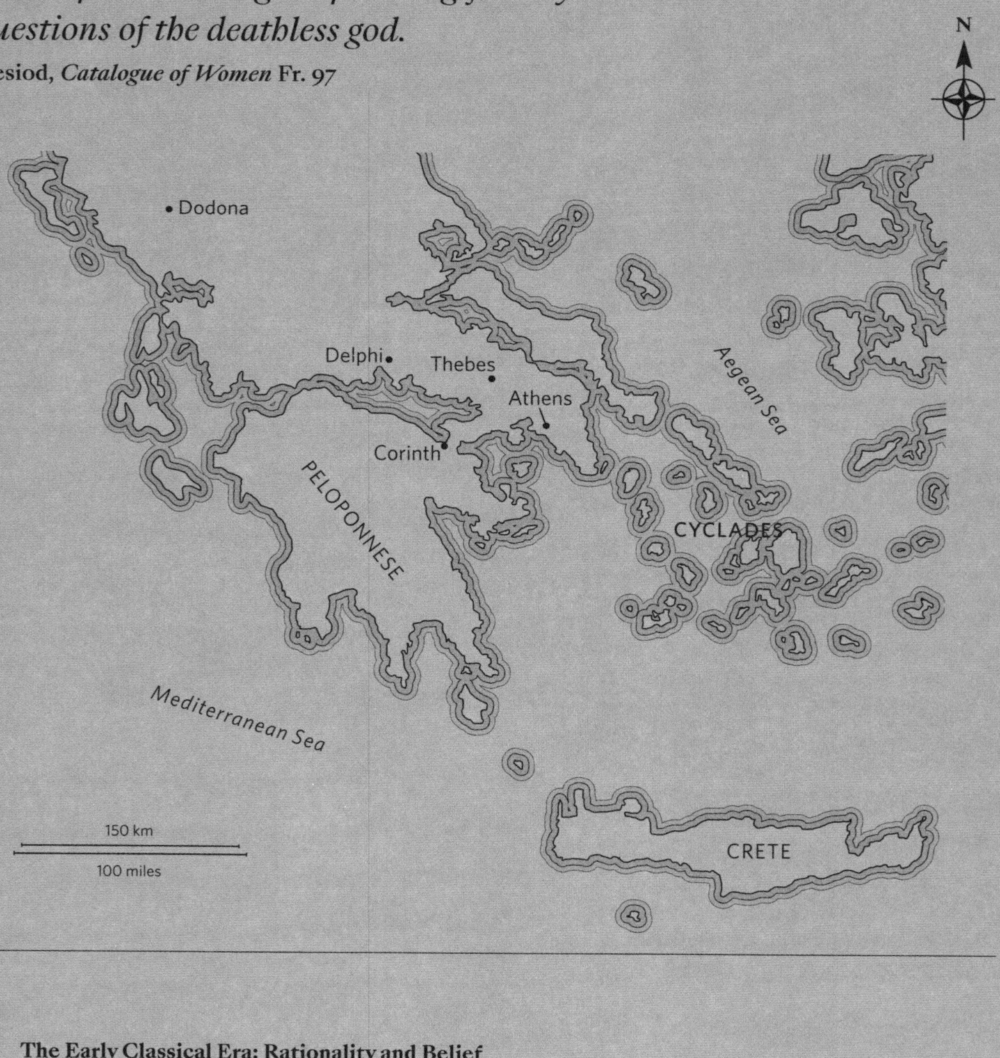

When the poet Hesiod wrote of Dodona twenty-eight hundred years ago, the oracle there was already ancient. The oldest offerings found at the site date back to six hundred years before Hesiod, but the place was almost certainly sacred even before then. In fact the ancient Greeks believed that Dodona was established by Deucalion and Pyrrha, the two proto-humans who restarted the human race after Zeus decided to wipe it out with a great flood.

The sacred oak grove of Dodona is located in Epirus, in the northwest of modern Greece – which many Greeks of the Classical era did not regard as being Greek at all. Yet it was here, according to the authority of Aristotle, who was himself drawing on sources already ancient, that the race of Hellenes (that is, the Greeks) originated.

## The great goddess

Before the Hellenes the area was inhabited by an early people, called the Pelasgians. Not much is known of this mythical folk, but they may be associated with the prehistoric people whom some twenty-first-century scholars believe worshipped an earth-mother divinity

A bronze statue of Zeus holding his primary weapon, the thunderbolt, in his right hand. The eagle, his sacred companion, often symbolizes the power of the lightning.

A terracotta statue of a goddess used as a votive offering. Such statues have been found at several Greek religious sites, showing the goddess in a *polos* headdress and long flowing gown.

at this location. Indeed, even in Classical times Zeus shared the sacred site at Dodona with a goddess. Her name is given as Dione, which is not particularly helpful as this simply translates as 'the great goddess'. To differentiate her from the other great goddesses of ancient Greece, the Dione at Dodona was referred to as Dione Naïa.

For the Classical Greeks Dione was one of the Titans, a race of beings from the primordial past who also counted Zeus among their number. Dione's sisters were associated with other oracular sites in the ancient world, but Dione arguably had the best location – a pleasant oak grove on the eastern slopes of Mount Tomaros overlooking the lush countryside of Thesprotia.

It is uncertain at what point Zeus, king of the gods, also took up residence, but it was certainly early in Greek history, for characters in Homer's *Iliad* and *Odyssey* already knew he was there. Beneath the walls of Troy the hero Achilles prayed at the funeral pyre of his friend Patroclus, addressing 'Lord Zeus, god of the Pelasgians who far away rules over winter-bound Dodona where your soothsayers dwell, with their feet unwashed and their beds made upon the ground' (Homer, *Iliad* 16.233–35).

## Talking trees and barefoot priests

These priests at Dodona were called the Selli, and even in later years they still went barefoot with unwashed feet, in order to be closer to the earth of the sacred grove, on the ground of which they also slept. They shared the grove with priestesses, probably of Dione, who were called the Peleiades ('doves'). The latter were three in number and usually elderly at the time of their appointment.

In his *Phaedrus*, Plato (*c*. 429–347 BC) has the philosopher Socrates remarking wryly to the young men with him:

> *The first prophesies were uttered at the sacred grove of Zeus at Dodona. The people of that time, not being as wise as you young people consider yourselves today, were simple folk who were prepared to listen even to an oak or a rock, provided only that it spoke the truth.*
>
> (*Phaedrus* I. 275b)

The 'listening' described by Plato was just that. Those wishing to understand the future or the will of the god took themselves to Dodona. There, after making a suitable offering and being taken through preparatory rites by the priests, worshippers came to the sacred grove to hear from Zeus himself. The god spoke to

A seventeenth-century engraving showing rituals around a sacred oak at Dodona. The Enlightenment saw a (not always well-informed) resurgence of interest in the Classical era.

these seekers after truth through the breeze blowing through the leaves. While all the oaks in the grove were sacred, the voice of Zeus could be heard best from one particular oak. Exactly what distinguished this tree is uncertain, but it may be that the god's voice was amplified by wind-chimes placed in the branches, or by breezes blowing over the mouths of cauldrons placed about the tree. However, while archaeologists have found pottery, tools, votive offerings and prayers inscribed on lead tablets, no such acoustic enhancements have been found. As Plato wrote, perhaps the simple whisper of the wind in the branches was all that pilgrims required.

It was to here that Odysseus came as he neared the end of his decade of wandering the seas on his long voyage after the fall of

A lead tablet (*lamella*) from Dodona, now in the Archaeological Museum of Ioannina. Hermon asks to which god he should pray to have useful offspring by his wife Kretaia.

Troy. 'He had gone to Dodona to hear the will of Zeus from the god's high-crested oak, there to learn how, after so long an absence, he best should return to his beloved homeland – and if this should be done openly or in secret' (Homer, *Odyssey* 19.300).

Another oak from the grove was quite capable of speaking for itself. This was the tree taken – by special dispensation – from the grove to form the prow of the good ship *Argo*, with which Jason and his heroes set sail in their search for the Golden Fleece. This outspoken item frequently gave its opinion as to how the voyage was going and critiqued the performance of the heroes.

## Sacred tourism

Relics discovered at the site by modern archaeologists include bronze tripods, pre-Iron Age weaponry and jewelry dated to the Mycenaean era (around 1300 BC). The first inscriptions recovered from Dodona date only to around 550 BC. This is not surprising because until then there were no buildings for words to be inscribed upon. It was only as Dodona became a major religious centre for visitors from all over the far-flung Greek world that the first temple, the Hiera Okia ('Sacred House'), was added. Thereafter they sprouted like mushrooms, so that by 300 BC Dodona boasted temples to Zeus, Dione, Aphrodite and Hercules plus shrines to numerous other deities.

Dodona reached its apogee in the third century BC under the rule of King Pyrrhus of Epirus (319–272 BC) – he who won those 'Pyrrhic victories' over the Romans. He established a festival to Dione Naïa, which included athletic events and drama contests, the latter staged in a purpose-built theatre which was one of the largest in Greece.

## Destruction

Sadly, greater political significance carried risk. By way of making a statement to the Epirots, the rival Aetolian people sacked the site in 219 BC. The buildings were carefully restored, only for the Romans to destroy them again in 167 BC as they rampaged through Epirus during the Macedonian wars. However, the Romans considered themselves a gods-fearing people and the site remained sacred through the *Pax Romana*, with the Naïa festival, though diminished, still held regularly. Emperors from Augustus to Justinian dropped by when they visited Greece.

This ended with the reign of the Christian emperors, for in AD 393 Theodosius sent his men to burn down the sacred grove and uproot the oak of Zeus. In the fifth century a Christian basilica was placed there instead. Thereafter Dodona slumbered in obscurity until Classically minded researchers relocated the site in the early twentieth century and archaeologists arrived to dig for its treasures. Most of these treasures can now be seen in the National Archaeological Museum of Athens, though some are in the Archaeological Museum of Ioannina, the nearest modern town.

The oak trees have grown back and even today one can come across visitors who have propped their backpacks against a tree, shed their footwear and lie listening for voices in the leaves.

*c.* 1400 BC – AD 390

# The Telesterion at Eleusis

## Secrets Never to be Revealed

*We celebrated what is rightly called the most blessed of Mysteries. As initiates we beheld that which was perfect and simple...serene apparitions bathed in the pure light. Visions in which beauty shone in brilliance.*

Plato, *Phaedrus* 250c

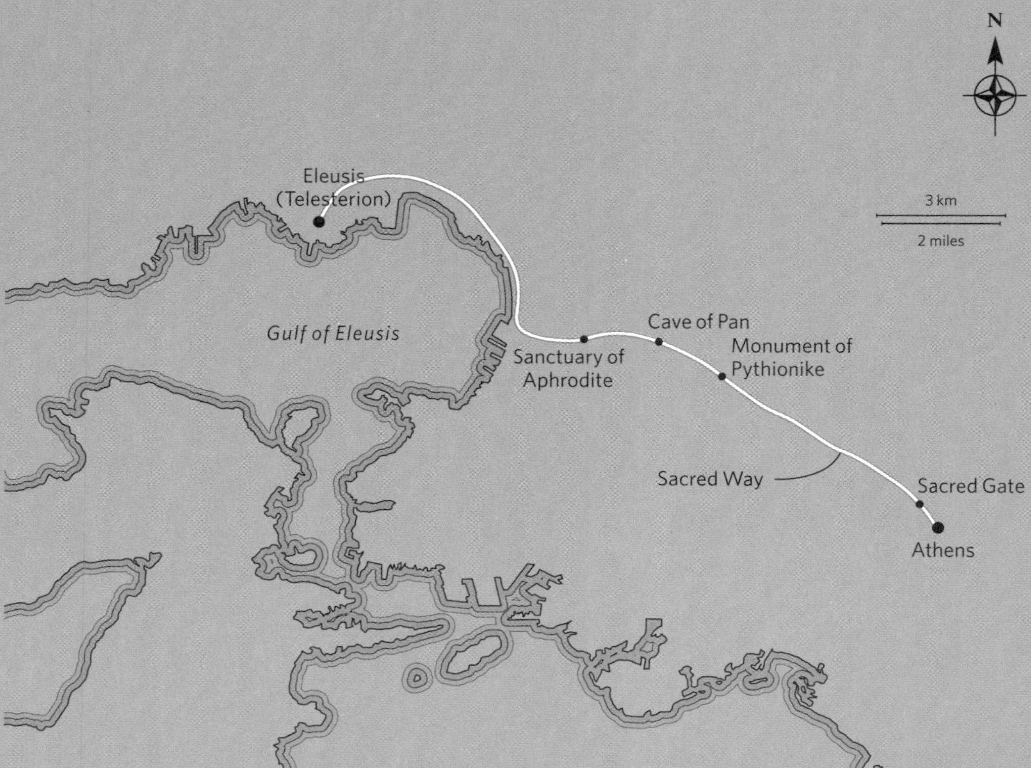

The place where Plato – along with many other great names of the ancient world, including Plutarch, Cicero and the Roman emperor Marcus Aurelius – underwent a sublime and deeply moving religious experience was the Telesterion, 'the Place of Fulfilment', in Eleusis beside the waters of the Saronic Gulf outside Athens.

## The queen of Hades – and her mother

Eleusis was the centre of the cult of the goddess Demeter and her daughter Persephone. The Mysteries of Eleusis were rituals in honour of these deities. The sacred rites were performed twice a year and reached their climax at the Telesterion at Eleusis. In this large hall, those waiting to be initiated into the Mysteries gathered after a 22.5-kilometre (14-mile) procession from Athens, there to sit for an all-night vigil as they beheld rites sacred to the corn goddess and her daughter. That daughter, Persephone, had been kidnapped by Hades to be his queen in the Underworld. Yet every year she returned to her mother, who celebrated her daughter's return by restoring life and fertility to the world at the start of a new season, a return celebrated with the rites at Eleusis.

These sacred rites were celebrated at the Telesterion for over a thousand years. Their performance may have originated as a private

A nineteenth-century reimagining of how the Telesterion may have looked. The picture is more evocative than accurate, though the colonnaded porch with twelve Doric columns is portrayed exactly.

The Thesmophoria was a women-only festival dedicated to Demeter and Persephone, here depicted by Francis Davis Millet in the late nineteenth century in a painting today in the Brigham Young University Museum of Art.

family function in Mycenaean times. Modern excavations have revealed that the Classical-era Telesterion was built over an even more ancient private dwelling.

## Priestly families

The most sacred part of the Telesterion was the *anaktoron*, a place which only certain priests were allowed to enter. The architecture of later versions of the Telesterion (the hall was rebuilt several times) was somewhat skewed to centre on this *anaktoron*, which suggests that at least the location, and possibly the form, of this sacred structure remained the same through the ages. Beside the *anaktoron* was a raised podium for the hierophant, the priest who celebrated the Mysteries.

Another sign of the antiquity of the rites was that every generation of priests came from three ancient families who traced their origins to Erechtheus, the legendary king of Athens. There were the 'heralds' of the Ceryces clan and the Philleides family who supplied the torch-bearers and the Telesterion's Priestess of Demeter. The Hiera, the high priest who exhibited the sacred objects, was from the family of the Eumolpidae.

## The mysterious Mysteries

There were actually two celebrations of the Mysteries. The celebration of the 'Small Mysteries' took place in Anthesterion (the first month of spring). The actual nature of that celebration within the Telesterion has been the subject of speculation for thousands of years (they are called 'Mysteries' for a reason). It is known that the rite had three parts – 'things said, things done and things shown'. However, these 'things' were *aporrheta*, 'matters never to be disclosed'. The Athenians were generally fairly relaxed about blasphemy, believing that offended gods were perfectly capable of doing their own smiting. But anyone who so much as hinted as to what went on inside the Telesterion was promptly executed.

Admission was open to all, men and women, slaves and free men. The only exclusions were those contaminated by the blood-guilt of an unexpiated killing and those whose Greek was too poor for them to understand what was going on. Those who had previously been initiated were welcome to attend on further occasions, but most preferred their original initiation to take place at the 'Great Mysteries' which were held six months after the Small Mysteries.

Thus the rituals of the Great Mysteries were celebrated at the start of autumn. Once the Athenian state had taken over the management of the Mysteries in the Classical era, this took the form of a ten-day festival. The climax began with a procession which started at the Eleusinion, a temple at the foot of the Acropolis. From there celebrants walked the 23 kilometres (14 miles) along the Sacred Way, crossing the plain of Thria, to arrive at the precinct at Eleusis, where they immediately consumed a drink made from barley and *Mentha pulegium* (pennyroyal) to prepare them for a night-long vigil in the Telesterion.

As with all Greek religion, the celebration of the Mysteries was a communal experience. The Telesterion could hold around three thousand people, and being part of so large a group certainly would have heightened the experience. Also, the Telesterion itself was designed to amplify the awe of the crowd. There was a forest of columns that faded into darkness at the edge of the lamplight, making shadowy aisles down which the torch-bearers and priests could approach. The air was fragrant with incense and (modern researchers have speculated) smoke from herbs with a psychotropic effect.

Whatever those in the Telesterion experienced, it had a profound effect. 'These mysteries are the means by which crude barbarians become smoothed and polished into civilized beings,' remarked Cicero. 'Initiations they truly are, because through them we are introduced to a love of wisdom and learn not only how to live properly, but to die with hope' (*De legibus* 2.36). These principles were inculcated into initiates not only by the intense, emotional overnight experience in the Telesterion but in a series of further rituals (the *mystes*) over the final three days of the festival.

## An international rite

As the celebration of the Mysteries grew from a family affair to an event of international significance, the site attracted enemies. In 480 BC, after their victory at Thermopylae, the Persians went out of their way to destroy the Telesterion (they were somewhat bitter about the Athenians having earlier done the same to their sacred sites in Sardis).

In the following decades the Telesterion was rebuilt on a grander scale and then on a grander scale again in the second century AD, when the building was again destroyed, this time during a raid by Sarmatian barbarians. The Roman emperor Marcus Aurelius (r. AD 161–80) took a personal interest in the reconstruction and was rewarded by being the only non-hierophant ever to be allowed to enter the *anaktoron*.

The Mysteries continued to be celebrated at the Telesterion until they were banned in AD 390 by a decree of the Christian Roman emperor Theodosius. It is possible, though, that furtive celebrations continued for another five years until the building was destroyed by soldiers of the Visigothic general Alaric (who went on to sack Rome fifteen years later). Thereafter the ruins of the Telesterion were left to moulder into the soil.

---

## The unknowable past

Interest in the remains of the Telesterion revived in the nineteenth century. By this time the area of Eleusis was flourishing as an industrial suburb of Athens. The Greek Archaeological Society, keen to preserve the nation's heritage, began excavations at the site. These have continued with the use of ever more sophisticated technology up to the present day. These explorations have told us much about the structure of the Telesterion in its various forms over the ages. However, we still know almost nothing of the arcane rituals that went on within.

The 'Ninnion' tablet, a red clay tablet discovered at Eleusis in 1895. It is the only known ancient depiction of the rites celebrated there.

# *c.* 1400 BC – AD 1451

# The Tomb of Achilles

## A Buried Myth

*That morning, Achilles, we collected your bleached bones* [and mixed them] *with perfumes and undiluted wine....Glorious Achilles, your white bones are interred there... on a headland beside the wide waters of the Hellespont.*

Homer, *Odyssey* 24.72–84

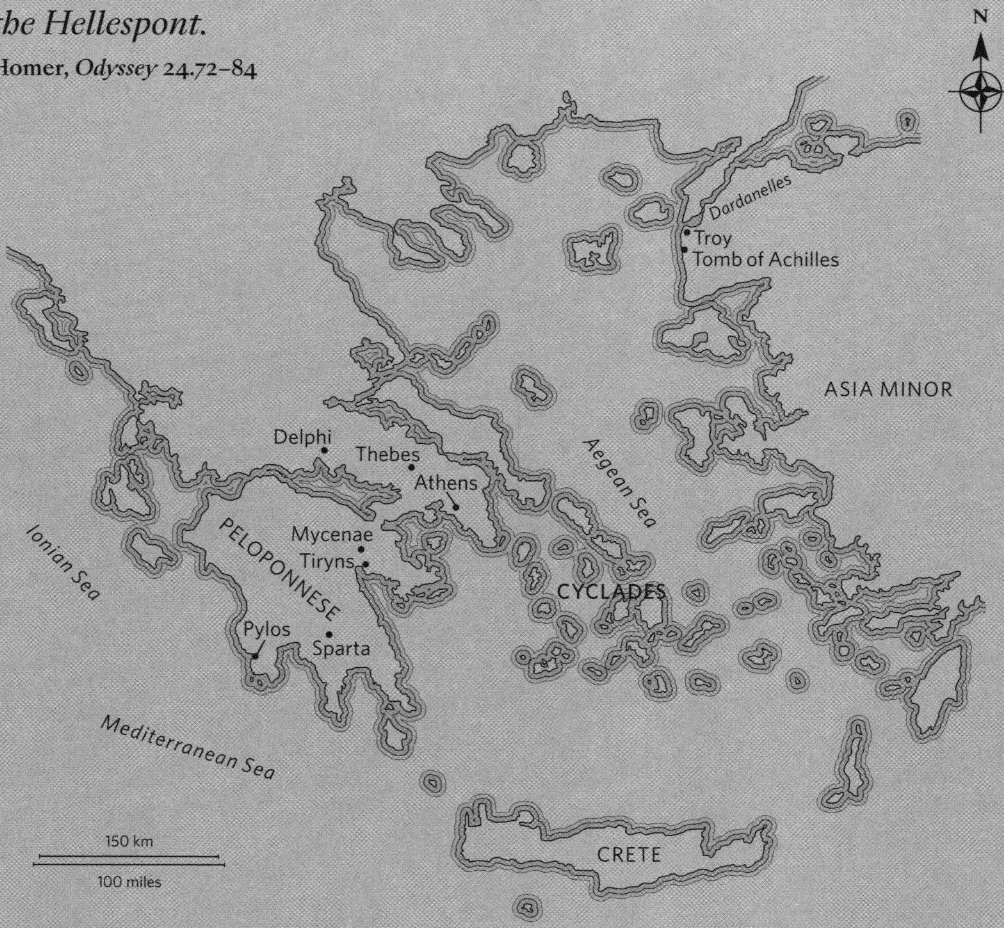

For centuries the stories in Homer's *Iliad* and *Odyssey* were regarded as pure fiction. Then a single-minded, and unfortunately rather unscientific, nineteenth-century archaeologist called Heinrich Schliemann set about finding the lost city of Troy. In fact, if one started with the premise that Troy was a real place rather than an invented one, the city turned out to be reasonably easy to locate, because Homer provided geographical detail so precise that he still surprises and delights archaeologists today.

Troy, Homer informed his listeners, lay on the Asian side of the Hellespont close to Mount Ida near the river Scamander. This, together with various other clues, led Schliemann to a mound which the locals called Hisarlık. While Schliemann's approach to archaeology resembled that of a bull in a china shop, the buried city which he excavated is almost certainly Troy – a discovery which required considerable rewriting of early European history.

Once Troy moved from myth to solid stone fact, some began to wonder – if Troy really did exist, might perhaps some of the characters in the *Iliad* have existed also? Was there a real Hector, a real Agamemnon, and above all a real Achilles? Homer composed his epic at least four hundred years after the events which he describes, but it is reasonably certain that his great achievement

Troy as the site appears today after extensive excavations have revealed different stages in the long life of the doomed city.

The fallen Achilles, dying from an arrow in his heel, by Filippo Albacini, 1825.

was not in literary invention but in collating pre-existing myths into superb lyric poetry.

In an oral culture, stories passed down through the generations tend to maintain a kernel of truth, not least because a well-informed audience is quick to correct any deviations from well-loved tales. Furthermore, modern archaeology has shown that the name 'Achilles' has solid roots in the Bronze Age, and indeed was relatively common in those times.

## The grave: part 1

Of all the lost heroes of the *Iliad*, Achilles should be the easiest to find, for as the passage at the start of this chapter shows, Homer has been his usual helpful self in describing the hero's resting place. In the Classical era there was a site in the northwest of present-day Turkey, an area historically known as the Troad, which was generally believed to be the location of the tomb of Achilles, and which may well have contained the remains of a Bronze Age warrior.

So well known was this grave that two hundred years or so after Homer a town was founded there, which Pliny describes: 'There was also in ancient times the town of Achilleon. This was founded close to the tomb of Achilles by the people of Mytilene' (*Natural History*, 5.33). The problem lies in Pliny's statement that the town was 'there in ancient times'. The location of the town, and therefore of Achilles' grave, already lost almost two thousand years ago, has become much harder to find in the millennia since, especially as the coastline of the Troad has changed considerably in the meantime.

Nevertheless, modern researchers reckon that there is a good chance that lost Achilleon is a settlement unearthed at Cape Burun, a headland (as specified by Homer) which juts into the sea near Besika Bay on the Hellespont. Even more encouragingly, near the ruins of the town is a cemetery, the Tepe Bisik, dating to the Mycenaean era and a large mound called Sivri Tepe, the appearance of which can be shoehorned into matching the description given by Homer.

There are, however, some severe problems with this identification. The first of these is that the Mycenaeans in the cemetery mostly appear to have died peacefully and to have got on well with the local Trojans. Also, while extensive investigation of Sivri Tepe has found signs of usage dating back to the Neolithic era, there is no helpful inscription referring to Achilles or indeed any trace at all of a Bronze Age Achaean warrior burial.

Bronze swords recovered from the site of Troy. Many are Mycenaean-style weapons attesting to the city's cultural links with the Greek world.

## The grave: part 2

If we are to seek the reason for the absence of Achilles in mythology, the answer may be found in an epic about the Trojan War which may be even older than the *Iliad*. This is the *Aethiopis*, which mainly related the travels of the hero Memnon, who came from Africa to fight by the side of the Trojans before he suffered an untimely death at the hands of Achilles.

Homer says: 'They marked off the mound [for Achilles and his comrade Patroclus], made a foundation for it about the pyre, and promptly piled earth upon it. Having heaped up this mound they returned [to their camp]' (*Iliad* 23.243ff). According to later myth the Greeks also performed a human sacrifice before they departed. The victim was Polyxena, the youngest daughter of King Priam. Legend says that she was betrothed to Achilles, so his son Neoptolemus sent her to join the dead hero in the Underworld.

Yet according to the *Aethiopis* the bones of Achilles (and Patroclus) did not remain within the tumulus. The verses of the *Aethiopis* are lost to us and what few fragments of the story we

The 'Achilleon' in the Troad, one of several burial mounds suggested as the site where Achilles was laid to rest by his fellow Greek warriors.

have are the result of an (also largely lost) summary by a later writer, which reads: 'The Achaeans lay out the body of Achilles, but then Thetis [the mother of Achilles] arrived with the Muses and her sisters. After mourning her son she removed him from the pyre and took his remains to the White Island' (*Homerica: The Aethiopis* Fr. 1).

This White Island has been identified as the present-day Snake Island in the Black Sea. Its modern heroes are the members of the garrison who told Russian warships to get lost (in obscene terms) at the start of the Ukraine–Russian war in 2022. There was indeed an ancient structure dedicated to Achilles on a headland on the island until the nineteenth century. That was when the Russian navy decided to build a lighthouse there and almost completely obliterated it.

## Paying respects

Empty or not, the tomb of Achilles on the Troad attracted numerous tourists. The most famous of these was Alexander the Great. Plutarch relates that 'He went to Troy...and placed a wreath on the column which marks the grave of Achilles' (*Life of Alexander* 15).

Another famous visitor was the Roman emperor Caracalla (r. AD 198–217). Festus, a favourite freedman of his, died while he was there and was buried with Homeric honours – which caused some disappointment in the modern era, when the probable grave of Festus was discovered at Uvecik Tepe, briefly raising hopes that Achilles had been found.

The last recorded visitor to Achilles' grave was in the fifteenth century when the Ottoman ruler Mehmed II (died 1481) came to pay his respects after his conquest of Constantinople. It is uncertain which of the possible grave sites of Achilles he visited.

# *c.* 1500 BC – *c.* AD 550
# The Altis at Olympia
## Of Gods and Games

*The throne* [of Zeus] *is adorned with gold and with jewels, to say nothing of ebony and ivory. Upon it are painted figures and wrought images.*

**Pausanias, *Guide to Greece* 5.11**

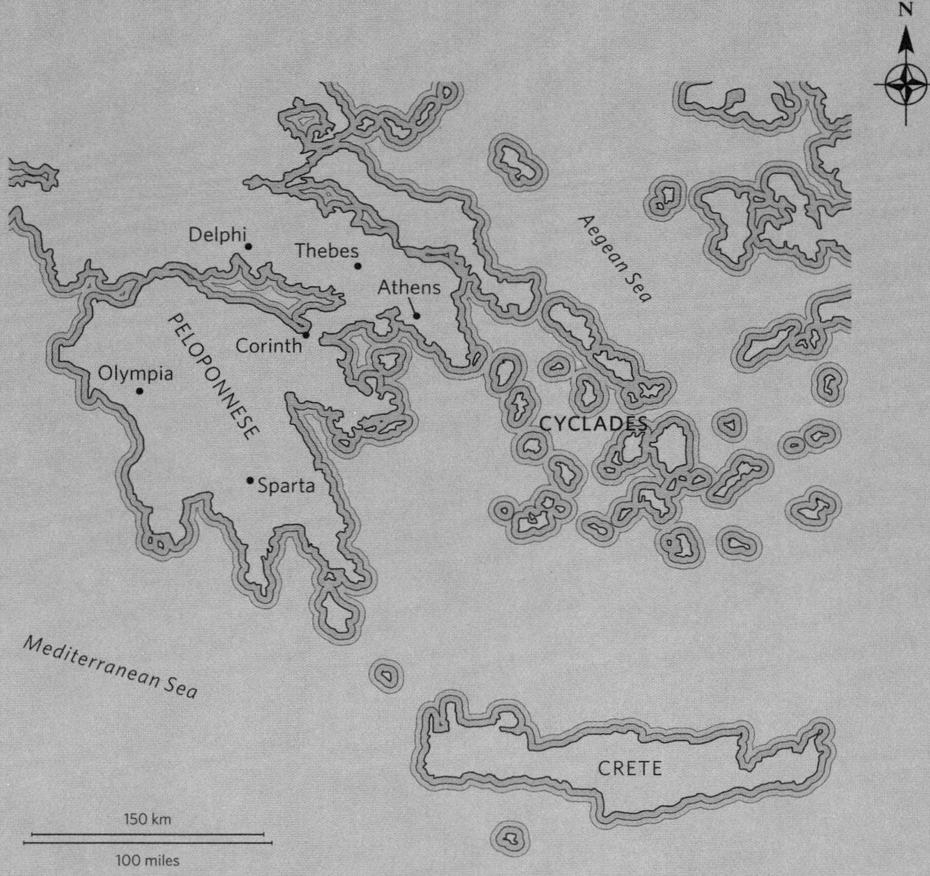

The history of the sacred temple area known as the Olympian Altis begins with a chariot race between the mythical hero Pelops and the homicidal King Oinomaos. The prize for the winner was the beautiful Hippodamia. (She was actually the daughter of Oinomaos, but this did not curb the king's incestuous lust.) The penalty for the loser was death. Pelops won – he cheated, but that is another story. The hero thus won the love of Hippodamia and the kingdom of the now-late and unlamented Oinomaos. In later years Pelops expanded his kingdom so that it dominated southern Greece to the extent that even today the region is called the Peloponnese.

After his death Pelops was given a memorial at the foot of Mount Cronos, though his actual bones were stored in the temple of Artemis in the nearby city of Elis. The memorial became a *heroön*, a place where sacrifices were made to figures not divine but believed to have power in the afterlife. Among those who came to honour the dead hero was a descendant of Pelops – none other than the mighty Hercules.

According to the poet Pindar, Hercules was distressed that the *heroön* lay in the burning sun. Therefore he planted the Altis, a grove of trees, about the monument. And, in order that the site be regularly maintained, Hercules instituted athletic events in honour of Zeus, to be held at the grave every four years. The location of the games

A first-century AD terracotta plaque showing Pelops beside a chariot – presumably the one with which he won his bride Hippodamia in his infamous chariot race.

was called Olympia as a reference to the home of Zeus on Mount Olympus, and the games thus came to be called the Olympics. 'That pinnacle of all contests, that which Heracles founded by the primordial grave of Pelops' is how the fifth-century BC lyric poet Pindar puts it.

## The sacred Altis

While the Greeks of the Classical era believed this story, modern archaeologists are not so sure. There are signs that the area around the Altis was in use as early as 1500 BC, in the Bronze Age, and the Altis definitely was sacred to the gods before 1000 BC, though to which gods is uncertain.

The monument to Pelops is still there today, and is certainly very ancient even by Greek standards. The *heroön* was in the Archaic style, formed of a mound of hard-packed earth (it has eroded somewhat in recent centuries), rather than the stone altars of the Classical era. It was surrounded by a pentagonal stone fence and every year at the top of the mound a black ram was sacrificed to appease the shade of Pelops. In honour of the memorable victory that won Pelops his bride and his kingdom, the chariot race in the Olympic Games was dedicated to his memory. Hippodamia fell out with her husband in later years but had her own sanctuary, the Hippodamion, within the Altis.

## Ancient temples

While the monument to Pelops is probably the most ancient in the Altis, the temple to Hera is a close second. Certainly it was among the oldest, if not the oldest, temple to the goddess in Greece. In fact so ancient was it that the upper parts of the walls were made of dried mud bricks and the columns of the temple were not made of marble but from tree trunks. As these trunks aged and decayed they were gradually replaced with stone columns, with the last trunk – an aged oak – being swapped out some time after AD 170, after around a thousand years of service.

The temple was originally dedicated to both Zeus and Hera but the site received a substantial upgrade in the fifth century when Zeus was given a temple of his own, which stood beside hers in the Altis. Hera's temple played a prominent role in the 'Women's Olympics' – the Heraean Games – which were held every four years, two years after the Olympic Games, with no male participants or spectators allowed.

At around the time that Zeus' temple was constructed, the Altis was closed off with a low stone wall called the *peribolos* (except on the north side where the slopes of Mount Cronus made this unnecessary). The wall enclosed an area of some 3.3 hectares (8 acres) and now had an entrance that led towards the Olympic *stadion*, the running track from which modern stadiums get their name. Here there was an altar beside which stood a gold statue of Zeus holding thunderbolts. This altar featured prominently in the opening event of the Olympics, the Contest of the Heralds. These heralds (and trumpeters also) stood on the altar and demonstrated their skills, with the winning competitors becoming the official announcers for the rest of the Games (Pausanias, *Guide to Greece* 5.22).

The remainder of the area within the Altis was packed with shrines, altars and votive monuments of greater or lesser size, two of the main ones being dedicated to the primordial goddesses Rhea and Gaia.

## A Wonder of the world

In the Classical era, the grandest building within the Altis was the temple of Zeus. This made the ancient temple of Hera look slightly

The Altis at Olympia reimagined in its prime during the mid-Classical era. The temple of Zeus dominates the centre with the smaller temple of Hera to the left, the circular Philippeion beside that and the colonnaded Gymnasium in the foreground.

*Following pages* This aerial view of the Altis today shows how the site became increasingly packed with temples and monuments as the Olympics gained in international renown.

shabby in comparison. The home of Olympian Zeus gleamed in marble (even though this marble was only a veneer to hide the inferior local stone which actually held the place up). It was roofed with tiles of Pentelic marble sliced so thin as to be translucent, so that light flooded the interior of the temple during the day. The building itself was the epitome of classic Doric temple architecture and the eastern pediment was carved with a bas-relief showing Pelops winning his epic chariot race. The altar before the temple was in the Archaic style, made not of stone but the compacted ashes of earlier sacrifices.

Sadly most visitors would have spared this impressive exterior barely more than a glance as they hurried within to behold the most famous occupant of the Altis – the statue of Zeus that was one of the Seven Wonders of the ancient world.

Even with Zeus sitting enthroned, the statue was impressive, estimated to be 14.5 metres (48 feet) high. It was chryselephantine, meaning that the body was made of carved ivory and beaten gold mounted upon hidden wooden scaffolding. The sculptor of this

The lighting of the modern Olympic flame enacted by women in Doric robes at the temple of Hera. Sunlight is used to light the flame.

monumental edifice was none other than Phidias, who stands with Myron as the greatest sculptor in ancient Greece. However, while Myron confined himself to near-life-size images, Phidias was inclined towards the monumental. Before creating the Wonder within the temple of Zeus he had made the famed statue of Athena in the Parthenon of Athens. (Jealous rivals had accused him of stealing gold from that statue, which is why Phidias was in exile in Elis and available for further commissions.)

The dank, humid air of much of the Altis grove meant that Phidias' masterwork was a high-maintenance affair and priests had to regularly coat the ivory with olive oil to prevent it warping. This oil was kept in a pool in front of the statue so that visitors first saw Zeus reflected upside down in the oil and then again upright, towering over them in all his majesty.

---

## The eternal fire

In ancient times a sacred flame was maintained in the northwest of the Altis within a small temple to Hestia (goddess of the hearth) which may have been built for this purpose. Sadly, this delicate wonder has not survived – in late antiquity it was taken to Constantinople where it was destroyed, ironically, in a fire. In the early fifth century AD a violent earthquake badly damaged the temple of Zeus and the rest of the Altis. By then Christianity was getting a grip on the Roman empire. Being a pagan festival, the Olympics had already been banned by imperial decree and fewer visitors were coming to the Altis in any case. Two further earthquakes in the sixth century completed the ruin. Thereafter, regular flooding (the sanctuary of Olympia lay in a valley created by the confluence of the Alfeios and Kladeos rivers) led to the Altis being buried in silt which has only recently been scraped away by archaeologists.

One result of this modern re-emergence is that Hera's ancient temple is in use again. Just as it was at the ancient Olympics, a flame is kept burning there through the course of the modern Olympic Games. The present-day flame is ignited by the sun's rays reflected by a parabolic mirror, in a ceremony held in the Altis beside the ruins of the temple of Hera.

# *c.* 900 BC – AD 262
# The Temple of Artemis at Ephesus
## Built Back Better...and Better

*When I beheld the house of Artemis soaring toward the clouds, other marvels lost their splendour and I said, 'Apart from Olympus, never was there a sight so grand under the sun.'*

Antipater of Sidon, *Greek Anthology* 9.58

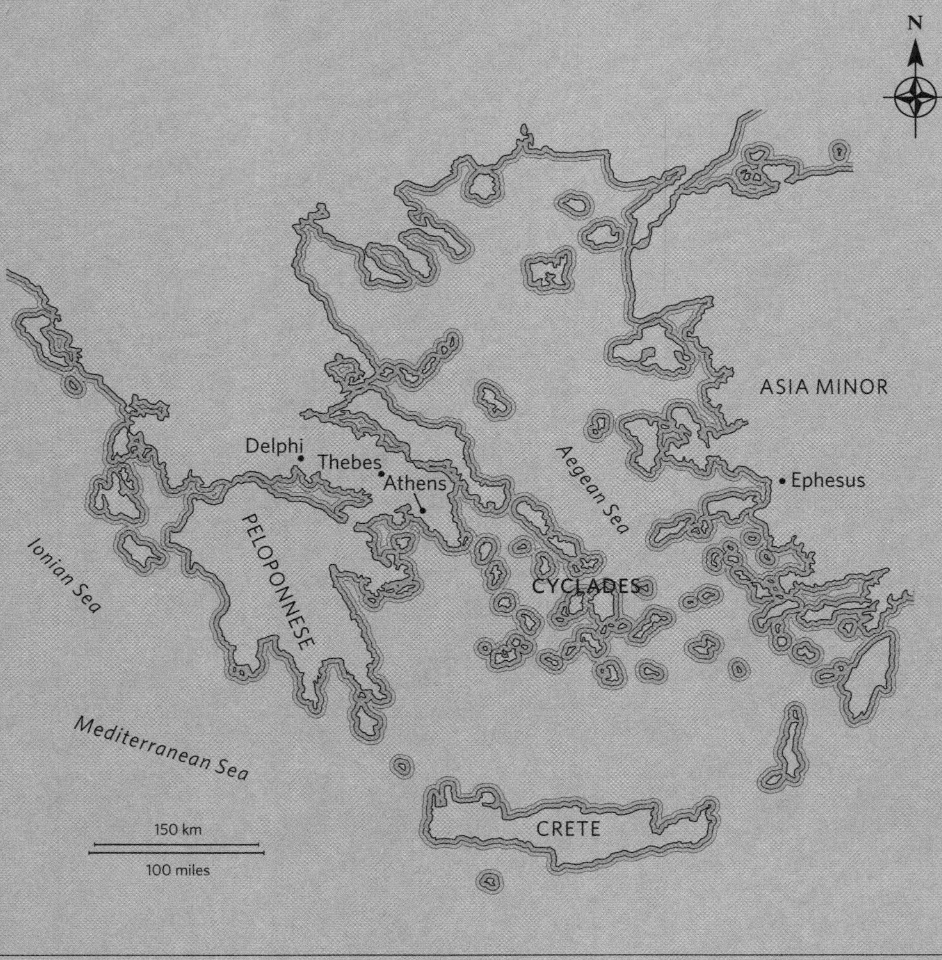

In Greek myth, the Titan Leto was mother to twins fathered by Zeus. These twin gods were in many ways mirror images of one another. Apollo was male, and the god of the arts and civilization. Artemis was female and the goddess of wild things. Appropriately enough, the most famous temple to Artemis was founded by the female race of Amazons outside the (then tiny) settlement of Ephesus.

The third-century BC poet Callimachus says, in his *Ode to Artemis*: 'At Ephesus beside the sea the warlike Amazons established your image beneath the trunk of an oak tree and there performed your holy rite' (3.237).

The name 'Ephesus' probably comes from *Apasa*, from the Hittite people who were dominant in western Anatolia three and a half thousand years ago. It is not known at what point the worship of Artemis began at the sacred site – or, more probably, at what time the goddess of the sacred site was first identified with Artemis. However, pottery from the Geometric period found in the temple remains suggest that Artemis was worshipped there as early as 900 BC.

The goddess Artemis viewed through the portico of her temple, reconstructed at reduced scale in Miniatürk Park in Istanbul, Turkey.

## Ancient worship

A statue of Artemis from Ephesus, the city where she was most revered. Exactly what is depicted on her chest has been hotly debated.

Over time the worship of Artemis in Asia Minor became widespread and entrenched, with the goddess seen as a protective deity for much of Anatolia and its peoples. The centre of her cult was at Ephesus, at that site allegedly first established by the Amazons. The Roman travel writer Pausanias adds this information:

> *The sanctuary of Apollo at Didyma and his oracle there date from before the coming of the first Ionians* [western Greeks]. *However, the cult of Ephesian Artemis is far more ancient still.*
> (*Guide to Greece* 7.2.6)

One issue with the holy site was that, although the soft, almost marshy soil was good for the oak tree which was allegedly the first site of worship, it was less than ideal for the sacred buildings that were later raised at this location. The first Bronze Age temple was destroyed by flooding some time in the seventh century. By now Artemis had enough of a reputation for many of the notables of Anatolia to chip in for the rebuilding and to pay top gold *stater* for the architects (the renowned father–son team of Chersiphron and his son Metagenes).

## A splendid rebuild

The historian Herodotus notes particularly the contribution of King Croesus, who used some of his fabulous wealth on the project. 'The work was funded by Croesus of Lydia, and took ten years to complete. He paid for the [statues of] oxen of gold and most of the columns' (*History* 1.92).

These columns were particularly costly because the temple of Artemis was one of the first – if not the very first – to use the peripteral style, in which the temple is completely surrounded by a columned portico. In recognition of its legendary founders, bronze statues of Amazons were placed at the temple. These (as with most bronze statues from antiquity) have been lost, but were replaced in the Classical era and three Roman copies of these later statues survive, with perhaps the best of them – the 'Wounded Amazon' – now in residence at the Metropolitan Museum of Art in New York.

In 356 BC the very fame of the temple brought about its destruction. An individual called Herostratus decided that the best way to make his name immortal was to set the temple ablaze. (This plan had succeeded for 2,381 years, at the time of writing, but the Ephesians tortured him to death to discourage others who might

The Pleiades in a nineteenth-century painting. These legendary daughters of the Titan Atlas were companions of Artemis, with one daughter, Taygete, the favourite of the goddess.

have the same idea.) It was said that Artemis had been unable to prevent her temple from being destroyed because she was away assisting at the birth of Alexander the Great (356–323 BC) on the day that the temple burned down. It has also been suggested that the arson attack came at a very convenient time, as the temple would probably have had to be torn down and rebuilt anyway because subsidence had become a major problem.

So 'the citizens erected another and better temple yet. This was partly paid for by the sale of the jewelry of the women of the city and also by the sale of the surviving pillars of the previous temple' (Strabo, *Geography* 14.1.22). This time, the temple was rebuilt on the epic scale which was to make it one of the Seven Wonders of the ancient world.

## The latest and greatest

In his *Natural History* (36.21) the Roman writer Pliny the Elder described the construction of the Wonder in detail.

> *The next, greatest, and ultimate version of the temple was paid for by the Ephesians themselves. A truly wonderful testimony to*

*Grecian magnificence, the temple of Diana at Ephesus deserves our genuine admiration.* [The Romans called Artemis 'Diana']... *One thing which makes this building a wonder is the massive architraves which needed to be raised to so great a height. The architect did this by creating a ramp made of sandbags which reached just higher than the tops of the columns. Then he gradually let the sand out of selected lower bags to slowly let the architraves down into the exact position required.*

The architraves are the blocks of stone that lay lengthways across the supporting columns to form the base of the temple roof. The temple of Artemis had 127 columns and the architraves had to be raised almost 20 metres (66 feet) on to the top of these. It is probable that many of these stone architraves were heavier than the equivalent blocks in the Parthenon, which weighed in at more than 10 tonnes.

The rebuild took decades. Alexander the Great, in adulthood, offered to pay for the work. However, the Ephesians had no wish for their temple to become known as 'Alexander's temple to Artemis' and tactfully declined. Pliny adds that the temple had always been a place of sanctuary, though the limits of the sanctuary had varied under various rulers. At one point the sanctuary was packed with vicious criminals who terrorized the townsfolk of Ephesus

When rebuilt, the temple at Ephesus was one of the most imposing structures in the ancient world both because of its size and superb architecture.

to such a degree that the Roman emperor Augustus pruned the temple's sanctuary rights to the point of almost eliminating them. (Eliminating them completely would have insulted the goddess.)

Within the temple was a veritable art gallery of some of the greatest statuary of the day, though naturally pride of place went to the enigmatic cult statue of Ephesian Artemis. This statue, of which there are many surviving copies, has a chest covered with egg-shaped objects. Some have speculated that these objects are indeed eggs and others reckon they are bulls' testicles. Either interpretation would carry the same message of fertility and abundance.

## The Christians

The temple had a rocky relationship with Christianity almost from the start of that religion. When St Paul came to preach in Ephesus he was met by a crowd chanting 'Great is Artemis of the Ephesians!' (*Acts of the Apostles*, 19:34). Fearing civic disorder, the authorities ran St Paul out of town.

The reputation of Artemis took a blow, however, when she failed to protect her city from invading Goths in AD 262. 'They set fire to the renowned temple of Diana at Ephesus, which the Amazons built' recounts the Gothic historian Jordanes (*Getica* 107 [20]). The ancients always had a transactional relationship with their gods and because Artemis had failed to deliver the protection which was her part of the bargain, the locals gradually turned to Christianity. By one account, just as the women of Ephesus had helped to pay for the construction of the Wonder, now they paid to demolish it (*The Ecclesiastical History* of Theodoret, 5.29).

In reality it is uncertain whether the temple was in fact rebuilt after destruction by the Goths, or deliberately destroyed by the people of Ephesus thereafter. Certainly there are references to worship continuing at the site into the late imperial period, but these might have resembled the very first acts of worship here – conducted in the open air under the trees.

In time the tumbled blocks of stone that once made up the temple were reused in other buildings or burned for lime. Today all that remains of the great temple is a single column roughly reconstructed from retrieved parts and a monumental base depicting a draped woman. This is now in the British Museum.

## *c.* 3000 BC – *c.* AD 370

# The Sanatorium at Epidaurus

## The World's First Health Centre

*Antikrates of Knidon had been blinded in battle by a spear through both his eyes and had the spearhead stuck inside his face. Sleeping in the shrine he had a vision in which the god pulled out the missile and re-seated his pupils within his eyes. At dawn he left, cured.*

*Inscriptiones graecae* 4.1.121

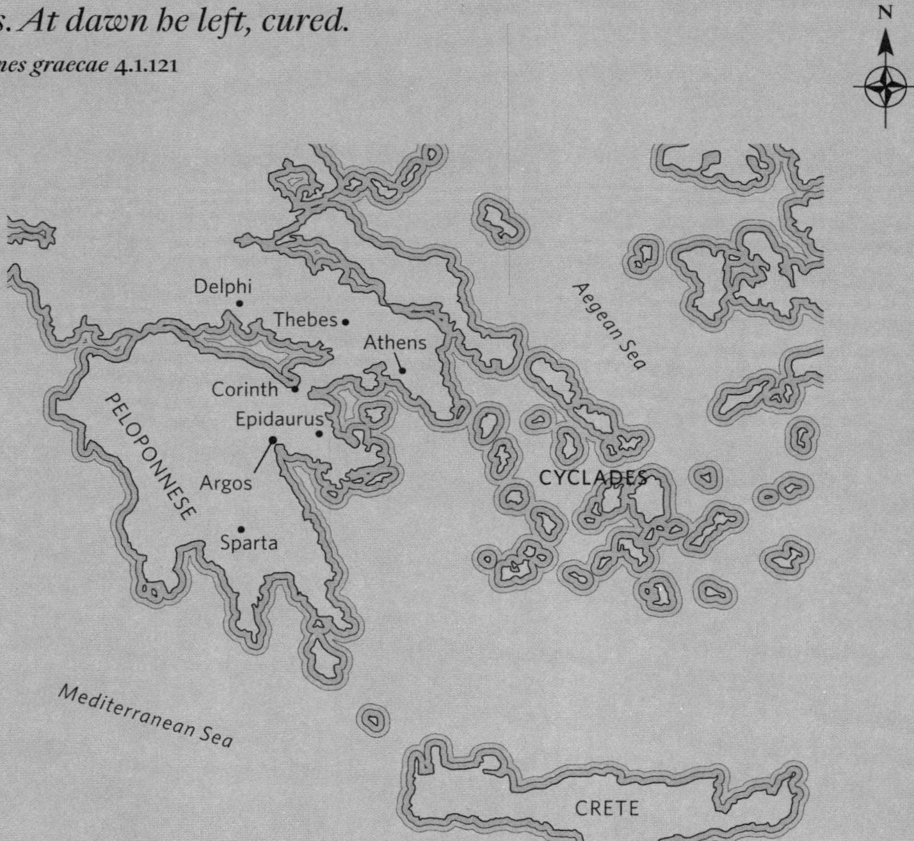

The intellectual revolution of the early Classical era saw a major shift in the way that the Greeks saw their world. Where once people had believed that everything was done by the direct influence of a god, the questioning minds of the pre-Socratic philosophers began to wonder – what if the world was more like a machine? If that were the case, then learning how that machine operated could bring substantial benefits.

One result of this change in thinking was to regard illness and health not as gifts or punishments by the whim of a god but as something that could be powerfully affected by careful maintenance of the human body. Accordingly medicine began to evolve from a matter of faith to an empirical science. The sanctuary of Asclepius at Epidaurus, close to the city of Argos in the Peloponnese, was at the forefront of this revolution and has a strong claim to be the world's first sanatorium.

Even gods sometimes need medical attention. In this nineteenth-century painting, Aphrodite asks Asclepius to remove a thorn embedded in her foot.

## The healing springs

Modern archaeology has revealed that the springs of Mount Kynortion were used for healing purposes as early as the third millennium BC. An unknown female deity was supposed to do the actual healing, and by the mid-Bronze Age a thriving little sanctuary had grown up on the mountainside. Some time before the sixth century BC the healing goddess was muscled out of her role by a pushy male usurper, namely the god Apollo in his healing aspect of Apollo Maleatas.

By now the Greeks were getting seriously interested in medicine as a science. Deciding that Apollo had too broad a portfolio (he also managed plague, music and prophecy among other things), the Greeks developed a more specialized god of healing. This was Asclepius (Latin name Aesculapius). Since the stories of the gods often reflected real-life changes in their worship, it was logical that Asclepius should be the son of Apollo. The same mixture of logic and myth gave Asclepius his children Hygieia, goddess of health, and Panacea, goddess of medicines. The rites of Hygiene are religiously practised in modern hospitals today, while laboratories all over the world still search for a full manifestation of Panacea.

The sanctuary at Epidaurus adopted Asclepius as its patron god around the start of the sixth century BC at the same time as the place was brought into the municipal control of the city of Epidaurus. Both benefited from this relationship, as little Epidaurus had a large harbour, and easy access to the sanctuary made it attractive to visitors from all over the Greek world.

## Divinely practical medicine

By that time the priests at the sanctuary could draw on over a millennium of experimentation and observation as to what medicines and practices were best for curing ailments. In a move that would be heartily recommended by any health practitioner today, the priests settled upon the curative powers of fresh air, exercise and a healthy diet, all taken in a low-stress environment.

Ancient cities were unhealthy places. By and large they were net consumers of people, requiring constant immigration from the countryside to prevent population collapse. Therefore, sometimes just taking a patient out of an urban environment was enough to effect a cure. (This was certainly true of one recorded case where a man was cured by being removed from the cooking of his mother-in-law, who was trying to poison him.) Other cases would be regarded today as psychosomatic, such as the mute

Roman bas-relief showing Asclepius and his daughter Hygieia.

boy whom the priests said would be cured if he promised certain services to the god. The boy promptly astounded his father by saying, 'Yes, I promise'.

When the efficacy of medicines failed and the doctors had exhausted all their remedies, supplicants turned to Asclepius to affect a miraculous cure against all the odds. These patients prayed at the temple of Asclepius which dominated the site. Though the foundations of this building remain, the columns and cult statue of the god have gone, surviving only through the efforts of that indefatigable reporter Pausanias, whose second-century AD description of the statue within the temple reads as follows:

> *The image of Asclepius is made of ivory and gold. The god is seated and holds a staff* [this staff with its entwined snake remains the symbol of the medical profession today]. *The other hand rests above the head of a serpent...When I asked why neither water nor olive oil is used to maintain* [the ivory] *on the statue the temple attendants informed me that the god and his throne were built over a cistern.*
>
> (*Guide to Greece* 2.27.2, 5.11.11)

How the temple at Epidaurus might have appeared to visitors in the Classical era in an early twentieth-century watercolour painting.

## Rest and exercise

Having followed a regime of diet and exercise and informed the god of their medical issues, patients retired to a place called the Abaton, there to literally sleep their troubles away. The walls of the Abaton were lined with inscriptions from grateful patients who had woken up healthy.

> *Hermodikos of Lampsakos suffered from whole-body paralysis. While sleeping in the shrine, he was ordered* [in a dream] *to bring into the sanctuary the biggest stone that he could carry. He awakened to find that he was cured. He went out and brought that rock which lies in front of the Abaton.*
>
> (*Inscriptiones graecae* 4.1.122)

A large dining hall provided visitors with healthy fare, and a gymnasium and stadium helped those needing to work off the effects of over-indulgence. Baths were fed by those same healing springs that had inspired the sanctuary thousands of years previously, with the waste water from the baths helping to flush a highly sophisticated sewer system.

There was also a theatre, said to be designed by the famed architect Polykleitos of Argos (active *c.* 460–410 BC). Sharing the experience of the great Greek tragedies in a communal setting helped the mental health of patients through catharsis (the purging of emotions). Today, this theatre is the best-preserved of the buildings at the sanctuary and indeed has been brought back into use. Performances have been regularly staged there since 1955.

## Faith healing, pillagers and tourists

During the Mithridatic Wars of the first century BC the sanctuary at Epidaurus was violently pillaged by the Roman general Sulla (*c*. 138–78 BC) – who, the Greeks noted, later died when the gods afflicted him with suppurating bowels. Nevertheless, the sanctuary went from strength to strength in the Roman era and finished with over two hundred franchise sanctuaries scattered about the Mediterranean world.

In the second century AD the site was given a particular boost by the emperor Hadrian (r. 117–38), who visited in 124. A dedicated micro-manager, Hadrian sorted out the cycle of athletic games held there and reorganized aspects of worship. The later Christian era saw the site still a centre of healing, but with the 'pagan' elements forcibly discouraged. Then, as faith-based medicine once again took hold, the sanctuary was allowed gradually to fall into ruin.

Today Epidaurus again hosts visitors from all over the world. Many are day-trippers from Athens, but others stay to enjoy the nearby beaches, take in a performance at the theatre and, perhaps, whisper a hopeful prayer in the ruins of the ancient temple of Asclepius.

8th century BC – AD 362

# The Oracle at Delphi

## Divine Information Broker

*'Know yourself'*

**Advice of the oracle to those seeking wisdom**

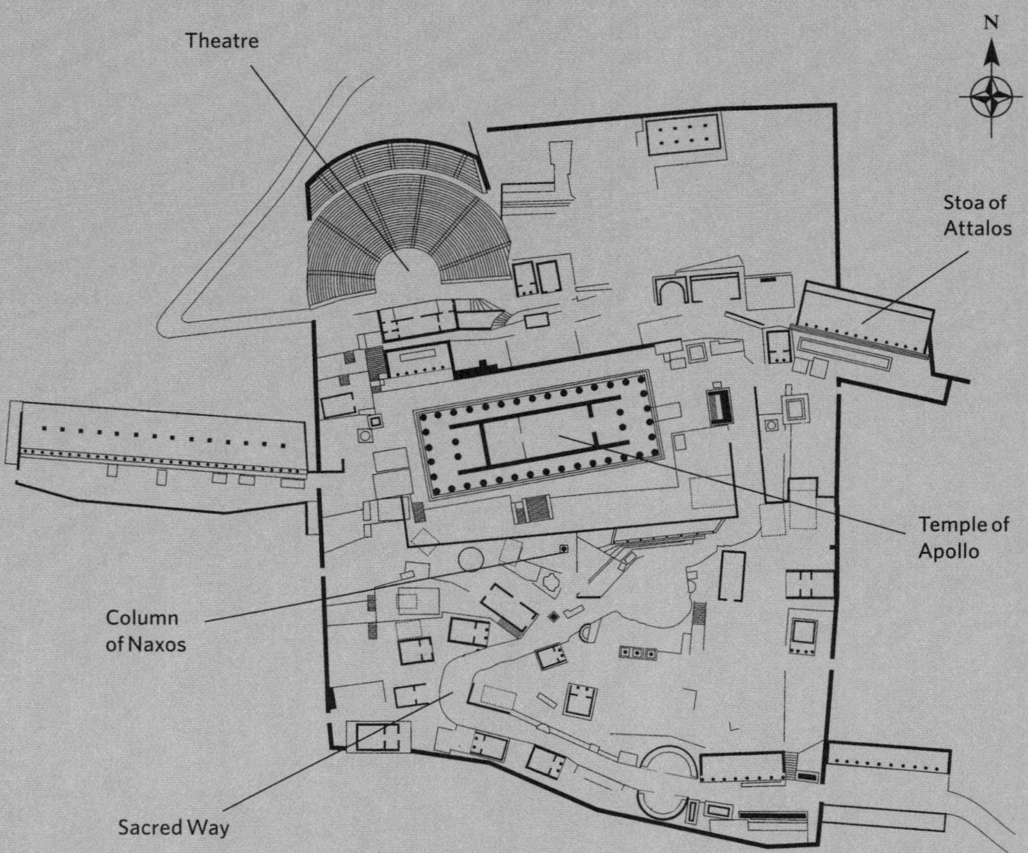

Today, a 'delphic' pronouncement is one which is deliberately obscure or hard to interpret. Yet for over eighteen hundred years people sought the advice of the Delphic oracle. Hard-headed kings, philosophers and lawgivers came so regularly to the shrine that they must have found it practically useful.

## The dolphin of Mount Parnassus

Delphi sits high in the mountains of Greece, on the slopes of Mount Parnassus some 10 kilometres (6 miles) from the sea. Yet, strangely, the Greeks associated the site with dolphins. An ancient poem explains that early in Greek prehistory a dolphin leapt aboard a merchant ship. Transforming into the god Apollo, this apparition ordered the startled sailors to proceed to the sacred site:

> *Pray there, standing around the altar....and as I was in the form of a dolphin when first I leapt upon your swift ship, so now worship me here as Delphinus, and for evermore call this holy place Delphi.*
>
> (*Homeric Hymn to Apollo* l. 494ff)

Modern academics reject this forced etymology and suggest that the name of the site actually comes from *delphys*, the Greek word

*Below* The Athena temple complex, including the tholos of Delphi. A circular temple which was built by the architect Theodore the Phocaean in 380–370 BC.

*Following pages* Reconstruction of Delphi, with the temple of Apollo in the centre, by the artist Albert Tournaire, 1894.

This sphinx was dedicated to Apollo in 560 BC by the people of Naxos to ensure that they would be granted the privilege of *Promanteia*, the right to consult the oracle first.

for 'womb'. Indeed, the Delphic oracle made pronouncements from the *adyton*, a room buried in the ground below the point that the Greeks believed was the navel (*omphalus*) of the world. The god Zeus discovered this by releasing two eagles, directing one to fly east and the other west. The eagles met at Delphi, demonstrating that Delphi was the centre of the world (and that Zeus knew that the Earth was round).

A sacred stone marked this spot, guarded by a monstrous snake called Python (from which a genus of constricting snakes get their modern name). This creature was slain by the god Apollo, avenging a wrong done to his mother. Apollo's penalty for taking life in the sacred sanctuary was to become guardian of the site himself and to hold four-yearly Pythian Games in memory of his victim.

## Delphi, the international information exchange

The Pythian Games were an important reason why Delphi became so famous as an oracle. They ranked just below the Olympics as one of the most prestigious sporting events in ancient Greece. Merchants, kings and politicians attended and were entertained by the local aristocracy – who took care to pick the brains of their guests.

Even in the years between the games, Delphi had many prestigious visitors from all over Greece who were compelled to spend a few days at the site. One did not just walk in and demand an oracular pronouncement – there were purifications and other rituals to go through first. As a result, people in Delphi regularly heard news of the economic, military and political situation in the eastern Mediterranean. These singularly well-informed persons included the Pythia, the priestess through whom Apollo made his pronouncements. It may be that some visitors to Delphi, religion aside, came mostly to get advice from the well-oiled political and military consultancy that the oracle had become.

Modern researchers and the ancients are in agreement as to how the oracle worked. After due preparation and sacrifice, the priestess descended into the *adyton* and sat on a three-legged stool, screened from visitors by a curtain. Because the room was only open for one day a month, it filled with the sweet breath of Apollo, which, when inhaled, allowed the priestess to become the vessel of the god. Or alternatively, the room held a concentration of the gas ethylene, which seeped in through an underground fissure and caused the priestess to become mildly intoxicated.

With her inhibitions lowered the priestess could draw directly on her subconscious, which was already primed with all the information

*Lycurgus Consulting the Pythia* by Eugène Delacroix, 1835–45. Lycurgus was a Spartan lawgiver who went to the Pythia to confirm that his new laws would benefit Sparta.

she needed to provide a cogent, well-informed answer. Far from delivering a drunken rant, she responded in a complex poetic metre called dactylic hexameter (according to Herodotus' *History* 1.65) – not easy even when sober. Nevertheless, the strain of making oracular pronouncements – or of inhaling the gas for a prolonged period – was described as comparable to running an endurance race. In later eras three women served as the Pythia, two alternating the duties and a third as a back-up.

## Oracular advice

When the Spartans came to Delphi to ask if they should go to war with Athens in 431 BC, 'Apollo' replied that he himself would fight on the Spartan side. The Athenian war strategy was to withdraw behind their city walls and obtain supplies from overseas. This, as the Pythia may have realized, was a sure way of introducing disease into an overcrowded city – and Apollo, the god of plagues, duly sent Athens a devastating epidemic.

When a city-state wished to found a new colony it usually consulted the oracle at Delphi about the viability of the site and whether it had divine favour.

Famously the oracle informed one visitor that Socrates was the wisest man in Athens. When Socrates heard the news he responded that this was probably because he was the only Athenian who knew the depth of his own ignorance.

The Greeks asked what should be done about a massive barbarian invasion in 275 BC, and Apollo's reply was the equivalent (in dactylic hexameter, of course) of 'I've got this!' The invaders were struck by landslides, snowstorms and plague and most died. Perhaps Apollo

The Charioteer of Delphi is a bronze statue dating to 470 BC. The statue was originally part of a larger group of sculptures which included a chariot, horses and child attendants.

intervened personally, or perhaps the Pythia knew local weather conditions better than the invaders.

At times prophecies were carefully ambiguous. When Croesus (he of great wealth) asked if his kingdom of Lydia should go to war with the Persians the oracle replied that doing so would destroy a great state. The state in question, it turned out, was Lydia.

### Later Delphi

Such was the prestige of Delphi that in later Greek history several wars – the so-called Sacred Wars – were fought for control of the oracle. These local squabbles were ended when Delphi came under the suzerainty first of the Macedonians and later of the Roman empire.

Delphi retained its importance in the Roman era, with persons such as the orator Cicero visiting the shrine. Cicero was told that the path to fame lay in being true to himself. The emperors Nero, Hadrian and Domitian consulted the oracle, though the ill-fated Nero, somewhat unwisely, expropriated from Apollo several hundred of the statues that adorned the site. With the advent of Christianity the oracle fell into disuse, and the last oracular pronouncement took place in AD 362. In the 380s the emperor Theodosius ordered that the temples and sanctuaries be destroyed.

---

## The Delphi that never was

Centuries later, the Victorians helped to restore Delphi to international prominence – even if their interpretation was deeply flawed. Nineteenth-century paintings such as *Priestess of Delphi* by John Collier, or Heinrich Leutemann's even more overwrought engraving *The Oracle at Delphi*, embody the early modern view of the oracle. In a shadowy underground cavern a semi-demented priestess raves and mumbles in a drug-fuelled stupor while fumes billow from the ravine beside her feet. With her are priests who cynically 'interpret' her incoherent rants into messages that suit their own purposes. This is a powerful image and one which fitted well with the Gothic fantasies of the Victorian era. It is also incorrect in almost every detail.

Today the site receives more visitors even than it did in its heyday. The Pythia has long hung up her sacred laurel, but the spectacular views from the mountain and the remains of the ancient monuments still have a powerfully evocative appeal.

*c.* 1750 BC – *c.* AD 31

# The Menelaion of Sparta

## Worshipping the Divine Helen

*Sparta preserves ancient traditions with the greatest fidelity. Even today at Therapne in Laconia, they follow the traditions of their ancestors by offering up holy sacrifices.*

**Isocrates, *Helen* 63**

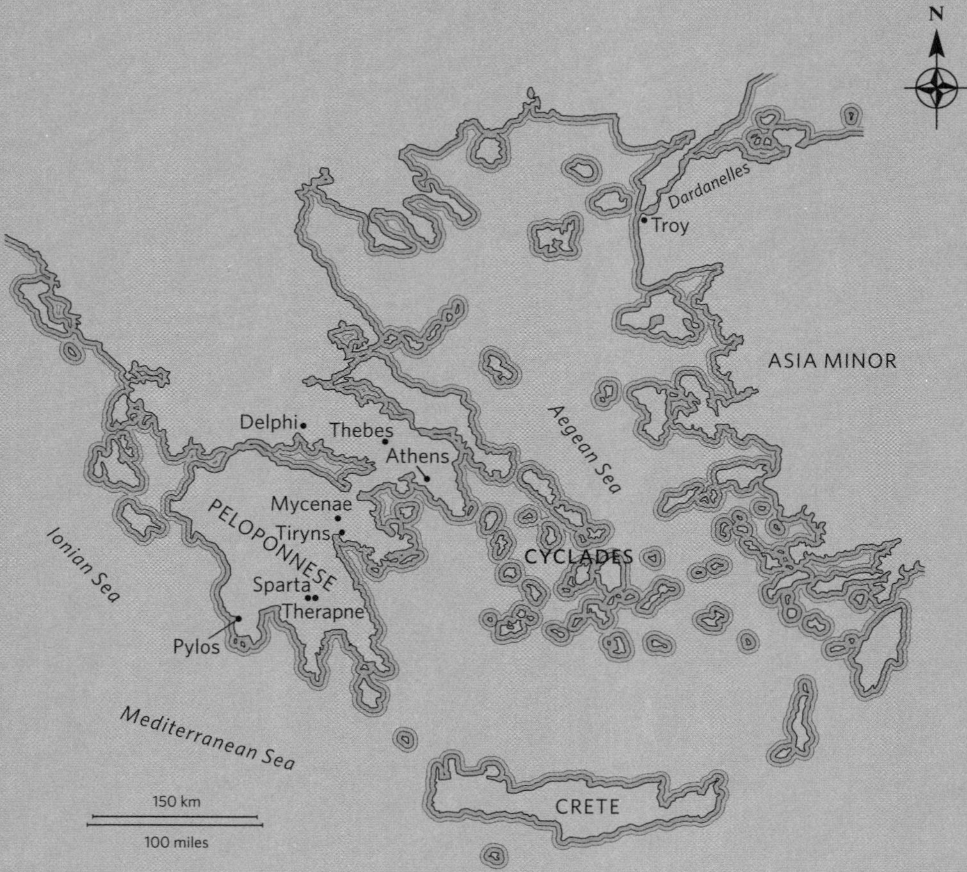

Even for the famously austere Spartans it was possible to enjoy a good day out. For the Festival of Helen, Spartan women would pile into carriages and travel from the city to make offerings at the Menelaion at Therapne. Thereafter it was possible to picnic amid the pine trees and enjoy spectacular views across the valley of the river Eurotas with the snowy Taygetos mountain range looming beyond.

## The odd couple

It may seem strange to the modern mind that the Spartans so venerated Helen, a woman who abandoned her native city – and her husband – to elope to Troy with her lover Paris, and in the process start the bloodbath of the Trojan War. Also venerated at the shrine at Therapne was Menelaus, the husband abandoned by Helen. From the ancient sources he appears to have been an amiable and, as it turned out, a very forgiving character. But he was hardly the sort of person one would consider today as being the subject of deep reverence.

Yet the Spartans more than revered Menelaus and Helen; according to the Athenian writer Isocrates the pair were 'worshipped

Paris and Helen as shown on a fresco discovered in Pompeii, Italy. While Helen is dressed in traditional Greek style, Paris is shown in 'foreign' attire to emphasize his non-Greek status.

Lead cult offerings such as these from Sparta were often left at shrines by those seeking the favour of the god or hero to whom the shrine was dedicated.

almost as gods'. One reason was that Helen was indeed divine in more than her looks. She was a demi-goddess, being a daughter of Zeus and the sister of Castor and Pollux (the twins who today make up the constellation and zodiacal sign of Gemini). Therefore, Spartans of all walks of life would give offerings to Helen and pray at her shrines (she had another in downtown Sparta) in the hope that her divine connections would bring health and fertility to both mothers and crops. This diversity of worshippers is reflected in offerings found at the shrine, which range from the ornate to crude little lead figurines.

The historian Herodotus gives an example of prayers being heeded when he tells the story of 'The most beautiful woman, by far, in Sparta':

> *She was once the most ugly. Her nurse...carried the child every day to the sacred precinct of Helen at Therapne and placed her beside the image* [of Helen]. *There she prayed for help for the afflicted child. One day, as she was leaving the sacred precinct, a woman suddenly appeared and demanded that the nurse show the child to her....The woman stroked the child's head and prophesied that she would become the most beautiful in all Sparta.*
> (*History* 6.61)

The Spartans also revered Helen and Menelaus as the ancestors of their people, thus gracing the Spartans with a lineage that went back to the distant heroic past even before the legendary Trojan War. The shrine to the pair was built at Therapne because the Spartans believed that this was where the mythical couple had made their home and where they were buried. The second-century AD Roman travel writer Pausanias says that the name of Therapne originally belonged to the daughter of a legendary pre-Spartan king who made that place her own (*Guide to Greece* 3.19.9).

## History and legend

Because of these beliefs modern archaeologists investigating the site have been intrigued to discover that, before it became a place of worship, Therapne was the site of a luxurious mansion which was regularly renovated between the fifteenth and thirteenth centuries BC, the latter being about the time when legend says that Menelaus was king of Sparta.

Several centuries elapsed between the destruction of the mansions (by earthquake and fire) and the building of the first

shrines, but from offerings excavated at the site it appears that it became a place of worship no later than the early Iron Age (around 1100 BC). This makes the Menelaion the oldest known *heroön* (hero shrine) dedicated to any characters of the Trojan War.

Some time around 750 BC a shrine was built at Therapne. It is generally believed that this was originally dedicated solely to Helen, but as Menelaus was her husband and the monument was called 'the Menelaion' because it stood on the remains of his house, cult worship was gradually extended to a man whom the Spartans already revered as their ancestor. Later this shrine was renovated, using limestone blocks from the original and perhaps also the remains of the mansion which had once stood on the site.

In the fifth century BC Sparta rose to become the most powerful state in the Peloponnese and the shrine at Therapne was upgraded to reflect the city's new status. The new shrine stood on a mound held in place with ashlar blocks and a retaining wall. It is the remains of this shrine that can be seen on the ridge today, with the view across the Eurotas Valley still as beautiful as ever.

## Rise and fall

The fortunes of the shrine of Helen rose and fell with the fortunes of Sparta as a state. The site appears to have been at its most magnificent around 450 BC after the Persian Wars, a time when Sparta was at the height of its power and fame. In later years, after Sparta suffered a number of severe setbacks, especially after the disastrous defeat at Leuctra in 371 BC, the Spartans seem to have lacked the resources and the will to properly maintain the shrine.

Later yet another earthquake inflicted further damage. There may have been a slapdash attempt to patch things up in the Roman era but by the time that Pausanias was in the area he considered the location worth mentioning but not visiting. Then, as the centuries passed, the site became a curiosity known only to the locals, its name and original purpose forgotten.

The nineteenth century saw renewed interest in Classical Greece, and as early as 1833 archaeologists considered that the mound might be the site of the Menelaion mentioned in the ancient texts. Confirmation had to wait until the twentieth century when archaeologists found a small bronze *aryballos* (a flask used for storing oil or perfume) with an inscription saying that one Deinis had dedicated the flask to Helen, the wife of Menelaus. Another find bore an inscription saying that it was dedicated 'By Euthikrenes

The Menelaion today. Though the shrine is somewhat dilapidated, the views of the Eurotas river from Therapne remain almost as unspoiled as they were three thousand years ago.

to Menelaos'. This and later discoveries have led to the site being identified with a high degree of certainty.

Today those making the pilgrimage are advised to park at a signposted location some 5 kilometres (3 miles) from the modern town of Sparta and then take a ten-minute walk uphill. Travel guides advise that, as well as appreciating the evocative remains of the shrine, one of the main reasons for making the trip would be to appreciate those same magnificent views that the women of Sparta enjoyed over two millennia before.

440 BC to present day

# The Temple of Poseidon at Sunion

## Shining Temple by the Sea

*...on Sunium's marbled steep,*
*Where nothing, save the waves and I,*
*May hear our mutual murmurs sweep...*

**Lord Byron, 'The Isles of Greece'**

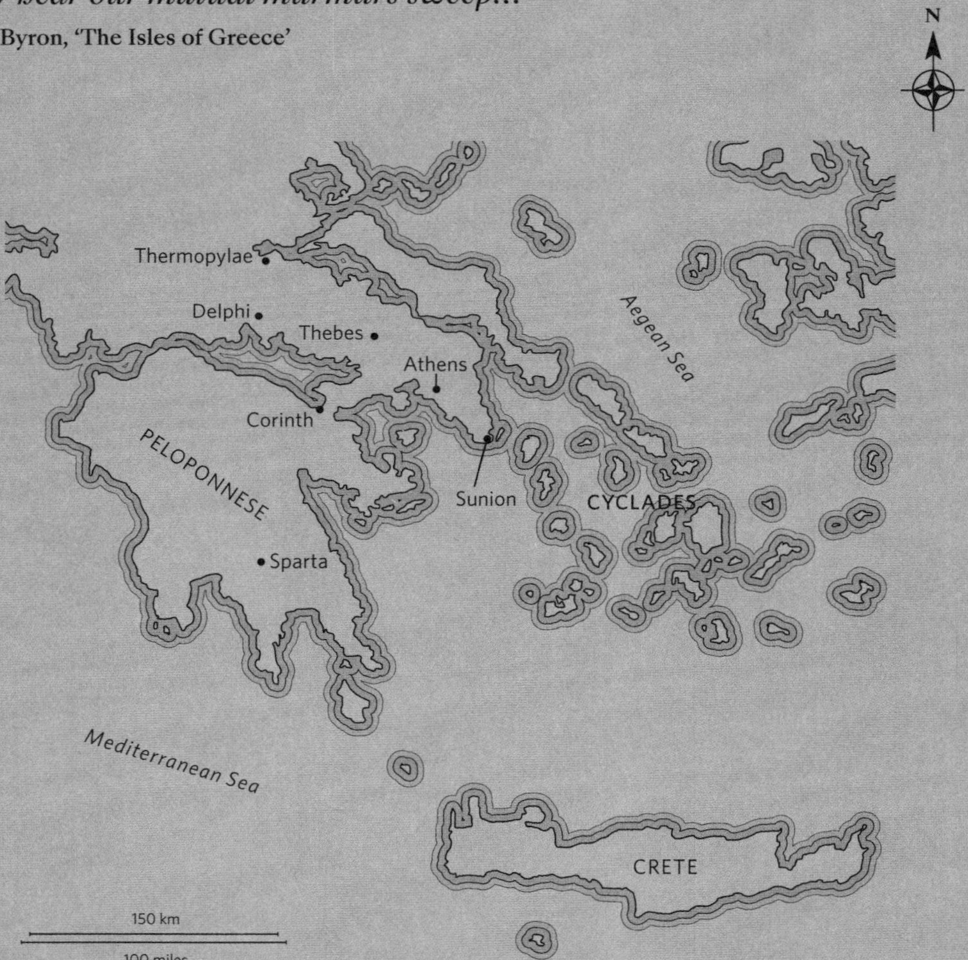

The rocky headland at Sunion is the southernmost point of Attica, the territory controlled by Athens during the Classical era. Even before the first temples were raised here, the headland had deep significance for the Athenians. According to myth, it was here that the ship of Theseus was sighted as it returned from Crete after he and other young Athenians had been sent as sacrifices to the carnivorous Minotaur of the Labyrinth.

Uncertain whether Theseus had succeeded in his mission to slay the dreaded Minotaur, or if he had been slain by it, King Aegeus waited anxiously at Sunion. He had arranged that should the ship return with black sails this would signal that his beloved son had been killed. Sadly, as Theseus returned in safety, that beloved son 'forgot' to change the sails to white. Consequently, the grief-stricken Aegeus threw himself to his death off the cliff into the sea which now bears his name (the Aegean) and the conniving Theseus became king of Athens.

The remains of the temple at Sunion, which inspired Lord Byron to verse when he visited it in 1810 (he also carved his name into one of the columns).

## The sacred lookout post

A mosaic depiction of Poseidon, now in Sousse Archaeological Museum, Tunisia. His chariot is drawn by hippocampi (from the Greek for 'horse' and 'sea monster'). This has given the name to part of the human brain with a roughly similar shape.

In historical times the Athenians appreciated the fact that a watcher at Sunion would be the first to observe ships approaching their city, so they set about installing a lookout post to keep an eye out for hostile fleets. With a cynicism that Theseus would have appreciated, the Athenians opted to secure this lookout spot from enemy attack by making it a temple to Poseidon, the god of the sea.

Destroying a temple to a notoriously bad-tempered and fickle god would have been a dangerous act of sacrilege. However, this did not deter the Persian invaders who rampaged across Attica in 479 BC after they had swept aside Leonidas and his 300 Spartans at the battle of Thermopylae. They were worshippers of Ahura-Mazda and had little respect for the gods of Greece. The temple of Poseidon at Sunion was not even finished before the Persians levelled it to the foundations.

An Archaic *kouros*-style statue found at Sunion. Pre-dating the Classical era, this statue is probably older than the temple in front of which it later stood.

Poseidon may have been taking notes, because soon thereafter Persian might was shattered in a sea battle at Salamis just a few kilometres from Athens. By way of thanks the Athenians dedicated a captured Persian trireme to Poseidon, placing it as a trophy on the shore below the headland where they planned to rebuild Poseidon's temple anew and on a grander scale (Herodotus, *Histories* 8.121).

## New and improved

Since they already had a decent base to build on, the Athenians shifted away the debris and began to raise their new temple on the old foundation. Modern archaeologists have found evidence for all this. The tufa and limestone blocks on the original foundation are discoloured, probably from burning by the Persians. A large pit (*bothros*) has been found filled with debris and fragments of marble statuary, which is assumed to be where the Athenians swept the rubble before beginning to rebuild.

While they were at it, the Athenians also honoured their patron goddess by rebuilding a temple to Athena which stood on a slightly lower prominence to the west. The original temple appears to have dated back to the Bronze Age but was rebuilt on a more modest scale than the temple to Poseidon. (Since Athena was also getting a splendid temple on the Acropolis in central Athens, she could hardly complain about this.)

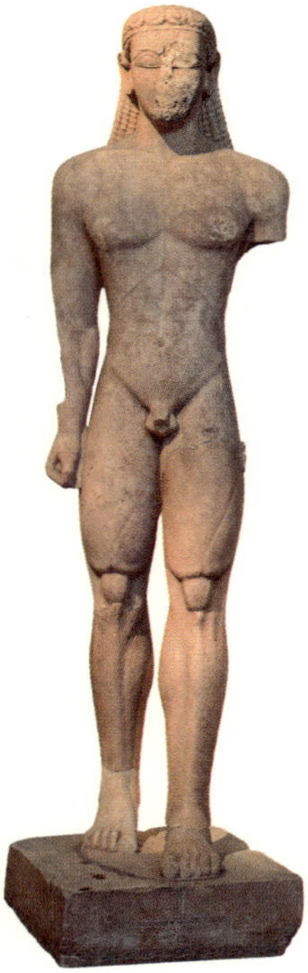

## The white temple

It seems that the Sunion temple architect was also in charge of other temples in the project of the politician Pericles (*c.* 495–429 BC) to build a new and better Athens once the Persians had been driven back to Asia. Architecturally minded archaeologists have noted that distinctive features of the temple of Poseidon match those of the temples of Hephaestus, near the Athenian agora, and of Nemesis at Rhamnos.

The temple at Sunion had a peripteral design, meaning that there was a single column on each corner and a colonnade running along the sides. The Doric-style columns were slightly slimmer than the standard model, which had the effect of making the temple look taller. Overall the temple was surrounded by some thirty-four columns, which would have given it a light and airy appearance.

As was usual with Greek temples, though, the core of the structure that housed the god himself was a windowless room.

The temple has inspired artists and photographers from different cultures and eras. Here it is depicted by the nineteenth-century British landscape artist J. M. W. Turner.

(There was a practical reason for this. Votive offerings to the gods were often valuable pieces wrought in gold or silver and not every Athenian of a larcenous inclination was particularly religious. The more secure the room containing the offerings, the better.) Poseidon himself was represented within this room in the form of a bronze statue 7 metres (23 feet) tall.

The stone for the building was quarried from Agrileza, near Cape Sunion. Agrileza marble is slightly more porous than the builder probably would have liked, but its dazzling white hue more than compensated for this. Standing in the sunlight, high on the headland, the gleaming temple at Sunion became the first sight of Attica for generations of sailors, be they on warships or merchantmen.

The rebuilt temple at Sunion came into use around 440 BC, both as a sacred site and as a lookout post for those watching for hostile navies. The latter role became of particular importance three years later when Athens went to war with Sparta and control of the sea became vital for the city's survival.

## Twilight of the temple

Archaeological examination of offerings and coins found at the site shows that worshippers attended the temple of Poseidon throughout the Classical era, but with the Christianization of the Roman empire the temple fell into disuse. Some of the stone from the ruins found its way to the small coastal town of Lavrio, whose people appreciated a handy source of dressed stone as building material.

In the late nineteenth century a revival of European interest in Classical Greece turned attention once more to the temple at Sunion, where the philhellene poet Lord Byron came to brood over the ruins. A more scientific visitor was German archaeologist Wilhelm Dörpfeld (1853–1940), whose 1884 investigation revealed much of what is known about the temple today. Sadly not all the interest in the temple was benevolent. Several of the column drums were hauled away – one to serve as the base for a bust of the sixth Duke of Devonshire in the gardens of Chatsworth in England. Another column drum is in the British Museum, a further Greek artefact that the original owners would rather like to have back.

Today the archaeological site at Sunion is fiercely protected by the Greek Archaeological Society and those wishing to explore the ruins must purchase tickets to do so. Despite the ravages of time, fifteen of the original columns remain standing, so Poseidon still does his ancient duty of guiding ships towards the Piraeus harbour of Athens. Visitors at sunset report feeling here that same awe and wonder that worshippers must have felt centuries ago when they came to the shining temple by the sea.

# *c.* 550 BC – *c.* AD 800

# Sacred Sites at Paestum

## Temples of Hera

*Holy Imbrasos, Holy Parthenie, Holy Parthenios*

**Temple inscription from the second century at Paestum, celebrating Hera as a river deity and protector of maidens**

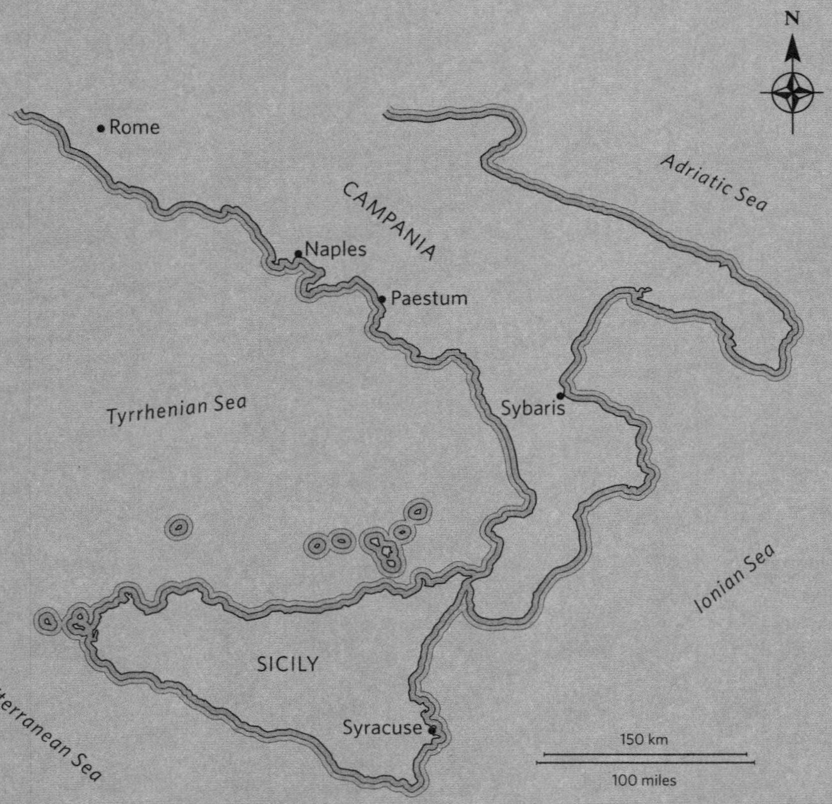

When Jason and his Argonauts went in search of the Golden Fleece, their journey took them around much of the Mediterranean Sea. In fact they would have voyaged even further if the goddess Hera (who considered Jason something of a protégé) had not perched atop the Rock of Gibraltar and urgently warned the Argonauts not to head out into the Atlantic Ocean.

## The sanctuary of Hera

Perhaps by way of thanks, Jason built a temple to Hera as he voyaged back east. The indefatigable geographer Strabo gives us the precise location, writing: 'On passing the mouth of the [river] Silaris [the modern Selo in Campania, Italy] one comes to Lucania, and the temple of Hera of Argos, built by Jason, and fifty *stades* beyond, to Poseidonia [Paestum]' (*Geography* 6.1.1).

Mythical origins aside, there can be no doubt that Hera, wife of the great god Zeus, was deeply revered in the region of Poseidonia – much more so, in fact, than the sea god after whom the town was originally named. Hera was not a very nice person even by the capricious standards of the ancient gods. She added her own vicious

The Doric temples at Paestum are among the best preserved in the modern world. Dating from around 500 BC, the contemporary city walls are also partly intact.

persecution to women already recovering from the trauma of being raped by her husband, and made miserable the life of Hercules for no other reason than that he was born of one such rape. She went one further with the beautiful Libyan princess Lamia, by making her kill and eat the child she had conceived with Zeus.

Hera also had a positive aspect, however. She was the protector of marriages, which were considered sacred to her. This was reflected also in Hera's Roman manifestation as Juno and is why June weddings are considered particularly auspicious even today.

Many of the metopes found at the site of the sanctuary which developed around 'Jason's temple' depict maidens dancing or wedding-related themes. (Metopes are panels found in the decorative friezes that run above temple colonnades.) Jason specifically dedicated his temple to Hera of Argos, in her aspect as a goddess of fertility. It appears that local cult also identified Hera as The Lady (which is what 'Hera' means in Greek) of the River.

The sanctuary was in use for around eight hundred years. Thousands of votive offerings were left there over the centuries by those hoping for happy and bountiful marriages – so many, in fact, that it seems to have been the practice of the priests to bury older offerings to make room for newer ones. These older offerings were

Hera, guardian of the sanctity of marriage and wife of Zeus, is here imagined by Carel Fabritius in a seventeenth-century oil painting.

A statue of Hera enthroned. Found in 1962, Hera is shown holding a *patera* (offering dish) and a pomegranate (symbolizing fertility and the cycle of life and death).

interred in pits alongside the site, to the delight of archaeologists who retrieved them some twenty-five centuries later.

The decline of the sanctuary in the second century AD was not due to the presence of rival temples to Hera situated more conveniently at Poseidonia (or Paestum, as the city became known), but rather due to the silting up of the river Silaris. This made the sanctuary less accessible and eventually led to its abandonment.

## Paestum

The city of Paestum went through a number of changes of ownership over the centuries that the goddess was worshipped there. The original settlers were Greeks from the city of Sybaris, that place so infamous for its people's decadent and luxurious lifestyle that 'sybaritic' is still used as an adjective today. These settlers built their temples to Hera in the sixth and fifth centuries BC. (Temple-building was a slow business that could easily take a generation or three from start to finish.)

The founder of the city is probably the unidentified person commemorated by the *heroön* located on the low hill on the other side of the city from Hera's temples. (A *heroön* was a monument dedicated not to a god but to some particularly noteworthy mortal who might yet have influence in the afterlife.) The sacred spot consisted of a tumulus (a low earth mound) which modern archaeologists have removed to reveal a small roofed stone chamber furnished with clay and bronze pots. The honey in some of the pots is probably still edible.

Worship of Hera continued unabated when the city was taken over by the Lucanians of southern Italy in around 400 BC. In fact it was probably they who finished building the second of the temples to the goddess. This stood beside the first, which has a reasonable claim to be among the oldest known Greek temples in Italy. The builders of both temples shared a common problem, which is that the local stone is coarse-grained. The builders had to make do with it, however, as their city was far from any decent source of marble. As a result the temple bas-reliefs were somewhat flatter than the ideal, and have eroded more swiftly.

The builders still did their best to make the temples as impressive as possible. For example they made considerable use of an optical effect called *entasis* on the columns. When we look up at something, perspective makes it appear narrower towards the top. The temple builders exploited this to make their columns seem taller by making them wider at the bottom and thinner higher up. Since each temple had some fifty columns, each of which had to be built of giant drums of stone, a construction period measured in decades begins to seem more reasonable – especially as the temples were so well built that most of the damage they have suffered over the past two thousand years has been inflicted deliberately, by those looting the stones for building.

There were two large altars and a third smaller one outside the second Hera temple. Unlike modern churches, worshippers did not usually go into the temples, and sacrifices were performed outside. However, the three altars suggest that the second temple housed a triad of divinities. Examination of votive offerings indicates that Hera shared the building with her husband Zeus. The third divinity is unknown, but perhaps the authorities had finally decided to acknowledge Poseidon, the god after whom the city was originally named.

A *hydria* from Paestum. *Hydriai* were used to carry water from the fountain to the home, often on the head of the bearer. They were sometimes given as prizes in athletic events or used in ritual.

## Deities not called Hera

When the Romans took over the city in 273 BC they added their own cultural stamp to a settlement already ancient. They reconstructed the town centre into that most Roman of institutions, a forum. There they built a small temple to their own sacred triad – Juno, Jupiter and Minerva. This temple could afford to be modest because, as Zeus, Jupiter already shared a grander temple with his wife Juno/Hera. Minerva was the Roman name for Athena and that goddess also was already well represented in Paestum with another magnificent temple which stood on the other side of the city near the *heroön*.

Paestum also contains numerous tombs, and is even today renowned for those of the Lucanian people who lavishly painted the interiors with frescoes, many of which still retain much of their original freshness. Today many of these can be viewed at the local museum.

---

## Later Paestum

The sacred sites at Paestum owe their preservation to the fact that the city was largely deserted before late antiquity, so there were few Christians in the locality to take offence at the pagan structures. Indeed there are signs that the temple of Athena served for a while as a church. However, the river which had for so long served as the lifeblood of the town began to silt up and flood. According to the geographer Strabo the site was never healthy in the first place and now pestilence forced the people to translocate to healthier environs.

Paestum and its temples were largely forgotten until they came to the attention of Italian engineers who were driving a new highway through what turned out to be the centre of the ancient town. (They carried on regardless, anyway.) The temples had never been entirely forgotten – the artist Giovanni Battista painted them in the eighteenth century – but now the Italians realized that they were in possession of some of the best-preserved Greek temples in the Mediterranean world.

Today the site is popular with tourists who benefit not only from contemplating these ancient places of worship but also from enjoyment of the magnificent beaches of the nearby modern town.

# *c.* 2300 BC – AD 529

# Grove of Academus

## Haunt of the Original Academics

*I was eager to distinguish the straight from the crooked and to seek the truth in the groves of Academe.*

Horace, *Epistles* 2.2.41

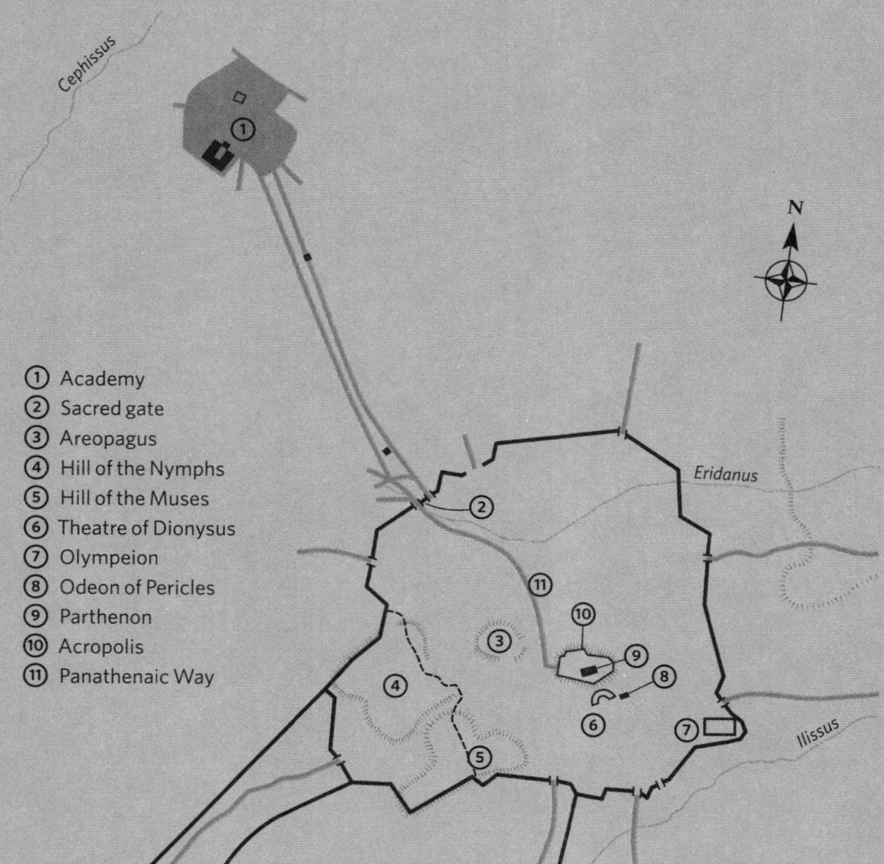

Discussion of the Academy in Athens covers two different yet largely overlapping entities – the School of Philosophy founded by Plato and the actual grove, sacred to Athena and the Muses. While the grove remains today as a small park with a litter problem, 1.5 kilometres (1 mile) from the city centre, the only worshippers in attendance are devotees of Helios catching a tan.

## Legendary origins

The grove has long been considered sacred, as is shown by a building recently discovered there. This structure dates back to the Bronze Age and is the oldest yet discovered in Athens. This – if we consider the Heroic Age of myth as contemporaneous with the Late Bronze Age of archaeology – is also when we get the first reference to the grove in our sources.

The name of the Academy is indirectly due to Theseus, the mythical hero who united the towns of Attica under the control of Athens. For all his heroic status, Theseus was an altogether

Plato in Pompeii. This mosaic, uncovered at the villa of one Stephanus, probably dates from the first century BC. It shows Plato (centre) instructing students at his Academy.

despicable character. One of the low points of his career came when he kidnapped an exceptionally beautiful prepubescent Spartan girl. This was an unwise, as well as morally repugnant, move because the girl was none other than that Helen who later became Helen of Troy. Her two brothers, Castor and Pollux (today the Gemini twins of the zodiac), took grave exception to this and followed Theseus to Athens. While Theseus wisely made himself scarce, the twins started ripping apart the city in search of their missing sister (Plutarch, *Theseus* 32.1).

A major war was averted when one Academus took it upon himself to track down the missing girl and inform the vengeful brothers of her location. Thankful for being bailed out of a crisis, the Athenians awarded this man custody of a plot of land outside the city which was sacred to Athena. Thereafter this area beside the Cephissus river was known as 'the Academus'. Later, among the other shrines and altars in the grove there was one dedicated to the memory of Academus. This was partly because, some six hundred years after his death, when Athens was at war with Sparta, the area was spared devastation by Spartan troops in recognition of the favour Academus had done for their ancestors all those centuries ago.

## Upgrade

For many years, despite its riparian location, the Academy was remarkably groveless, being an 'arid and waterless spot' (says Plutarch in *Cimon* 13.6). The vegetation consisted of a single olive tree, reputed to be the second oldest in Athens. This tree was said to have been installed by Athena herself, and to be a relative to the oldest-ever olive tree, which she had placed on the Acropolis.

The Athenians were a lot more successful in their wars with the Persians than they were at fighting the Spartans. In the early fifth century they organized the people of Ionia into a defensive League and used the profits to beautify their city. One beneficiary of this was the Academy, which the Athenian leader Cimon (510–450 BC) transformed into a pleasant grove by building a large cistern to irrigate the grounds. He also added running tracks and walkways, later to be shaded by the olive trees that he planted at the site.

It is uncertain how much of the Academy was in private hands at this point. The Athenians built a public gymnasium at the location and put a wall around the park, yet we know from a later reference by the writer Diogenes Laertius that some of this land was still privately owned. The new olive grove, like the solitary tree which had preceded it, was sacred to Athena.

The famous 'School of Athens' in the Vatican, Italy. The fresco, by Raphael *c.* 1510, shows Plato (probably modelled on Leonardo da Vinci) surrounded by scholars and stands opposite another fresco with a theological theme.

When the Roman travel writer Pausanias came to visit the Academy in the second century AD he reported that 'in my time this is a [public] gymnasium though it was once private property'. Within the Academy was an altar to Eros, allegedly the first such erected in the city, and there was a matching altar in central Athens dedicated to Anteros, the god of requited love. (It is Anteros, incidentally, who stands atop the pillar in Piccadilly Circus in present-day London.) Athenian youths had a nocturnal race where they ran from the altar of Prometheus in the Academy to the altar of Anteros (the Athenian one) each carrying a lighted torch. Letting the torch go out was grounds for instant disqualification (Pausanias, *Guide to Greece* 1.30.3). The race started at the altar of Prometheus because Prometheus, in Greek myth, was the being who had first given fire to humans.

## The School of Plato

The reason for Pausanias visiting the grove was not to witness Athenian fire ceremonies but because it had become famous as a haunt of philosophers. Which was unsurprising since the whole area was dedicated to Athena, the goddess of wisdom, strategy and

Plato outside the modern Academy in Athens. This statue sits with Socrates to its right and Athena and Apollo towering behind.

cool logic. The first of these 'lovers of wisdom' was Socrates (469–399 BC), who was in the habit of walking to the Academy and there taking on all comers in wide-ranging debates.

One of the most devoted followers of Socrates was a young man called Aristocles, who is better known today by the nickname derived from his broad shoulders – 'Plato' (*c.* 429–347 BC). After the death of Socrates Plato went on to make a name for himself as a philosopher, to the extent that he was invited to Sicily to discuss philosophy with Dionysius I, the ruler of Syracuse. The conversation did not go well. Dionysius accused Plato of talking like a senile old man, to which Plato retorted that the other talked like a tyrant (which he actually was). For speaking truth to power Plato was arrested and after various misadventures ended up being ransomed from slavery by his friends.

One of these friends purchased a small plot of land in (or adjacent to) the Academy and on his return to Athens Plato made his home there and established his famous School. The School's most famous alumnus was Aristotle (384–322 BC), who studied at the Academy for over a decade before founding his own school, the Lyceum, and then going on to become tutor to Alexander the Great. Another philosopher who studied at the Academy was Zeno (335–263 BC), the founder of the Stoic school. Plato was buried at the Academy. Modern technology has enabled the reading of carbonized scrolls from Herculaneum and one of these seems to have revealed the exact location of his grave (alongside the shrine of the Muses).

## The later Academy

The Academy continued to thrive for centuries, though the olive trees of the sacred grove of Athena were radically pruned by the Roman general Sulla, who in 87 BC – with his usual disregard for religion – chopped down trees and used the wood to build siege engines. (He was besieging Athens at the time.) The Academy – both the School and the sacred grove – flourished during the Roman empire with various notables attending the School and a large complex being built beside the gymnasium.

With the advent of Christianity worship ceased at the grove and the school was closed when the teaching of philosophy was banned by imperial edict in AD 529. The sacred grove reverted to being the small dusty patch of land it had once been, but the seeds of thought planted there by Athena have spread and taken root in Academies which now flourish all around the world.

## 13th century BC – AD 435

# The Cecropia

## Sacred Heart of Athens

*The whole land is sacred to Athena...but the most holy is the image of Athena which is on what is now called the Acropolis.*

**Pausanias, *Guide to Greece* 1.26.6**

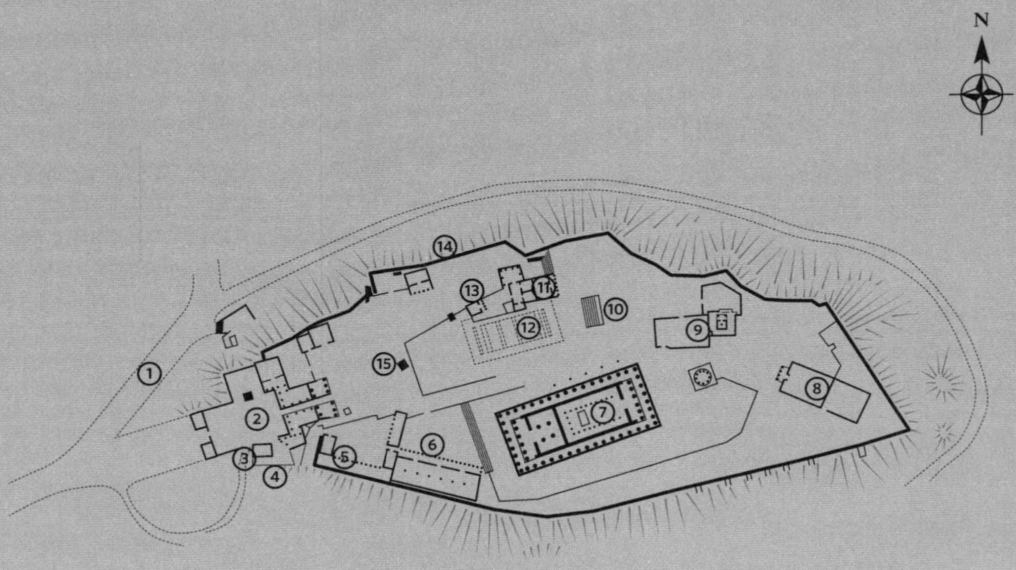


100 yards

100 metres

① Panathenaic Way
② Propylaea
③ Temple of Athena Nike
④ Eleusinion
⑤ Sanctuary of Artemis Brauronia
⑥ Chalkotheke (bronze store)
⑦ Parthenon
⑧ Sanctuary of Pandion
⑨ Sanctuary of Zeus Polieus
⑩ Altar of Athena
⑪ Erechtheum
⑫ Older temple of Athena
⑬ Pandroseion
⑭ Aglaureion
⑮ Statue of Athena Promachos

While '*The* Acropolis' is used to describe the complex of buildings that constituted the municipal, defensive and religious heart of Classical Athens, the ancient Athenians probably did not always use this term. It was too general. Almost every contemporary Greek city had its own Acropolis ('high city') but only Athens had the Cecropia.

## Pre-Classical origins

The name 'Cecropia' is derived from the mythical first king of Athens, a half-human, half-dragon individual called Cecrops. Rather like the later Romans' mythical King Numa, Cecrops was credited by the Athenians with stabilizing their society through just laws and organized worship. He was said to have been the first to recognize Zeus as the king of the gods and he ordered that no living thing should be sacrificed to him. (His more bloodthirsty descendants got around that by making the killing of the sacrificial animal a different part of the ceremony.)

Cecrops was also witness to the planting of the first olive tree by Athena on the Acropolis, and in recognition of the benefits of the olive Cecrops decreed that Athena should become the patron goddess of Athens.

A sixth-century BC *kylix* (drinking cup) from Athens. It shows scenes from the myth of Cecrops (bottom left) who is depicted as having the tail of a giant serpent instead of legs.

The famous caryatid porch on the Erechtheum on the Athenian Acropolis. Caryatids are pillars shaped as a female form, of which these are the most famous examples.

Modern archaeologists agree that settlement on the Cecropia is very ancient, as pottery sherds found there are over six thousand years old. By the time of the Late Bronze Age in 1300 BC, when legend has the Athenians as part of the force besieging Troy, 'the strong-built house of Erechtheus' described by Homer (*Odyssey* 7.81) was a Mycenaean city perched atop the 3.2-hectare (8-acre) rocky crag that dominated the local landscape. Erechtheus was the legendary successor to Cecrops.

## Sacred Athena

Being closest to the heavens, the Acropolis of almost every Greek city had a sacred aspect, but the Athenians took matters further. At the end of the Bronze Age the citizens turned their Acropolis into a combined fortress and temple serving the city which had developed on the flatter land some 150 metres (nearly 500 feet) below. The Acropolis became the home of Athena Polias ('Athena of the City'), who was given a dedicated temple, and its priestess held the highest religious office in Athens.

This temple was built on the northeast of the Acropolis, contrary to the later tradition that buildings sacred to Athena were to be mostly on the southern side. Other gods such as Poseidon and Artemis had to crowd into shrines and altars in the remaining space. Access to the sacred space was restricted by a gate (*propylon*) at the foot of the hill.

The people most responsible for the Acropolis as we know it today were the Persians of the Achaemenid empire. In 498 BC the Athenians attacked the Persian city of Sardis in Asia Minor and burned it to the ground, thus infuriating the Persian king Darius I. In 480 BC, the Persians had their revenge. After they had defeated the Spartans at Thermopylae, their army swept down upon Athens, captured the city's Acropolis and flattened every building upon it.

## A new and improved Acropolis

Subsequent successes against the Persians and the establishment of a maritime hegemony in the Aegean Sea gave the Athenians the wherewithal to rebuild. The surviving relics and ruins of the old Acropolis were solemnly gathered together and ritually interred in caves and pits on the hill. Then the hill itself was given a reinforcing wall and thousands of 2-tonne blocks of limestone were used to create a secure foundation. Then the serious building began.

Athena in her many manifestations was celebrated as never before. A giant monumental statue was raised to Athena Promachos ('Athena of the Battle-line'). Athena was also a war goddess, as her helmet indicates. One of the first colossal statues raised by the Athenian genius Phidias, Athena's was some 9 metres (nearly 30 feet) tall. The tip of her spear appearing over the horizon was the first sight of Athens for those approaching by sea.

In the southwest corner of the Acropolis stood the small but exquisitely designed temple of Athena Nike ('Athena of Victory'), in its own walled enclosure, separate from the main complex of the Acropolis and approached by a different stairway.

Next was the complex and beautiful but enigmatic building known today as the Erechtheum, its front porch decorated with the caryatids that still delight visitors today. (A caryatid is a supporting column carved into the shape of a woman.) The building is named after King Erechtheus, and was built upon the shrine dedicated to his memory. For reasons still hotly debated the Erechtheum does not have the format of a Classical temple, and present-day academics are uncertain which god (or gods) were worshipped there.

## The Parthenon

'Earth proudly wears the Parthenon as the best gem upon her zone,' remarked the nineteenth-century poet Ralph Waldo Emerson. This jewel of the Acropolis was the temple to the Maiden Athena (*parthenos* was Greek for 'virgin'). As Emerson observed, this building is considered among the finest, or even foremost of, the sacred buildings of the ancient world. Like the temple to Athena Nike, it was built with profits resulting from the Persian Wars and no expense was spared in the construction. The foremost architects, stonemasons and sculptors of the day were set to work on a design that used top-quality Pentelic marble. The building appears to soar lightly towards the heavens, because the designers used a variety of optical effects to make it seem larger than it actually is (for example the columns toward the rear are built slightly closer together to mimic the foreshortening effect of distance). Because a smaller building is less affected by gravity, by appearing larger the Parthenon also looks lighter.

Within the temple of the maiden goddess was another statue of Athena, also by Phidias. It was chryselephantine, meaning that it was apparently composed of gold and ivory (probably with a core of solid cypress wood). This gigantic statue had a golden cloak, indicating that the Parthenon was not just a place of worship but also the ancient equivalent of the Reserve Bank of Athens. That cloak of solid gold was designed so that it could be dismantled at need for the Athenians to meet extraordinary expenses (to be later repaid with interest).

Most Athenian religious ceremonies, sacrifices and processions either took place on the Acropolis or began or ended there. Who had what role in these events was an indicator of the participants' social standing in the city. The most important event was the Panathenaea, held annually to honour Athena. It included a grand procession, athletic contests, sacrifices, and musical and poetic competitions. The *Canephorus* – the aristocratic girl who carried a basket of first fruits to be dedicated to Athena during the Panathenaic celebration – would boast of it all her life, and on occasion for centuries thereafter in a memorial inscription. A more arcane rite was that of the Arrephoria, celebrated at a site on the Acropolis called the Pandroseion. This involved young girls carrying sacred objects hidden within a closed basket through a cave in the hill down to a hidden spring – even though the spring ceased to flow after an earthquake in the early Classical era.

The Acropolis at night with Mount Lycabettus in the background. This picture shows why, as well as being a religious centre, the Acropolis served as the Athenian fortress of last resort.

## Later eras

The Athenian Acropolis lost some of its sacred functions when the temples were closed by Roman imperial decree in AD 491, though several temples reopened as churches. (The temple to the Virgin Athena became the Church of the Virgin Mary in *c.* AD 435.) The Acropolis retained its role as a fortress in the Ottoman era (1456–1833). The Parthenon became an ammunition dump, and the temple of Athena Nike was dismantled and built into a defensive wall.

Most of the present dilapidated state of the Parthenon happened when the ammunition dump exploded while Athens was under attack by the Venetians in 1687. Later, a British aristocrat transported many of the remaining friezes to the British Museum – to the great indignation of modern Athenians who would really like to have them back.

The temple of Athena Nike has been more fortunate. After liberating their city the Greeks extricated the temple bits from the rest of the defensive wall and carefully rebuilt it on the original foundation. In fact the Committee for the Conservation of the Monuments on the Acropolis is still engaged in the painstaking process of preserving and restoring the ancient site – sometimes to the frustration of modern tourists who travel great distances to see towers of modern scaffolding and plastic sheeting.

PART THREE

# The Coming of Rome

## Roman religion

In the Roman imperial era religion was both a dividing and unifying force, but in every case it was deeply embedded into the civic and private lives of the empire's people. Sacred spaces were not just huge temples built at government expense, but also part of ordinary homes, where families set a space aside for a *lararium* at which the gods of the household were worshipped. (Even today, step into the courtyard of an older Italian house, and you are likely to find a small shrine to the Virgin Mary or a local saint.)

In the Roman Republic, politicians harangued crowds from the forecourts of temples in the Roman Forum. Because the early Forum flooded a lot, temples were built on high bases, which made them so useful for speakers that the word for a Roman temple base – *podium* – has now moved into the modern language in that context. Another example of the close relationship of Roman religion and political life was that the Senate House (Curia) was itself technically a temple to Nike (Victory). Though Julius Caesar was not murdered in the Curia (it was being refurbished), the temporary meeting place would also have been consecrated. As his last act on Earth, Julius Caesar did as a devout Roman should do and covered his head with part of his bloodstained toga, for no Roman came into the presence of the gods bare-headed.

## Temples as cultural tools

Roman religion was highly inclusive. Indeed the Romans had a rite called *evocatio*. When besieging a hostile city they would call on that city's gods to abandon the inhabitants and take up residence in superior quarters in Rome, where they could enjoy a better class of worshipper. Of course, once within Rome, such gods tended to do as did many of the city's cosmopolitan inhabitants and become increasingly Roman. An independent god might be conflated with one in the existing Roman pantheon and finish in genteel retirement as an aspect of that god. The Romans also used this technique as a means of domesticating deities in their native environment. Thus for example Magusanus, the warrior god of the warlike Batavi, became the romanized Hercules Magusanus, just as the Batavi went from being enemies to auxiliary soldiers in the armies of Rome.

Thus religion became an instrument of romanization rather than a point of friction. Local peoples were welcome to build shrines or even temples to their own gods, and even do so when they brought their gods with them to Rome – but usually with the unspoken proviso that the deity adopted a suitably Roman guise. Where this was impossible the Romans could be merciless, as demonstrated by the destruction of Germanic sacred groves and the devastation of the Druidic isle of Anglesey in Britain.

Peoples of the Hellenic world had long accommodated their rulers' desire to be worshipped as gods, and they had no inhibitions about extending this to Roman emperors. In many cities, and especially those with a large population of Roman colonists, the temple of the current divine overlord served as a focal point for civic rites and ceremonies. The emperor himself was Rome's also chief priest – the *pontifex maximus*, who embodied in his sacred self the union of state and religion.

### Christians and pagans

It is often pointed out that there were no pagans before there were Christians. There were worshippers of Baal, Isis, Mithras and the Olympian gods, but none of these religions considered themselves as 'pagan'. The term itself existed before Christianity but in a different context. *Pagani* were villagers, unsophisticated rednecks unaware of the refinements of urban life. They were outsiders from the group in the know. Roman legionaries referred to civilians as 'pagans' because they knew nothing about army life.

The term has been enthusiastically adopted by Christians and now refers – in somewhat derogatory fashion – to anyone who has not adopted the gospel of salvation. The persecution of the early Church caused a rethink of sacred spaces. When worship could be fatal, religious rites were best performed within the House of God rather than publicly outside it.

As Christianity gained momentum and became the dominant religion of the empire its practitioners proved themselves just as intolerant as – though considerably less violent than – those who had persecuted them. Shrines and sanctuaries were closed or demolished by imperial decree, and those buildings which survived did so by being purged of their ancient divinities and repurposed as churches. So, for instance, in Rome one can attend Mass in the Basilica of St Mary and the Martyrs (the Pantheon), or the church of San Lorenzo (the temple of Antonius and Fausta in the Forum). Until the 1930s worshippers could sit where Roman senators had once sat in the church of St Adrian in the Forum (formerly the Senate House), and even today those attending Mass in the city of Assisi can do so in a repurposed temple of Minerva.

Now it was paganism's turn to go underground, or at least to retreat to the groves of its origins. One of the last gods to succumb to the tide of Christianity was the woodland god Pan – immediately recognizable today in his demonized form, with the goat legs and horned head of the Prince of Darkness himself. Likewise the crossroads, sacred to the goddess Hecate, continued to see mothers furtively bringing their babies there to be blessed, despite the extreme measures taken by the medieval Church to stop this.

13 BC – 2nd century AD

# The Ara Pacis

## Augustan Altar of Peace

*The senate decreed that an altar of the Augustan Peace should be consecrated next to the Campus Martius...and that the magistrates, priests and Vestal virgins should sacrifice there.*

**Augustus, *Res Gestae* 12**

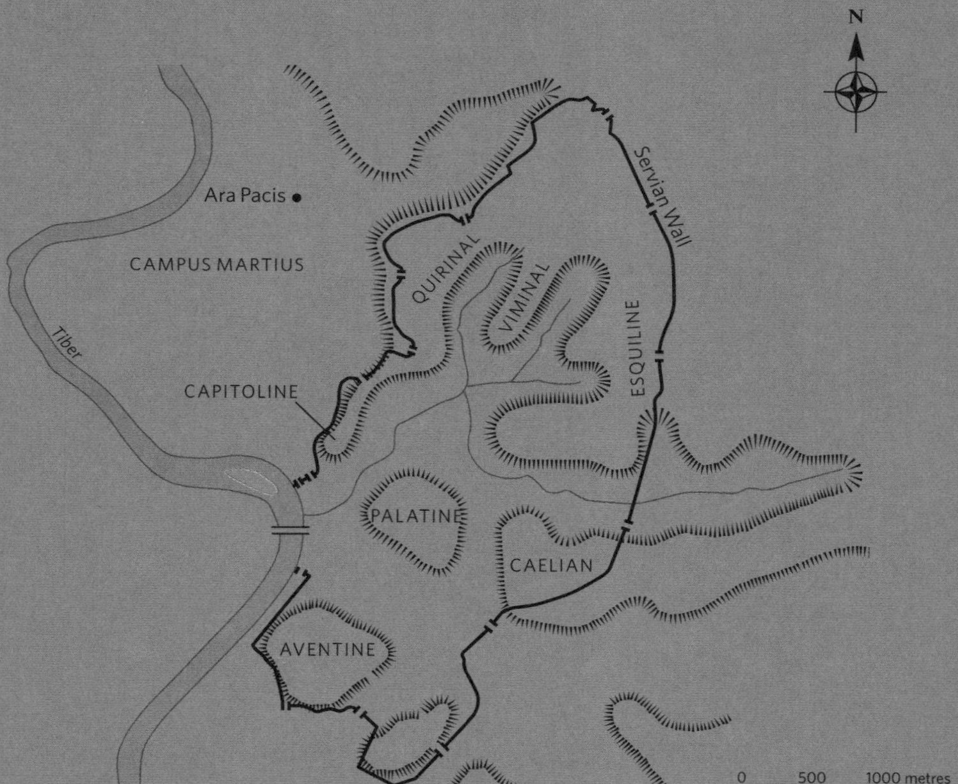

## Why an altar to peace?

Bust of the emperor Augustus wearing a civic crown given to soldiers who had saved Roman citizens during warfare.

From a secular perspective, if anything is to be sacred then peace and prosperity ought to be very high on the list. And indeed, there is an altar dedicated to peace. It was built in Rome between 13 and 9 BC to celebrate the end of the civil wars that had raged for over a century and ended the Roman Republic. The winner of the latest conflict and Rome's first emperor, Caesar Augustus, wished to persuade the Roman people that life under his sole rule was a huge improvement on the chaos that had gone before.

The Altar of Peace was part of that effort of persuasion. In one monument this altar combines religion, propaganda and sublime art. As such it illustrates the cultural mood of the Augustan era and provides a trove of complex symbology for later artists and historians to untangle.

It should be noted that, although Augustus claimed to have brought peace to the peoples under his rule, this peace came at a price to those who were being brought into the Roman empire by force and conquest even as the altar was commissioned. At that time Augustus was returning in triumph after subjugating parts of Iberia, and his legions were busily expanding the empire in all directions, from the Balkans to the Danube. In a way, then, the Altar of Peace was as much a representation of Augustan aspirations as a statement of existing fact. (On his deathbed Augustus warned that the empire was large enough and his successors should focus on ruling well the lands they already commanded. They did not listen.)

## A monument to calm and prosperity

The altar itself is not large. It stands within box-like walls; each wall is just short of 11 by 12 metres (36 × 39½ feet) and less than 5 metres (16½ feet) high. The whole monument would fit within a large room – as in fact it does today, in a purpose-built museum. As one might expect of an edifice designed to please an emperor, the Ara Pacis is made of the finest marble, in this case Carrara stone from Tuscany, which the Romans called 'Moon Stone' for its pale, blue-white colour. Like most Roman sculptures, it was originally colourfully painted. However, the paint has worn away over the centuries (Roman paint was not that colour-fast to begin with). Many art critics feel that the present monochromatic beauty of the stone only adds to the feeling of serene tranquillity which the altar exudes.

Among the many superb bas-reliefs on the sides of the monument is the so-called 'Tellus Panel'. The central figure is a seated woman holding a toddler on her lap with another at her side. This figure has

been variously described as Roma, the female personification of Rome; Gaia, the female representation of the entire Earth; or Venus, the goddess of love, whom Augustus claimed as a distant ancestor. Whomever she may be, her figure is superbly carved in bas-relief so deep that it is nearly three-dimensional. Her body is covered in a loose mantle and the sculptor has skilfully shown the outline of the figure beneath.

Garlanded nymphs appear beside her, probably depicting the land and the sea (one nymph sits on a grassy tussock, the other on a sea-snake) while a goose, a sleeping ox and a grazing sheep suggest bucolic tranquillity. The rural theme is emphasized by the upper sections of the panels, which feature vegetable motifs symbolizing growth,

A Renaissance depiction of sacrifice to a Roman emperor by Giovanni di Stefano Lanfranco, c. 1635.

renewal and fertility – all developments that Augustus earnestly wished for his empire (and which, to his credit, he largely delivered).

## Propaganda in stone

To make sure that his admiring public directly associated their emperor with this testament in stone, Augustus had himself depicted in another of the most significant panels. This is the 'processional' frieze. It shows the imperial family, priests and courtiers, clad in formal robes and togas, walking in a solemn ceremonial procession. Their expressions are serene; the presence of children adds to the family feeling; and the overall effect is to associate the imperial family and government with the peace and prosperity that Augustus has created.

This frieze has also inspired a modern guessing game, whereby archaeologists and art historians debate the identity of the minor figures and children depicted. The main protagonists are clear. For example, Augustus' henchman Agrippa (with his head suitably covered, as Romans did in the presence of their gods) is certainly at the head of the procession. But is the woman just behind him his own wife, Julia, or Livia, the wife of Augustus? And the nearby child, once thought to be Gaius Caesar, is now considered a barbarian hostage princeling on account of his longer hair and necklace. In a nice touch, the foot of one of the participants projects beyond the edge of the panel, as though the figure is about to step out of line and off the frieze altogether.

The carved panels enclose the altar itself, which was approached by one of two doors, usually the one to the east. (Most Roman temples faced the sunrise.) The altar is stepped so that those entering the enclosure would have a good view of the rites taking place within. As was usual for Roman altars the Ara Pacis was open to the sky – most Roman sacrifices took place at altars outside a temple. Even when done expertly, animal sacrifice was a messy business. Also, the temples were not places of worship that the public could enter, but literally dwelling-places for a god.

The Ara Pacis as it currently stands in the Ara Pacis Museum in Rome.

## Disappearance and reappearance

The Ara Pacis was originally situated in the Campus Martius, a grassy area to the north of Rome where young men practised military drills. Owing to a lack of public space within Rome, Augustus increasingly used the Campus Martius for his propaganda in stone. Here were erected a splendid voting area (the Saepta Julia) for a people whose votes were no longer relevant, a temple to all the gods (the Pantheon) with a statue of Augustus right outside, Rome's first public baths (built by Agrippa) and ultimately Augustus' own monumental mausoleum.

After the fall of the western Roman empire in AD 476, poor riparian management led to the Tiber river repeatedly flooding and the Ara Pacis was largely buried in silt. Rediscovered centuries later in the Renaissance, it was taken apart by aristocrats eager to display parts of the splendid artwork in their own mansions. This rediscovery and display of the bas-reliefs had a considerable impact on neo-Classical art, not only in Italy but Europe as a whole.

In the twentieth century the fascist dictator Benito Mussolini (1883–1945) made the aristocrats return the missing parts (some remain to be tracked down). He wanted to reassemble the altar as a propaganda statement symbolizing his intention to recreate the Roman empire. The monument was largely reconstructed in 1937–38.

Today, located in the Ara Pacis Museum in Rome, the altar stands not only as a monument of ancient art but also as a symbol of the enduring legacy of Roman culture and of humankind's quest for peace and prosperity. Visitors are invited to reflect upon this and also upon how these eternal ideals can be twisted for propaganda purposes.

From 8th century BC

# Grove of Egeria

## A Divine Romance

*The water which filled the pool was declared holy and its use reserved for the Vestal Virgins.*

**Plutarch, *Life of Numa* 13**

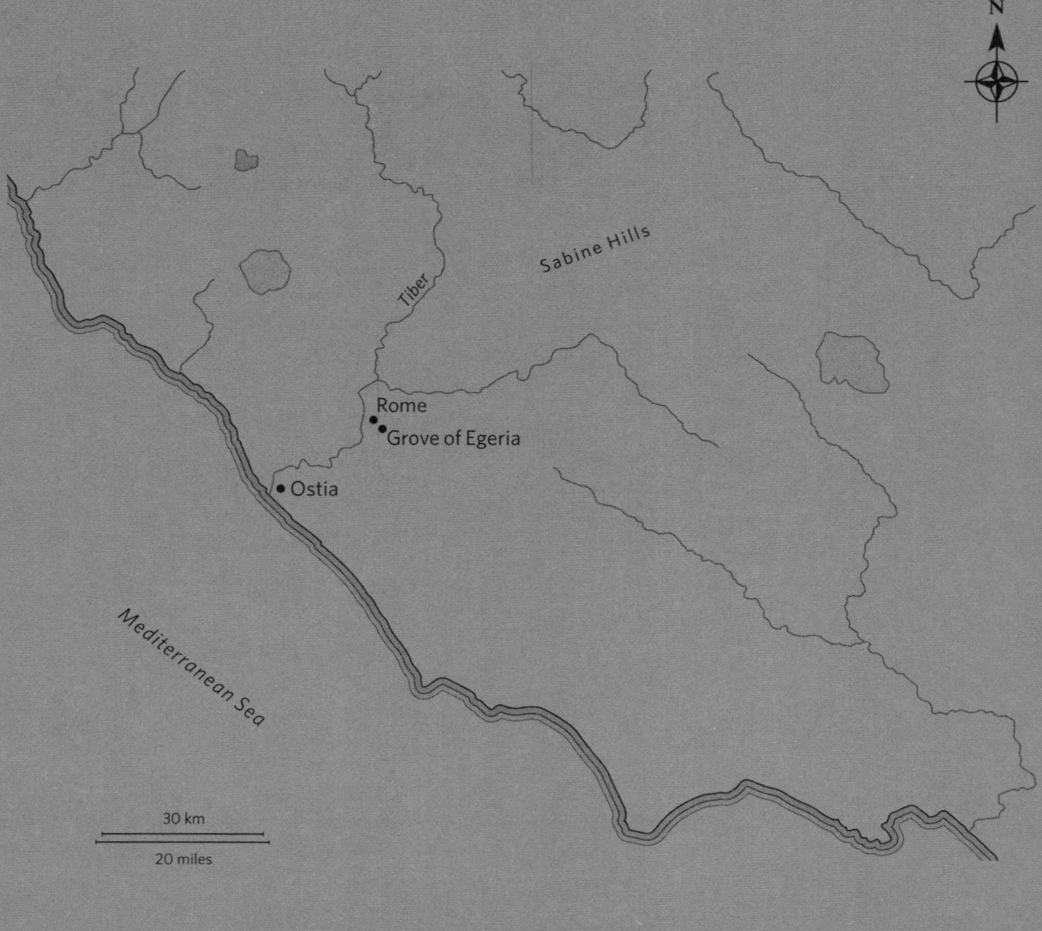

Being the second king of Rome was no easy job. Numa Pompilius, the Sabine aristocrat who had reluctantly assumed the throne, was well aware that his subjects were rightly considered by the neighbours as a violent gang of ruffians who might well have murdered his predecessor Romulus, the founder of the city.

Under the circumstances Numa (probably a legendary figure, but traditionally given the dates 715–673 BC) needed all the help he could get and he got it from his lover. No ordinary woman she, but the divine Egeria, who is variously described as a nymph, a dryad or minor goddess who had the ear of great Jupiter himself. Numa worked hard to convince his unruly subjects of his relationship with Egeria and maintained that he conversed deeply with her on topics concerning the city and its destiny. These conversations (and more) happened near the Porta Capena, one of the city gates, which stood close to a quiet grove of trees watered by a nearby pool.

It was at this grove (says Numa's biographer Plutarch) that a bronze shield suddenly dropped from the heavens. Egeria explained to Numa that this was a sign that if Numa followed her instructions carefully then he could lift the pestilence that was currently afflicting Rome. Numa did as he was told, ordering that the waters beside which the shield had touched down be used exclusively by the Vestal Virgins to purify their shrine, and that copies should be made of the shield to make it harder to steal. 'The truth of all this became clear when the plague immediately ceased' (Plutarch, *Numa* 13.3). And indeed, for the rest of their history a selected Vestal Virgin went daily from the sisterhood's shrine in the Roman Forum to the grove to draw water from the pool of Egeria.

Numa and Egeria share an intimate moment in her grotto. An eighteenth-century relief by Bertel Thorvaldsen, a Danish sculptor most famous for his statue of Jason with the Golden Fleece.

## Spring time

Numa died, as mortals do, which left the immortal Egeria with the rest of eternity to mourn her deceased beloved. Egeria took herself to nearby Aricia and sought solace at the shrine of the goddess Diana. 'But others could not ease the sadness of grieving Egeria... until moved by her faithful sorrow, Diana out of pity changed her to a spring with her limbs becoming a clear flowing stream' (Ovid, *Metamorphoses* 15.457).

Elsewhere (in the *Fasti* 3.259) Ovid relates that he had tasted the sacred water himself 'in little sips'. Regrettably, though, Ovid neglected to describe exactly where the transfiguration of Egeria took place. Was it at Aricia, where locals attributed a spring which flowed into a nearby lake to the transformed Egeria? Or back at the sacred grove where she had spent so much time with her lost love? Or at another site, also near the Porta Capena, where a spring ran some 400 metres (nearly a quarter of a mile) through a grove before joining the river Almone?

Later Romans partly sidestepped the issue by making all three sites sacred to Egeria. It is probable that the site near the Almone was previously sacred to water deities called the Camoenae, and so the Romans inducted Egeria into this group. Thus, if she had not been so before, Egeria became a minor goddess and she, as did the Camoenae, protected pregnant women during childbirth. She also granted wisdom and prophetic pronouncements to those who poured libations at her sacred pool after performing the proper rites.

The three locations sacred to Egeria had much in common. They were cool, shaded areas nestling deep in a quiet grove of greenery with spring water sliding almost silently into a tranquil pool of green, cool water. That remains the case with the small pool that is still a quiet haven at the centre of the 1-hectare (2.5-acre) Park of Egeria in present-day Rome.

## Development and commercialization

The second-century AD poet Juvenal became quite exercised by 'improvements' which he saw as the desecration of the sacred pool near the river Almone.

> *When one goes down to the Valley of Egeria, the caves are totally unnatural. We would feel so much closer to the spirit of the pool if the waters had only a border of grass instead of this hideous marble! Here the Camoenae have been ejected and the Grove and Pool are rented out.* (*Satire* III, 3.1)

*Landscape with the Nymph Egeria* by Claude Lorrain, 1669, now in the Museo e Real Bosco di Capodimonte, Naples. The grander vista shows that Egeria has strayed from her grotto on this occasion.

It is probable that Juvenal was ranting about work done by the senator Herodes Atticus (*c.* AD 101–177), who obtained ownership of the sacred pool and surrounding lands through his marriage to the noble Regilla. This Regilla was later murdered by one of her own freedmen and Herodes Atticus was never able to shake off the suspicion that he had put the freedman up to it.

Once he was formally cleared of the charge of murder, Herodes set about transforming the natural beauty of the grove into a nymphaeum (a shrine to nymphs) with marble statuary, a large shrine and a series of landscaped pools leading down to the river. Despite the commercialization of the site that followed, the waters of Egeria retained their magical powers and the largest of the pools gained the name Lacus Salutaris ('The Lake of Good Health').

## The sacred waters today

The sacred pool and grove suffered along with the rest of Rome as the empire declined, not least because the nearby gates of the Porta Capena were a natural focus for rampaging armies attacking

the city, be those armies composed of barbarian hordes or Romans commanded by usurper emperors. It was only when Rome had fallen into early medieval decrepitude that the sacred pools regained a measure of serenity.

Even though Egeria was by then considered a demon by the Roman Christian Church, her waters were still considered beneficial. It is claimed that Pope Alexander VII (1599–1667) relieved the pain of his kidney stones by daily imbibing the waters of the pool, now redesignated as 'Acqua Santa'. (Rome's Mari family have run with this tradition, using it as the inspiration for their 'Egeria' brand of bottled mineral water – though they claim no miraculous health benefits from its consumption.)

Today the nymphaeum of Egeria is part of the larger Caffarella Park, of which the Park of Egeria is an adjunct. Egeria's grove shares the park with a magnificent tomb that Herodes Atticus erected for his deceased wife (though his motivation for building the tomb has been questioned both then and in the modern era). The ruins of the nymphaeum are still decorated with a statue personifying the river Almone, though now sadly headless. For much of the year the place retains the gentle serenity which first drew Numa and Egeria to picnic at the spot – as many couples still do today.

Egeria's grotto today. Converted into a nymphaeum (shrine to the nymphs) in Roman times, the grotto now sits in a secluded spot in a park in central Rome.

c. 660 BC – AD 408

# The Curia

## Senate House and Shrine to Victory

*Winged victory, Rome's faithful guardian, was in her temple with her golden feathers arched protectively over the sacred sanctuary where the senators meet.*

Claudian, *Panegyric for the Sixth Consulship of the Emperor Honorius* I.636

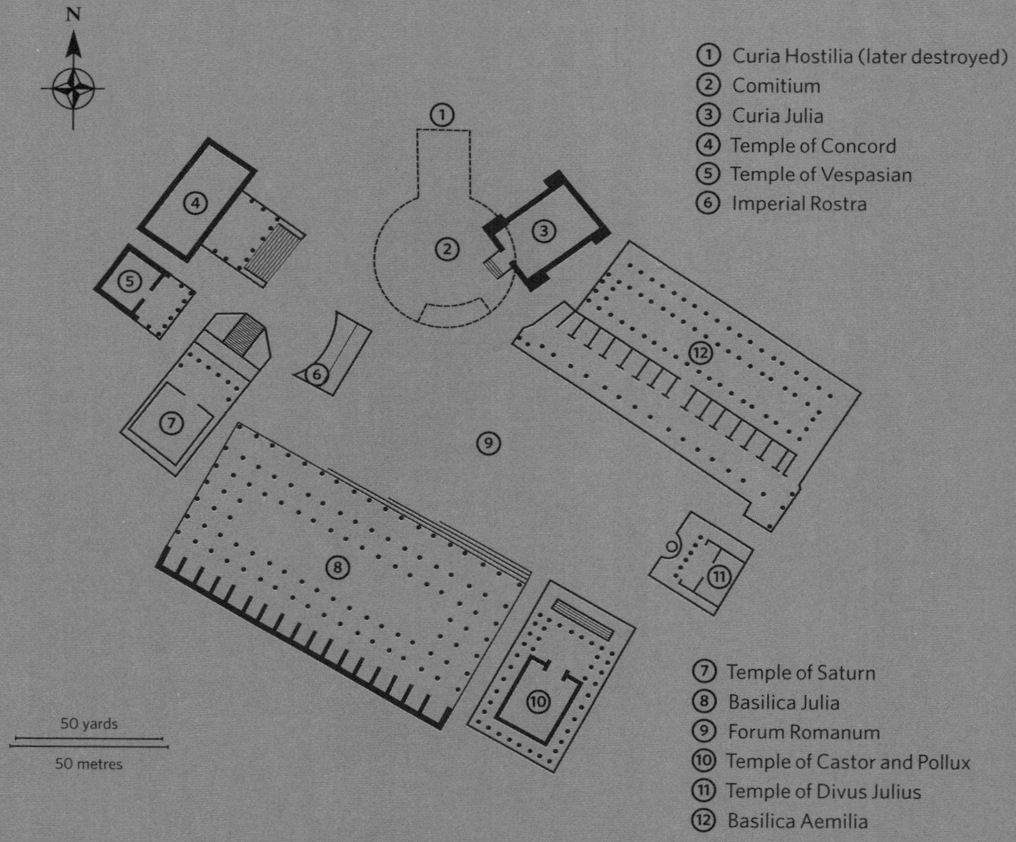

The Roman senate was a body of individuals, rather than a place. In fact the senate could meet anywhere so long as that place was sacred ground. Roman generals – and anyone else bearing weapons, for that matter – were not allowed within the boundaries of the city of Rome. Therefore the senate regularly used to hold meetings with a military theme outside the city in the temple of Bellona (Rome's ancient war goddess).

## The first Senate House

However, the main meeting place for the senate was at the place where the rest of the denizens of Rome naturally congregated, the Forum Romanum. The first mention of this dedicated meeting place in the Forum comes from Livy's substantial history *Ab urbe condita*, or 'Rome, from the Beginning'. In this he tells how Rome's legendary third king Tullus Hostilius (traditionally given the dates r. 672–641 BC) enlarged the number of Roman senators and 'built for them a sacred place, a senate house which...was called the Curia Hostilia' (*Ab urbe condita* 1.30.1). In fact, though the second part of the appellation changed over the centuries, the building was thereafter called 'the Curia', though *curia* simply means 'meeting place' in Latin.

Livy's reference to 'a sacred place' indicates that there was an earlier Etruscan temple on the site. Since the present Senate House is one of the few structures in the Forum not demolished by over-enthusiastic medieval builders looking for construction materials, no

The Curia today is one of the most intact structures in the Roman Forum. It was saved from demolition because it remained a sacred place as the medieval church of St Adrian in the Forum.

one has been able to excavate the site to check, but it is significant that the building was orientated on a precise north–south axis. This put it out of alignment with most Forum buildings, which generally skewed slightly more to the east, but was necessary for the strict rules of Etruscan temple-building. In fact even the present Curia, which was given its shape by the architects of Julius Caesar, still retains elements of Etruscan sacral architecture. (The Senate House survived by becoming a church. It was deconsecrated in the 1930s.)

The most famous feature of the Curia Hostilia was not the sacred shrine – in fact no one is certain to which god the Curia Hostilia was dedicated – but a splendid mural called the Tabula Valeria which depicted a victory of the Roman general Valerius Corvinus over the Carthaginians in the First Punic War (264–241 BC).

## Destruction and renewal

In the late Republic, appointment to the senate became a means of gaining adherents for the generals in Rome's civil wars, and the resultant doubling of the number of senators required the rebuilding of the Curia Hostilia on a much grander scale. This was accomplished in 80 BC by Cornelius Sulla, the victor in one of the earlier bouts of civil conflict. Civil unrest led also to the destruction of Sulla's Curia. When the demagogic politician Clodius Pulcher died in a street brawl in 52 BC his indignant supporters gave him a send-off on a funeral pyre of benches from the Senate House, and the entire building was destroyed in the subsequent conflagration.

The winner of the next round of civil wars was Julius Caesar, and he set about rebuilding the Senate House into the form it largely retains today. He also straightened the building to align it with the general axis of the Forum. Work on the Curia Julia was terminated in 44 BC at the same time as Caesar himself was terminated by his fellow senators on the Ides of March and it was only in 29 BC that construction was complete. This was accomplished by Caesar's heir Octavian, better known to posterity as the emperor Augustus, who boldly recorded this in his 'Record of Things Accomplished' (*Res Gestae* 19).

## The shrine of Victory

At this point the Curia was re-dedicated as a temple, this time to the goddess of victory. Victoria was the Roman equivalent of the Greek goddess Nike, and like her was depicted with wings – for the Romans knew that victory can be fleeting. Indeed the provenance

While Caesar was killed at a meeting of the senate, this did not happen, as many imagine, in the Curia but in the Theatre of Pompey about fifteen minutes' walk away.

of the statue reflects this, because it was originally captured from the people of Tarentum during the Pyrrhic War of 280–75 BC.

It is probable that Augustus chose Victoria in part to boost his own rather undistinguished military record. Newly installed in the Senate House, Winged Victory stood upon a globe (the Romans were very well aware that the world was round) holding a palm branch. The palm signified victory to the Romans, to the extent that the word *palma* was synonymous with it. With her other hand the statue proffered a laurel wreath. This was given to the victors of any major contest, be it at the Olympic Games or in a hard-fought war.

For the next four centuries this shrine to Victory stood in the Senate House. It was at this sacred shrine that senators swore their oaths of office and pledged their loyalty to each emperor as he ascended to the purple. It was here also that the senate collectively offered prayers for the well-being of the empire. Because the doors of the Curia were open while the senate was in session, these prayers and offerings presented ordinary Romans with a tangible link between their religion and their ruling class in action.

A bronze statue of the goddess of victory. Probably similar to that which stood in the Roman Senate House.

The golden statue was left unscathed in a fire which severely damaged the rest of the building in AD 94, and it also survived another fire in AD 283. Each time the Curia was conscientiously repaired by the reigning emperor, although by then the demands of a failing empire meant that rulers spent their time fighting on Rome's frontier and had little time to visit the Senate House and shrine in person.

### Decline and fall

Even as the empire became more Christian, the pagans in the senate argued strongly for the retention of their altar. 'Who gets on with the barbarians so well that he does not need an Altar of Victory?... And where else shall we swear to obey your laws and commands?' asked the pagan senator Symmachus (*c.* 340–402) in a letter to the Christian emperor Valentinian II.

Nevertheless, in AD 357 while on a visit to Rome, the emperor Constantius II ordered the statue removed (though there are indications that it was quietly replaced once the emperor's back was turned). Certainly it was back in place for the short reign of Julian (r. 361–63), Rome's last pagan emperor. In 408 the altar was dismantled for the last time in belated compliance with the edict of the very Christian emperor Theodosius I (*Codex Theodosianus* 16.10.19), which banned pagan religious statuary.

Rome's last pagans protested bitterly that removing the ancient altar from the Curia meant also removing the protection of the goddess from Rome. They would have felt gloomily vindicated two years later when a Gothic horde of barbarians captured and sacked the city.

## The Senate House today

Today the Senate House is closed to visitors, who can only admire the façade from the Forum. Apart from some statuary stored within, the interior is largely bare, with three broad stepped ledges running the 25-metre (82-foot) length where once the senators had their seating. The bronze doors that deny admission are replicas copied from the originals, which can still be found in the Basilica of St John Lateran, to where they were expropriated by the papacy in 1660. The golden statue of Winged Victory and her altar have both vanished without trace.

AD 120 – *c.* AD 180

# Sacred Places at Hadrian's Villa

## An Imperial Country Retreat

*His villa at Tibur was marvellously constructed, and he actually gave to parts of it the names of provinces and places of the greatest renown....in order not to omit anything, he even made a Hades.*

***Historia Augusta*, 'Life of Hadrian' 26**

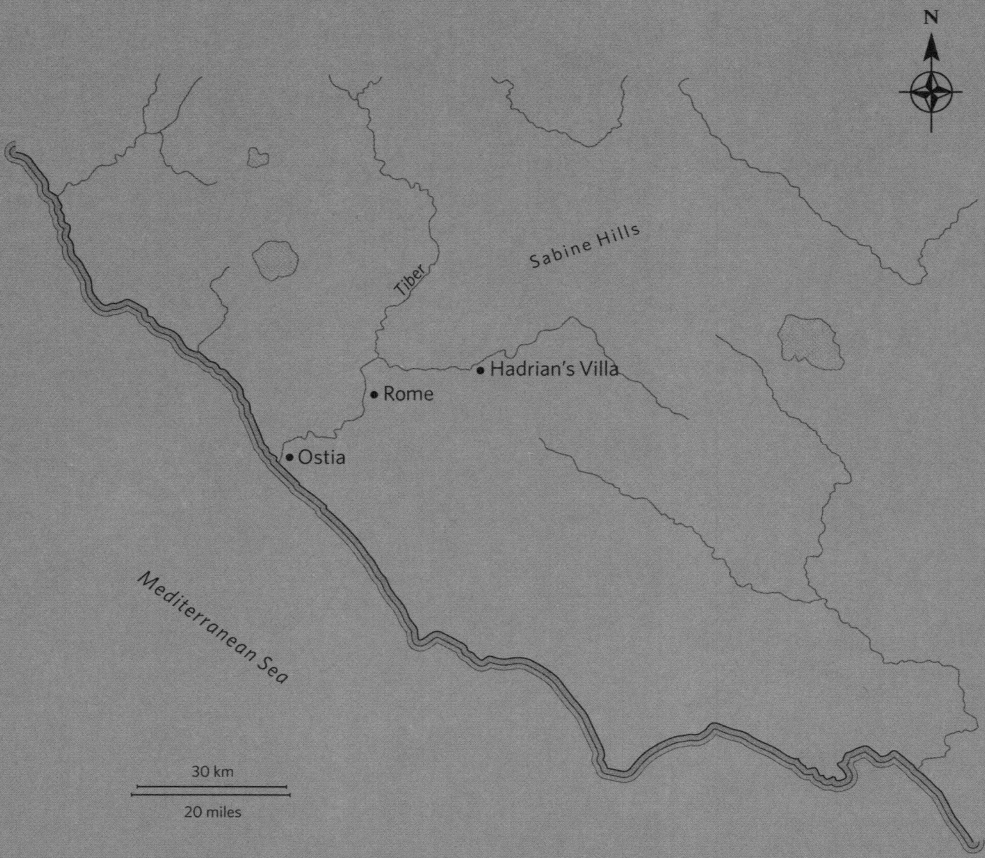

The emperor Hadrian (r. AD 117–38) ruled Rome while the empire was at the height of its power. Hadrian himself was an extremely cultured individual who had a great interest in the arts and architecture. He was personally involved in the construction of several monumental structures in Rome, including the Pantheon in the Campus Martius and the temple of Venus and Rome which was situated on the Velia, the ridge between the Colosseum and the Roman Forum.

Yet it was with his 'villa' at Tibur (modern Tivoli) that Hadrian really let his creative juices flow. He is generally believed to have been involved in every aspect of the design and indeed to have designed several parts of the complex personally. Calling the result a 'villa' is like describing a large aircraft carrier as a 'boat'. Hadrian's country house was larger than the entire city of Pompeii and was home to several thousand inhabitants. Some modern academics describe the place as being more akin to an idealized model city.

If not personally pious, for political reasons Hadrian had at least to appear so. Naturally his residence in Tibur included several places where he and the other denizens of his country retreat could

The Canopus at Hadrian's villa. This was lined with statues, including copies of the caryatids of the Erechtheum, and had a large grotto at the far end called the Serapeum, dedicated to the Greco-Egyptian god Serapis.

Now a World Heritage Site, Hadrian's 'villa' had a population of several thousand slaves, servants and visitors – the equivalent of a small town.

pay their respects to the gods. In fact, since by the time of Hadrian deceased emperors were routinely deified upon their deaths, it would have been very careless of Hadrian to have shown disrespect to those whose divine number he was scheduled to join.

## Nymphaea

A nymphaeum was an area sacred to a nymph (or nymphs) who acted as the *genius loci* of a particular location. Generally these were green places that included pools or springs. Where his villa was lacking in these Hadrian had his engineers supply them. Water features such as pools and fish ponds abound at the villa, and it was not hard for Hadrian to make a pious nod to divinity by designating some of these as sacred to the nymphs. (It is not known if each was sacred to a single nymph or just to the species in general.)

Their connection with the sacred did not prevent these places having a dual use. For example, the Cavea Nymphaeum had facilities allowing for al fresco dining on summer evenings. The 'Hades' referred to in the *Historia Augusta* was another nymphaeum. This was a long narrow crevice with a grotto at the southern end. It was considerably enhanced from its natural state with galleries, service corridors, fountains and pools. This was, in fact, a clever use of what had once been an open pit from which the tufa for other buildings in the villa was extracted.

## The temple of Venus

With vistas of the mountains to the east and with views toward Tibur, the temple of Venus was positioned in imitation of the temple which inspired it – that of Venus at Cnidus in Greece, which likewise overlooked a spectacular view. The central feature of the Cnidus temple was a statue of the goddess modelled as if she were preparing for her bath. This statue had been created by the famed sculptor Praxiteles in the fourth century BC.

According to no less an authority than the philosopher Plato, a popular contemporary story has it that the statue at Cnidus became so famous that eventually the goddess decided to see her likeness for herself. Having approached the temple she examined her effigy from every angle – the circular colonnade around the statue was designed to make this possible. So close was the resemblance that the goddess demanded indignantly 'So when did Praxiteles see me naked?' (Plato, *Epigram* 17).

The statue in question had not survived but several copies had, and Hadrian had one of these early deepfakes installed in his temple of Venus at the villa. While the statue was the undoubted star of the temple, it was accompanied by several herms and what appears to have been a depiction of Apollo. Toward the front of the temple a lower level seems to have been designated as a picnic area where those visiting the goddess could share a meal while taking in the scenery.

## The temple of Antinous

One of the most controversial aspects of Hadrian's private life was his relationship with a beautiful youth called Antinous. When Hadrian first met Antinous the lad was barely a teenager, yet Hadrian was immediately smitten with him. The pair were inseparable until Antinous died some time before his twentieth birthday. One theory was that the young man died to avert a scandal. The Romans saw no problem with having sex with boys (Trajan was noted for this) but affairs between adult homosexuals were frowned upon.

However politically convenient his lover's death may have been, personally Hadrian was devastated. He immediately had Antinous deified and even founded a city at the site of his death in Egypt, where annual games celebrated his short life.

At the Tibur villa Hadrian built a temple to the deified Antinous. This stood on a plaza near the main entrance from Rome to the grounds of the estate. There was an accompanying temple which may have been dedicated to Osiris, the Egyptian god with whom

Bust of Antinous, the youth beloved by Hadrian. After his lover's death, Hadrian had him deified, and a temple dedicated to the boy-god is located at the villa.

A pastoral scene depicted on a mosaic at Hadrian's villa. The highly cultivated Hadrian was a patron of the arts and architecture; he may have designed some of the villa's buildings himself.

Hadrian wanted Antinous identified. The two temples stood on a 30-metre (98-foot) columned semicircle, flanked with water features (and the inevitable nymphaeum). A question still debated today is whether the Antinoeion – the temple dedicated to Antinous – also housed the body of the deceased, or if it was only dedicated to his memory.

## The 'temple of Apollo'

Whether this temple was indeed dedicated to Apollo has been an open question since at least the eighteenth century, when the ruined structure was depicted by the famed Italian artist Giovanni Battista Piranesi. He expressed his doubts by entitling his work 'A view of the so-called Temple of Apollo at Hadrian's villa'.

Among his many attributes Apollo was a solar deity, and this may be why this building has been attributed to him. The nearby Academia Esplanade is aligned along the celestial axis. This means that at dawn at the winter solstice and at sunset on midsummer's day the sun shines through the main axis of the building, creating blades of light illuminating the temple. This definitely was an effect calculated to inspire religious awe, but some modern researchers think the divinity that viewers were supposed to be awed about was the Egyptian goddess Isis and not the Greco-Roman Apollo. It is also conceivable that both divinities were worshipped here – for example, in the sanctuary of Apollo in Cyrene, Apollo and Isis were worshipped side by side. It is also possible (though unlikely) that this structure was sacred to neither god. No Apollo-specific votive offerings or statuary have been found, and the building lacks aspects of architecture usually found in buildings dedicated to Isis, such as underground chambers and stone purification bowls.

Nevertheless, some aspect of the goddess would be in keeping with the Egyptian theme of many places in the Tibur complex, including the famous Canopus feature – a long pool surrounded by statues and a colonnade. The artificial grotto at one end of this feature is referred to as 'The Serapeum'. Despite taking the name of the most famed of Alexandrian temples it does not seem that this was a sacred spot. If it was dedicated to any divinity this would not have been the Greco-Egyptian deity Serapis, but the more obscure Egyptian fertility god Bes, whose statue is nearby.

## Hadrian's villa today

Hadrian's country retreat was a superb example of the application of Roman architecture to landscape features. Sadly the centuries that followed were too stressful for the complex to receive anything like the care needed to maintain it, and the place became overgrown and was allowed to fall into ruin. In the modern era interest in the site has revived and it is now one of the most visited historical sites in Italy. The authorities have been doing their best to make the experience as pleasant and informative as possible. Money from the EU has supplemented that from the National Lottery for programmes of investigation and restoration, so that even in the ruins today it is possible to catch glimpses of how beautiful the place must have been when Hadrian walked there in its prime.

509 BC – *c.* AD 500

# The Capitoline Temple

## A Great Temple for a Great God

*During the war with the Sabines king Tarquin vowed to build a temple to Jupiter. With prophetic anticipation of future grandeur he laid the foundations.*

Livy, *Ab urbe condita* 1.38.6

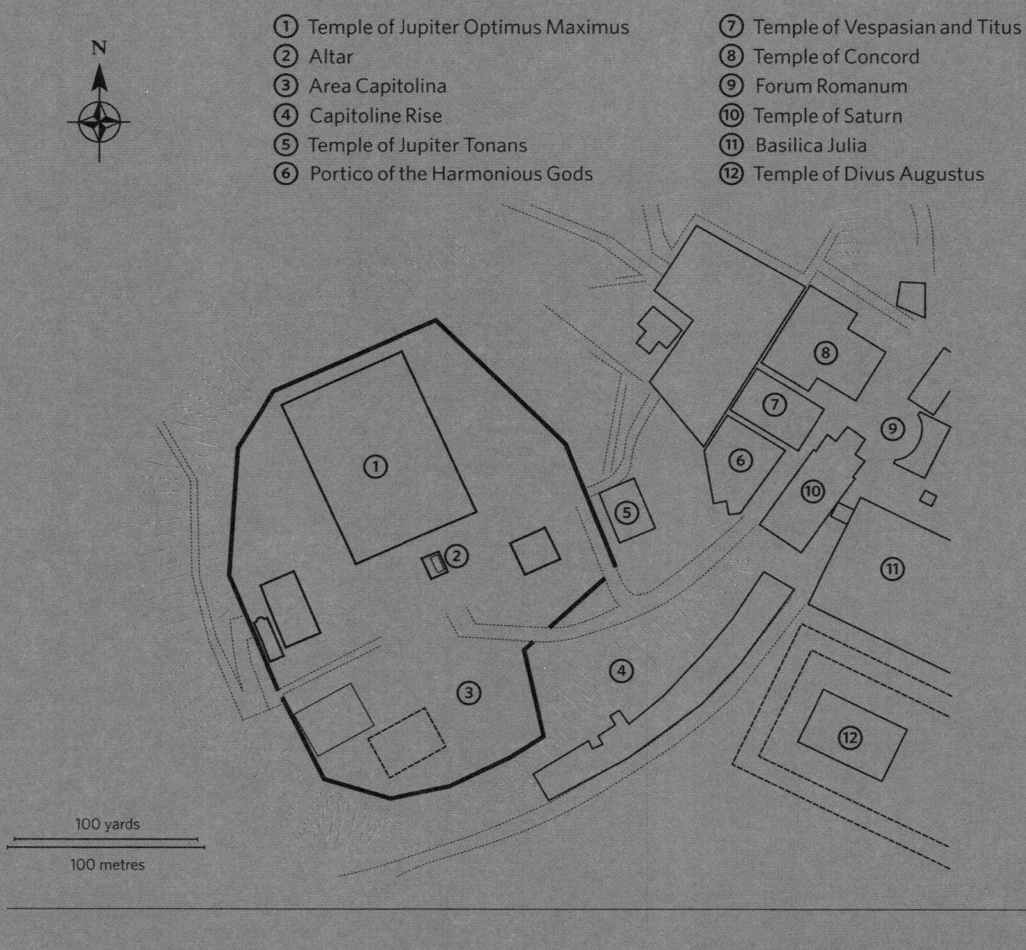

Roman legends reassure later generations of the piety of their ancestors. Many of these legends featured the patron god and protector of Rome. Unsurprisingly, given the huge empire over which Rome was later to rule, this god was none other than the king of the gods himself, Jupiter, or as the Romans familiarly referred to their mighty protector, 'IOM' – Iuppiter Optimus Maximus, 'Jupiter the best and greatest'.

The greatest god of the greatest empire needed a temple befitting that status and, according to Roman legend, the city's kings planned it that way from the start. That first temple vowed by Tarquinius Priscus (traditional dates r. 616–579 BC), fifth king of Rome, was planned on a scale that rivalled the temples of the wealthier and more sophisticated civilizations of Greece and Etruria. A warning, had those states only heeded it, of the scale of Rome's future ambition.

The temple of Jupiter Capitolinus was intended to awe tourists and worshippers alike. It succeeds in this watercolour by nineteenth-century artist C. R. Cockerell.

'Jupiter the best and greatest' is shown here in a statue from the second century AD with a thunderbolt in his right hand and his totemic eagle beside him.

Yet the auguries for the building of the temple were mixed, to say the least. For a start, the Capitoline hill on which the temple was to be built (at that time known as 'The Mount of Saturn') had been a sacred place since time immemorial, even before the foundation of Rome. Numerous other temples had accumulated on the hill, and their priests required careful consultation and incentives before the resident gods allowed their places of worship to be moved. (In the ancient world states routinely negotiated with their gods.) Despite the pleas of the secular authorities, the god Terminus refused to budge from his hilltop home.

## Omen-ous signs

Nevertheless workmen began cutting back the tufa atop the hill, both to level the ground and to use the material for later construction. Inexplicably, they came upon a head, so freshly severed that it was still bleeding. Since this head was found buried in the undisturbed tufa, evidently it had been placed there as a sign from the gods. But did it portend something good or ill?

Putting the proper public relations perspective on these unexpected developments took some imaginative work by the soothsayers, but eventually they came up with a suitable explanation. Terminus was an aspect of the ancient god Janus, the god who had ruled these lands before humans ever came to be. That the terminal aspect of the god of beginnings and endings refused to leave his perch on the hill signalled that the rule of Rome would be without end. As to the head – well, it signalled that Rome would one day be the head of the world. To hammer home this point with a dubious populace the hill was renamed with the Latin for 'head' – *caput* – so that it has forever thereafter been known as the Capitoline.

Because in the ancient world three was the number of the sacred and divine, the temple was built to house a triad – Juno, the wife of Jupiter, Jupiter himself, and his child the goddess Minerva. Each had their own separate *cella* (inner shrine) housing a cult statue – an arrangement which remained through later iterations of the temple, even though the building became known in the popular mind as the 'Temple of Jupiter Capitolinus'. Partly to accommodate the triple gods, the temple was built on a foundation of some 60 by 55 metres (197 × 180 feet), making it one of the largest in Italy at the time.

Now completely demolished, the temple is known to us only through contemporary depictions, such as on this coin now in the British Museum.

## The Republican temple

The amount of money and manpower needed for the massive building did little to help the growing unpopularity of the family member who succeeded Tarquinius Priscus. This was Tarquinius Superbus, who was overthrown in the revolution that made Rome a republic in 509 BC – the year the Capitoline temple was inaugurated.

It was just as well that the temple was built on a splendid scale, because over the centuries Rome went from strength to strength. Victorious Roman generals – and there were a lot of them – finished the extravagant ceremonial parade of a Roman Triumph at the temple, where they ceremonially handed over a portion of their spoils to Jupiter. Between the years of 220 and 70 BC alone Rome celebrated over one hundred triumphs. Consequently the temple became crowded with statues and its coffers bulged with captured booty.

This overcrowding may have led to the disastrous fire of 83 BC, when not only was the temple destroyed but also the sacred Sybilline books of oracles which had guided Rome to its greatness thus far. At the time Rome was under the domination of a dictator called Cornelius Sulla (*c.* 138–78 BC) and once again some nifty public relations 'spin' had to be deployed lest it seem that the fire signalled divine displeasure with the current administration.

In fact, explained Sulla, the fire did indeed signal divine displeasure. Firstly because Sulla had not returned to Rome sooner (he was busy with a war in Greece) and secondly because Jupiter was signalling that he was unhappy with his current accommodation. The efforts of the early Romans had been well-meaning, but admittedly somewhat crude. Rome was not now a tiny city-state but mistress of a Mediterranean-wide empire, and she needed a Capitoline temple to match. Sulla made it plain that he had taken the hint by expropriating the magnificent columns intended for the temple of Zeus in Athens and shipping them to Rome as part of the portico for a new and yet more splendid temple.

Sulla brought not only the columns, but also a number of Greek craftsmen to Rome to work on the new temple, which consequently had a decidedly Hellenistic appearance. However, temple-building was a painstakingly slow process (the temple in Athens from which Sulla looted the columns was finally finished in the reign of Hadrian two centuries later). Even with the resources of the Roman state behind the task the new and improved Capitoline temple was only completed in the 60s BC, well after Sulla's death.

Perhaps, though, the destruction of the ancient Republican temple did signal Jupiter's displeasure at the civil wars wracking the Roman Republic at that time. Certainly the temple was to be destroyed yet again in another bout of civil wars, this time the convulsion of bloody disturbances that saw the overthrow of the emperor Nero and his eventual replacement by Vespasian in AD 69.

## The final update

Until the death of Nero, Rome's emperors had all been of the highly refined clan of the aristocratic Julio-Claudians. Vespasian and the sons who succeeded him were distinctly more middle class (at one point Vespasian had made his living as a mule-trader) so they needed to work harder to impress the snobs in the senate. The new dynasty did this partly with a spectacular building programme – literally spectacular in the case of the Colosseum at one end of the Roman Forum, and more metaphorically in the magnificent temple which now crowned the hill on the other end. Even today we have some idea of how this temple looked in its prime, because Domitian, the youngest son of Vespasian, proudly advertised it on a series of coins.

For the next three hundred years this temple was the centre of religious life in Rome. As Livy (*c.* 59 BC–AD 17) had written earlier, 'Can we properly celebrate Jupiter anywhere but on the Capitoline? It is completely clear that the auspicious nature of this location cannot be shifted anywhere else' (*Ab urbe condita* 5.52.6). Even as Rome fell into decline in later centuries the last great historian of the western Roman empire, Ammianus Marcellinus (*c.* AD 330–395), could still write of 'the Capitoline, by which sacred Rome is raised to eternity, where the whole world beholds nothing more magnificent' (*History* 22.16.12).

Yet in the fifth century AD, just as the western empire was being taken apart, such was also the fate of its most iconic building. The bronze statues were melted down for weapons and armour, the gold stripped from the roof and doors to pay for armies, and the marble rebuilt into the new Christian basilicas. By the early Middle Ages, nothing remained but the foundation. By now the Capitoline was known only as 'cow hill' after the cattle which grazed where once the Caesars and generals of Rome had stood before their god.

## From *c.* 27 BC

# The Pantheon

## For All the Gods of Rome

*M*[arcus] *Agrippa L*[ucii] *f*[ilius] *co*[n]*s*[ul] *tertium fecit*
*'Marcus Agrippa, son of Lucius, made* [this building] *when consul for the third time'*
**Inscription over the entrance to the Pantheon**

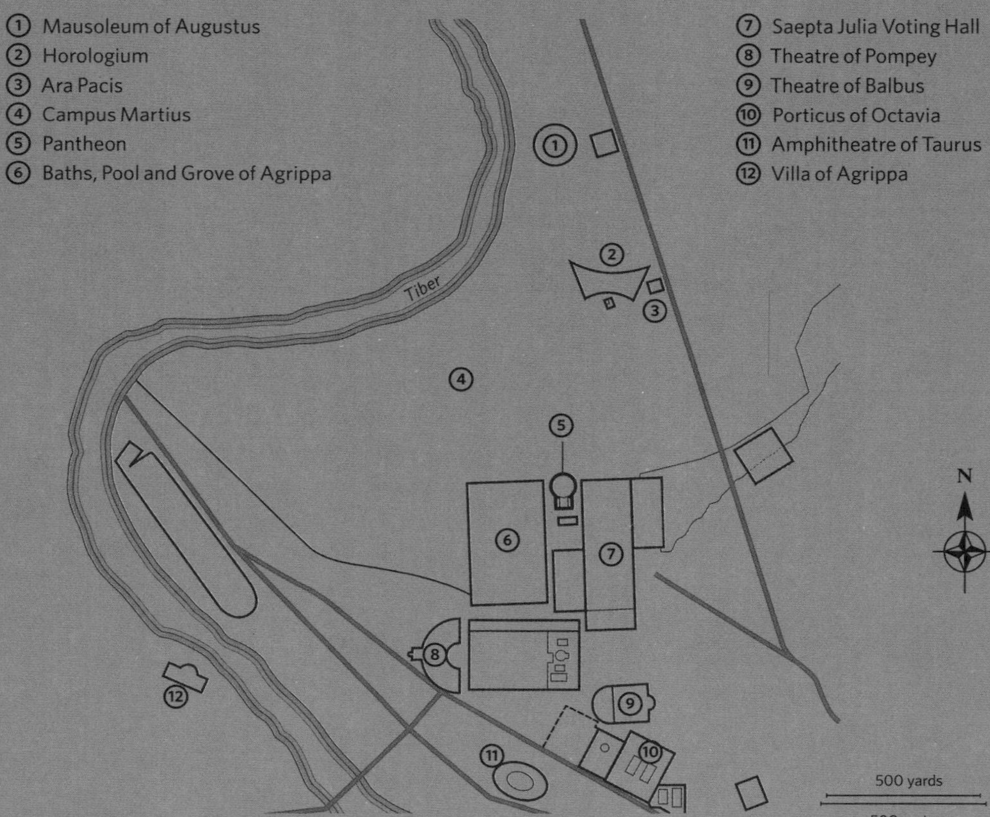

The name of this, one of the most iconic buildings in Rome, is actually Greek. It is the fusion of two words, *pan* meaning 'all' and *theoi* meaning 'gods'. Given that Roman religion alone recognized dozens of gods, this title is not strictly accurate – the first of many fudges related to this building. More precisely, this temple was a sacred space for the state gods of Rome, especially the gods of the Olympic pantheon. Deities such as Jupiter, Venus and Apollo had their own shrines within the building. Followers of minor deities such as Pomona, the apple goddess, or Laverna, goddess of thieves and fraudsters, had to do their worshipping elsewhere.

## Infringing on Mars

To a large extent the Pantheon has always been more about public relations than the gods within. Even its construction had an ulterior motive that was far from divinely inspired. The Pantheon stood on the Campus Martius – the 'Field of Mars' – which had, from the earliest days of Roman history, been dedicated to the war god Mars. Immediately adjacent to the fast-expanding urban conglomeration of Augustan Rome, the field served as a sort of green lung for the denizens of the crowded city.

The Pantheon, unchanged for centuries. Hadrian's 'modest' retention of Agrippa's original inscription on the new building was a propaganda masterpiece.

Marble head of the war god Mars. The elongated neck allowed the head, made by a skilled stonemason, to be slotted onto a body carved by a lesser craftsman.

'Chariot races and equestrian events can take place not only without interfering with each other but also yet leaving space for all the crowds who exercise by themselves by playing ball, rolling hoops or wrestling' remarked the contemporary writer Strabo (*c.* 63 BC–after AD 21) in his *Geography* (5.3.8).

All well and good, but the emperor Augustus had an ambitious building programme by which he intended to (literally) cement his reputation with posterity and he needed somewhere to put his new constructions. He was already getting some pushback to his ambitious plans to build himself a monumental mausoleum on the field, so he planned to get the public gradually accustomed to building work taking place on their favoured green spot.

Augustus was a master manipulator of public opinion. He first had his henchman Agrippa (*c.* 63–12 BC) build public baths on his own land beside the field. These, the first public baths in Rome, proved wildly popular. So the next step was to build a relatively modest construction on the Campus Martius itself, because who could object to something that honoured all the major gods of the city?

## Sacred, yes, but a temple?

It is uncertain whether this building was actually a temple, because the Romans preferred their temples to be dedicated to a single god. That way, any prodigies or omens could be correctly attributed to the divinity concerned. As with the name of the Pantheon, Augustus seems to have fudged its identification somewhat. Contemporary Roman writers agree that this was a sacred building but shy away from calling it an *aedes,* the formal name for a temple.

Agrippa stressed that Augustus had firmly refused to have his own likeness within the Pantheon, but had agreed to allow a large statue of himself to be placed immediately outside. Augustus thus gained fame as the inspiration behind the building while also very publicly demonstrating his modesty and restraint. The more cynical might have noted, though, that within the Pantheon pride of place was given to Venus, whom the family of Augustus claimed as the founder of their line.

Perhaps Jupiter, king of the gods, resented being given second place, because a fire destroyed the Pantheon seventy years later. It was rebuilt by the emperor Domitian (r. AD 81–96), but not long after completion another thunderbolt from the heavens caused such damage that work had to start all over again.

The view across the marble floor of the Pantheon towards the main altar. Like the Roman Senate House, the Pantheon survived destruction because it was converted into a Christian church.

## Building for the ages

Rebuilding started under the emperor Trajan (r. AD 98–117) but was enthusiastically taken up by Trajan's successor Hadrian. If one has a hobby as expensive as architecture it pays to have the resources of a great empire at one's disposal for putting ideas into concrete form. And concrete was exactly what Hadrian had in mind. The Romans used concrete as no civilization had done before. While the material was known to previous cultures, only the Romans had figured out how to get the stuff to set hard. (Before that, for example, it took almost a century for the concrete in the foundation of the temple of Zeus in Athens to set properly.) Roman concrete was so good – superior to many modern versions – that in some places today one can admire the fine latticework of mortar which is all that remains when the brick of a Roman house wall has eroded away.

Hadrian planned to rebuild Agrippa's 'temple' on a far grander scale (the Romans had by now become resigned to building work on the Campus Martius), and to use the opportunity to construct the largest concrete dome the world had ever seen or ever would see. The dome of the Pantheon still holds the record. This stunning gilded dome was a major landmark that impresses even today. So perfectly designed was it that, if the roof were to be extended

MINVM IN SANCTIS EIVS
LAVS EIVS IN

An eighteenth-century painting of the interior of the Pantheon. Apart from the clothing of those within and their lack of cameras little else has changed in three hundred years.

to a full sphere, the bottom of that sphere would almost exactly touch the floor of the Pantheon.

---

## Fame by restraint

It is speculated that the dome in the reconstructed building represented the heavens, and thus encompassed all gods great and small. We can be sure that prominence was given to the *Dii Consentes*, the major gods of Roman religion, including Jupiter, Minerva and Vulcan.

The inscription above the doors carefully omits mention of Hadrian as the builder. This 'modesty' is comparable to Augustus' refusal to allow his statue within the temple. The denial of self-promotion has spoken louder than any grandiose gesture. Even today most descriptions of the building stress Hadrian's self-restraint, when they would otherwise not have mentioned the inscription at all.

Thus, leaving his name off the inscription was a propaganda act. In reality Hadrian was inordinately proud of the building and would often hold court before the great bronze doors. These doors are themselves a marvel: over 7 metres (23 feet) high and 4 metres (13 feet) wide. Though they have a combined weight of 17 tonnes the doors are so perfectly balanced that they can be opened by a single person. The doors are remarkable for another reason also – modern investigation has shown that these are the same doors that were installed by Hadrian's engineers, a remarkable feat of survival through times when bronze was scavenged from almost every other ancient monument.

The Pantheon survived because it became a church at some point in the seventh century. Some items from the interior were removed – the glorious porphyry columns were replaced with granite and of course all the ancient gods had to go. In fact so comprehensive was the divine clear-out that no direct evidence exists as to which gods were there in the first place.

The pagan gods were replaced by several Christian altars of equal grandeur and, as one of the places where the Pope celebrated Mass on special church festivals, the building was well maintained. Indeed, the Pantheon remains a church today, though few of the tourists flocking its interior are aware of the fact. It is also one of the final ironies of the Pantheon that a building dedicated for the past 1,400 years to a monotheistic religion is still known to the general public by the original name dedicating it to 'all gods'.

PART FOUR

# On the Edge of the Empire

## Roman religion

The Mediterranean world was not closed to outside influences. Even in prehistory, trade routes stretched from Britain and the Baltic to the Middle East and Egypt. The flow of ideas and goods moved back and forth across these, and newer, highways for millennia. Then in the mid-fourth century BC the Middle East and Mesopotamia received an unexpected and not entirely welcome jolt of Hellenism, delivered by the armies of Alexander the Great. Alexander's empire fell apart soon after his death in 323 BC, but the contact between Eastern and Classical Mediterranean culture endured – and to some degree still does.

The frontier was not just a military or political border. It was also a zone where different societies met, clashed, merged and negotiated – politically, socially and in terms of religion. Modern historians point out that the space between the Mediterranean world and its 'barbarian' neighbours to the north was not a hard line with marble temples on one side and mud huts on the other. In many cases Classical culture became less pronounced close to the frontier and continued for a very substantial distance beyond it. What had been true in previous centuries became even more so with the dominance of the Roman empire.

Where Rome met The Other, be that Germanic warriors, Berber tribesmen, or Parthian merchants, sacred spaces – temples, altars, shrines and natural features of religious significance – became part of a wider cultural dialogue. The Romans used the divine both as an instrument of empire to control subject peoples and also as a means of reinforcing their own Roman-ness in the midst of people with alien ideas.

At the same time, at least at the local level, the Romans were open to religious negotiation. They accepted local gods, but even these in time – and with the enthusiastic backing of the authorities – gradually became more Roman. Even in areas beyond their control, such as the ever-recalcitrant Germans, the Romans tried to suggest that, in their worship, their enemies had basically the same, Greco-Roman, gods.

## The *interpretatio Romana*

This process of assimilation was a conscious one, which modern historians refer to as the *interpretatio Romana*. This is a spin on what the Romans themselves recognized that the Greeks had done previously, calling the Greek tendency to identify foreign gods with their own as the *interpretatio Graecae*. The Romans had long accepted the Greek view that the two cultures shared their gods, albeit under different names. Yet what the Greeks had done successfully with the Romans was but one example of this process; when foreign deities were too different to be shoehorned into aspects of existing Greco-Roman gods, they instead simply adopted them wholesale – Hecate of Caria being one example.

While discussing a Germanic tribe called the Nahanarvali, the Roman historian Tacitus explained to his audience: 'Among these people one discovers a grove sacred for time immemorial. The person in charge is a priest who wears female clothing, but the deities described are, from a Roman perspective, clearly [the divine twins]

Castor and Pollux and such indeed, are the attributes of their divinity' (*Germania* 43).

Well-documented Roman Britain offers an example of how the Romans managed the process of religious assimilation in lands under their control. Their approach to religious inclusivity allowed the water-goddess Sulis at (present-day) Bath to become an attribute of the Roman goddess Minerva, who was worshipped on the Capitoline hill in the heart of Rome. On Hadrian's Wall – the literal hard limit of empire in Britain – one finds numerous inscriptions dedicated to the Celtic god Belatucadrus, who had by then become a naturalized Roman bearing the name Mars Belatucadrus. This compromise allowed Roman legionaries and Celtic auxiliaries to worship the same god in the same place despite different religious perspectives.

The same approach was used across the empire. At the opposite end from Britain, the Egyptians were assured that their millennia-old god Ra-amun was actually Jupiter/Zeus and the emperor stood as his representative just as the pharaohs had done.

The historian and naturalist Pliny the Elder gives a first-century Roman take on this pragmatic approach, arguing that it was natural for humans everywhere to have similar gods because everywhere, humans are basically the same kind of people:

> *Being weak, fragile, and well aware of its own weakness, human nature has made these divisions* [of the divine into different deities]. *Thus we find that different people call these gods by different names; the inferior deities are arranged in classes, and that even diseases and plagues are deified because of our anxious wish to propitiate them...with Jupiter and Mercury, and the rest of the celestial nomenclature, everyone has to admit that they have reference to certain natural manifestations.*
>
> (*Natural History* 2.5)

## Statements in stone

Thus sacred sites formed spiritual bridges, legitimizing Roman rule by incorporating elements of indigenous belief systems, allowing the empire to cultivate loyalty within the very sacred sites that might otherwise have become foci of resistance.

Consequently, while Roman urbanized areas had temples with very standardized architecture and tightly regulated rituals, sacred spaces on the edge of empire could be more eclectic. Certainly there were Greco-Roman-style temples to be found, because nothing says 'Rome is here' like a well-placed temple to Jupiter, the emperor, or both, such as the temple of Claudius in Britain. These temples were not just places of worship – their very massiveness, and the time and expense needed to build them, solidly conveyed the permanence and power of Roman rule.

But, sometimes just yards from these monumental structures, soldiers, settlers and native peoples mingled their religious practices in a fascinating blend of iconography and dedications. Votive altars in Germania and the Danube provinces reflect this with inscriptions in Latin and local dialect – sometimes on the same stone.

# From 530 BC
# The Tomb of Cyrus
## A Conqueror's Resting Place

*I am Cyrus, son of Cambyses, who founded the empire of the Persians, and was king of Asia. Do not therefore grudge me this monument.*

**Inscription above the entrance to the tomb**

In the year 550 BC Persia was a small state under the control of the neighbouring kingdom of Media. Just over two decades later, in 529 BC, the Persians ruled an empire that stretched from the mountains of Afghanistan to the shores of the Mediterranean. This extraordinary period of conquest and expansion was largely the work of one man, Kurus II (r. 559–530 BC) – who is better known today by the westernized version of his name, Cyrus the Great. In 539 BC Cyrus conquered Mesopotamia and captured Babylon. He had already defeated King Croesus to add the kingdom of Lydia to his empire. A highly competent administrator, he generally respected the traditions of conquered peoples and is revered by Jews for restoring the exiled Hebrews to Jerusalem.

## Great conqueror, modest tomb

Yet the man who created one of the largest empires in the ancient world was buried in a relatively modest tomb some 650 kilometres (400 miles) south of Tehran in present-day Iran. His mausoleum is 11 metres (36 feet) high and covers some 163 square metres (175 square feet) of ground in what was the royal park of his capital of Pasargadae. Compare this with the famous Mausoleum in Halicarnassus, built some two centuries later for the ruler of a small patch of Asia Minor. This stood 45 metres (148 feet) high and covered well over 1,000 square metres (19,700 square feet).

*Alexander at the Tomb of Cyrus the Great*, Pierre-Henri de Valenciennes, 1796. While excellent in projecting mood and atmosphere, the painting is inaccurate in a number of details.

King Cyrus died in battle when seventy years old, and his remains were taken back to the capital city that he had founded. His tomb was described in detail by a Greek called Aristobulus, who worked on its restoration some two hundred years later:

> *Around his tomb was planted a grove with trees of many different types, watered by a nearby stream which also fed the tall grass in the nearby meadow. The base of the tomb was made of rectangular blocks of squared stone. And atop that a building and roof of stone. A door led within, so narrow that even a small man could only enter with difficulty and some discomfort.*
>
> *Within the body of Cyrus lay in a golden coffin and beside there was a couch with feet of hammered gold. There was a carpet of Babylonian tapestry and purple rugs...and swords, earrings and precious stones on a nearby table.*
>
> *Within the burial enclosure was a small house built for the guardians of the tomb, Magians who passed the duty from father to son....the king had ordered for them a sheep and a quantity of wheat flour and wine as a daily ration and a horse once a month to be sacrificed to Cyrus.*
>
> **(Aristobulus quoted in Arrian, *Anabasis* 6.29)**

## Desecration

Alexander the Great came upon the tomb in 330 BC and was distressed to find that the last request of Cyrus, that his tomb be left undisturbed, had not been honoured.

> *It had been dug through and stripped. Everything had been carried off except the coffin and couch. Even the King's body had been despoiled. The looters had ripped off the lid and tossed out the corpse. They had tried to make the coffin smaller by cutting off part of it and crushing it, but when this failed they left, leaving things in that condition.*
>
> **(*Anabasis* 6.29)**

Given that he was himself a conqueror, Alexander felt that the remains of men such as himself should be treated with more reverence, So Aristobulus, an officer in Alexander's army, was given the task of restoring the tomb to its former glory. Aristobulus' writings are mostly lost, but his description of the tomb is quoted at length in the later work of Arrian (*c.* AD 86–160), who wrote a description of the campaigns of Alexander in his *Anabasis*. This has survived to the present day.

## Recognized later

So also has the tomb of Cyrus – probably. In 1812 the former royal gardens at Pasargadae were visited by a British diplomat called James Justinian Morier (*c.* 1780–1849). He found the small edifice around 1,000 metres (3,300 feet) from the ruins of Pasargadae, and being something of a classicist, he recognized it from the description given by Arrian.

By then the body within had long since disappeared. Locals remembered only that this was the tomb of someone important and settled on the belief that it was the tomb of 'Suleiman's' mother. Which Suleiman is uncertain. If the Suleiman in question is the biblical King Solomon, his mother would be Bathsheba. More probably, however, the presumed mother was that of the revered eighth-century caliph, Suleiman ibn Abd al-Malik (*c.* 675–717), who was governor of Palestine in the Umayyad era.

As recounted by Aristobulus, there was a small stream nearby feeding a pool, the water of which was believed to be capable of curing those bitten by a rabid animal. There are some discrepancies

Tablet showing a winged figure, sometimes assumed to be Cyrus the Great, found at Pasargadae and now in the Persepolis Museum, Iran.

The tomb of the founder of the Achaemenid Persian empire stands in lonely splendour against a starlit background.

– the roof of the original tomb was described as a dome, whereas this monument is gabled, and there is no inscription bearing the last words of Cyrus. Nevertheless, most experts regard the identification of the tomb as reasonably certain, given how closely it otherwise matches the description given in the works of Arrian and confirmed by the Roman geographer Strabo in his *Geography* (15.3.7).

## Unique architecture

The tomb is built with blocks of ashlar (a type of off-white limestone) without the use of mortar. Instead the blocks were carefully fitted together by a process which the Greeks called *anathyrosis*, which smoothed adjoining blocks together for a near-perfect fit. Dovetail clamps and iron rods fitted into the stone enabled the building to remain in excellent condition even after thousands of years in an earthquake-prone region. (Iran is one of the most seismically active areas in the world.) These techniques are those of Ionian builders and are known to have been introduced into Persia during the reign of Cyrus.

The actual architecture is unique, in that though later imitations have been found, the tomb appears to have been the first of its kind, blending Elamite, Persian and Mesopotamian influences. This reflects the multicultural make-up of the Persian empire and the mixing of influences may well have been quite deliberate; Aristobulus says that clothing typical of different ethnicities was originally placed within the tomb.

This tomb today respects both the ancient Persian and Muslim traditions. It is honoured as the resting place of Cyrus the Great – whom his Iranian descendants hold in high regard – but it also now has a *mihrab* carved within. (A *mihrab* is the niche in the wall of a mosque that indicates the direction of the Kaaba in Mecca, which Muslims face when praying.) Ceremonies take place outside the tomb on Cyrus Day, an unofficial holiday in Iran celebrated on the 7th of Aban, or 29 October in the Western calendar.

Along with the other remains of Pasargadae, the tomb is now part of a UNESCO World Heritage Site. Today's visitors can reach it from the modern city of Shiraz, which is around two hours away by road.

## *c.* 200 BC – *c.* AD 300

# The Ploutonion of Hierapolis

## Gate to the Underworld

*Any beast that goes within that enclosure is doomed. Bulls that are led within fall, and the corpses are dragged away. I myself threw in sparrows and watched them breathe their last and drop.*

Strabo, *Geography* 13.4.14

The poet Virgil remarked in his epic poem the *Aeneid*, 'Anyone can enter the gates of Hades. But getting out again – that is another matter.' The ancient Mediterranean had a number of places from which a living being in desperate need could enter the Underworld. The Ploutonion at Hierapolis was different. The uninitiated could enter alive through the subterranean gate but would assuredly be dead soon thereafter. The reason for this is explained by an eyewitness, the geographer Strabo, who travelled to Asia Minor in the first century AD and personally witnessed the deaths of animals being sacrificed to Pluto (the Greek Hades), god of the underworld, within the deadly enclosure of the Ploutonion.

> *The Ploutonion is within a small ridge with mountainous ground above and behind it. The entrance is not very large, about enough for a single person to enter, but the space behind is quite deep. This space is a plethrum in circumference* [3.5 metres, about 100 feet] *fenced off by a four-barred handrail. The vapour there is so dense that one can hardly see the ground beneath.*

This oil painting from nineteenth-century Russia shows Charon taking souls across the river Styx. Those who lacked the fare for the ferryman were doomed to remain on the river's desolate banks for a century.

*In calm conditions anywhere behind the handrail above the enclosure the air is harmless, for the vapour is confined within the enclosure....but any beast that goes within that enclosure is doomed. Bulls that are led within fall, and the corpses are dragged away. I myself threw in sparrows and watched them breathe their last and drop.*

*But the Galli* [here, priests of the Underworld] *are eunuchs, and they venture into the enclosure unharmed. Indeed they even approach the portal and step inside.*
(Strabo, *Geography* 13.4.13)

The really interesting thing about the Ploutonion is that it was rediscovered in the 1960s and Strabo's account seems to be completely accurate. In an effort to determine exactly what happened at the Ploutonion scientists have been giving it serious attention since the start of the present century. If the modern identification of the site as the Ploutonion is indeed correct (and there is little doubt that it is) then visitors do indeed pass through a small stone doorway to an enclosed space. This is rectangular, open to the sky and with stone benches serving as seating around the edge. Carved into the hillside is a wall with false columns and in the centre of the wall is a small barred gateway.

Just as when Strabo visited, a stone statue of Hades and Cerberus stands in the original location, though the statue is a modern replica. And even today the enclosure is lethal to those who enter it, as the appearance of dead birds regularly testifies.

## Tourist attractions

The Ploutonion was one of two religious sites in the ancient city of Hierapolis, the ruins of which lie near the present-day town of Pamukkale in southwestern Turkey. Hierapolis was founded in 190 BC by King Eumenes II of Pergamon, who named it after Hiera, the wife of the founder of his native city.

At the time the main attraction was not the Ploutonion but the volcanic springs in the area, which were believed to have healing properties. As a result Hierapolis boasted a splendid temple to Apollo, who was considered a god of healing. (Actually he was originally the god of plague, but the ancients reasoned that if Apollo could start diseases he could also stop them.) Apollo was also the god of prophecy and in the remains of his temple some of his prophecies have been discovered carved into the stone of the walls.

Exactly what rituals were performed at the Ploutonion for the dread Lord of the Underworld is today unknown, because our two eyewitnesses – the geographer Strabo and the later historian Cassius Dio – were far more fascinated by the deadly gases which were used to sacrifice the offertory animals. It seems that, to some extent, the Ploutonion combined its sacred function with the role of deadly tourist attraction. We know that the Ploutonion was regularly visited in the third century AD because Cassius Dio's first-hand report is very similar to the comments of Strabo over two centuries before. After describing a similar phenomenon near Babylon, Dio remarks:

> *I saw another opening like it at Hierapolis in Asia and used birds to test its lethality. I also leaned over* [the handrail] *and personally observed the vapour. It is trapped within a sort of cistern and a viewing area has been built overlooking it. The enclosure slays anything living except castrated humans. I have no idea why this should be so – I am simply reporting what I have seen and have been told.*
>
> (Cassius Dio, *History* 68.17)

The entrance to the Ploutonion in Hierapolis. Even today this entrance to the Underworld remains lethal and care must be taken lest unwary tourists become unwitting sacrifices to Hades.

Hercules poses with the hell-hound Cerberus whom he captured for one of his famous Labours. He was among the few characters in myth who entered the Underworld (easy) and came out again (very hard).

The site seems to have been in use until the Christianization of the empire in the fourth century AD, at which point the entrance to the Underworld was stuffed with rocks. In the sixth century one of the frequent earthquakes that shake this tectonically active region destroyed much of Hierapolis, and the city, including the Ploutonion, was thereafter gradually abandoned.

## Unravelling the mystery

Today science is uncovering the secrets of the Ploutonion. The hell-hound Cerberus has yet to be discovered but his lethal breath has been exhaustively examined. It turns out that the deadly vapour issues from a deep underground fissure. It is mostly carbon dioxide, though there are other poisonous gases in the mix. The density of the gas is increased by a small subterranean spring which carries the vapour into the air above it.

The gas mixture which pours into the enclosure through the ancient portal is slightly heavier than air. As a result it pools on the floor of the enclosure and even today reaches concentrations high enough to kill a human within minutes. However, there was a reason why the priests performed their rituals at dawn and this had nothing to do with the religious significance of the sunrise. Once heated by the sun's rays the gas rises and dissipates.

So how did the priests survive when their sacrificial victims did not? The answer, according to researchers, is that most humans – with or without testicles – are taller than the average bull. Because the concentration of carbon dioxide diminishes exponentially with height, even less than half a metre (2 feet) makes the difference between being dizzy and being dead.

Also, as the bulls inhaled more of the gas, their heads would droop, causing them to breathe in the gas at ever more lethal concentrations. Birds and small mammals with their much faster respiratory rates were even more at risk. Nevertheless, it must have taken both careful timing and nerves of steel for the priests performing the sacrifices. When the priests actually crossed the dread portal to stand within the cave, it seems that their immunity was based on the simple fact that they held their breath.

'You could see the change in their faces as they struggled against suffocation', remarks the keen-eyed Strabo.

# Grove of Hercules Magusanus

## Hercules of the Batavians

*Valerius Nigrinus of the Cavalry Regiment of Tungrians set up this* [altar in honour] *of Hercules Magusanus*

Dedication to Hercules Magusanus, *Roman Inscriptions of Britain* 2140

The legendary hero Hercules was something of a wanderer. In his career he travelled to the shores of the Atlantic Ocean and to the Caucasus mountains east of the Black Sea. So perhaps it is less unlikely than it sounds that a Greek demi-god with mythical origins in ancient Egypt should end up as the principal deity of a people living on the northwest frontier of the Roman empire.

These people were the Batavi, a Germanic tribe who had moved westward to establish themselves on the banks of the river Weser in the modern Netherlands. The Batavi seem to have originally worshipped a god with the somewhat ambiguous name of Magusanus. Ambiguous because the name is a portmanteau word, combining the Germanic *senos* ('old') and *magus* ('young'). Puzzled modern linguists have decided that the name probably means that this deity combined the wisdom of an elder with the vigour of youth.

The Batavi had a strong warrior ethos. Once they made their peace with the Roman empire they supplied it with top-notch

Reconstruction of the temple of Hercules Magusanus at Empel. Like the god who was worshipped within, the temple is a cross-cultural fusion of Mediterranean and Germanic cultures.

A first-century AD limestone altar to Hercules Magusanus found in the Netherlands. While parts of the inscription have become illegible, the second line clearly reveals that it was dedicated to the god.

auxiliary troops. Once, deeply annoyed by official corruption, they became a major problem when they rebelled in AD 69. The Batavi counted their wealth in cattle and never really grew out of the habit of raiding the herds of their neighbours. Therefore it is unsurprising that they felt a considerable affinity for Hercules, who was both as macho as a demi-god could be and a pretty good cattle thief as well. (In fact his Tenth Labour had him travelling across the Mediterranean world to steal the herd of a monster called Geryon.)

## Two gods become one

The Roman pantheon was a somewhat flexible institution and the Romans themselves believed that most peoples worshipped the same gods as they did, even though they used different names for them. Therefore it proved easy enough to conflate Magusanus with Hercules to make one god out of the two. It also helped that the consort of Magusanus was a goddess called Haeva, which sounded close enough to the heavenly spouse of Hercules, who was Hebe, goddess of youth.

Magusanus was worshipped at Empel in a sacred oak grove on a sandhill which stood at the confluence of the Meuse and Dies rivers. That this location was a very deliberate choice is shown by the fact that oak groves are rare in this area – willow is the dominant species. Also the Germanic tribes attached great religious significance to rivers, and the place where two rivers joined was especially sacred.

By joining Hercules with their native god the Batavi showed the Romans that, far from being a barbarian tribe, they were a *civitas* (citizen community) on an equal footing with any Roman equivalent, and to hammer the point home further they upgraded the sacred grove of Magusanus by installing a proper Roman (well, Gallo-Roman) temple to their god.

## The temple

It has to be said that the temple of Hercules Magusanus at Empel was not a very grandiose affair, but then it was probably not the major cult centre of the god. There seems to have been another larger affair at Elst in Gelderland, also in the Netherlands, and there are the remains of an even greater temple in Kessel, which is reasonably close to Empel. Large pieces of religious sculpture have been found in the river Meuse, which may have belonged to either the Kessel or Empel temples.

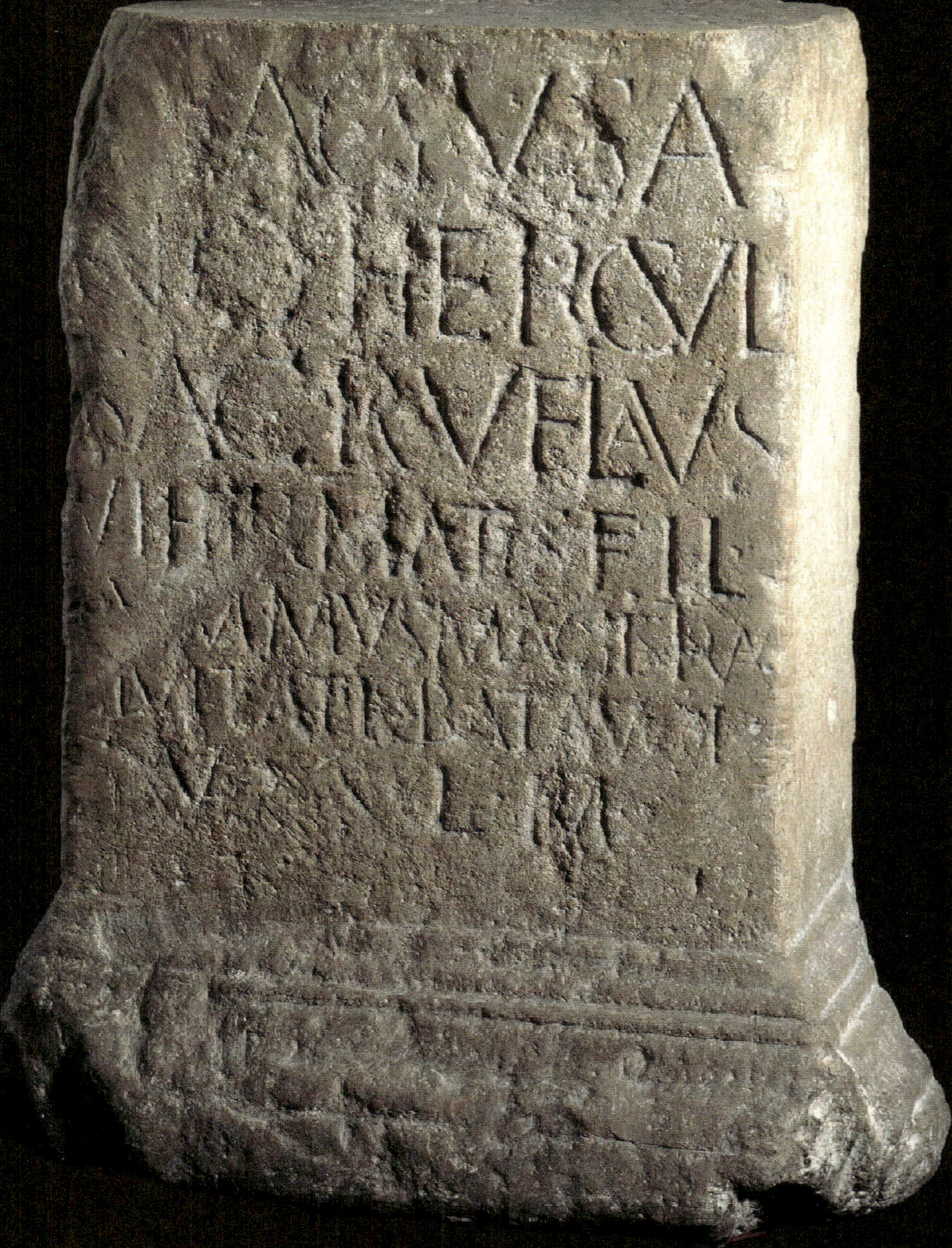
HERCVL

However, identifying the religious practices at ancient Germanic religious sites is notoriously difficult, and the temple at Empel is one of the few where the worship of Hercules Magusanus can be identified with a fair degree of certainty. Further confirmation of worship at the Empel temple comes in the form of a small cult statue of Hercules Magusanus, which was recently discovered at the site.

Quite a lot of the sacred oak grove had to go as the price for romanization. The temple precinct took up around 2,500 square metres (27,000 square feet) on the sandhill, with the temple occupying around 100 square metres (1,700 square feet) on the west side. That choice of orientation went somewhat against the grain of standard Roman practice (they liked their temples to face east) but the builders evidently felt the more impressive view from the west was adequate compensation. The building itself stood on a high stone base with a surrounding colonnade.

## Soldier's god

Batavian auxiliaries in the Roman army relied on the protection of Hercules Magusanus while on campaign. For example, Valerius Nigrinus, an officer in a Batavian cavalry unit, set up a stone dedicatory offering to Hercules Magasanus while serving in northern Britain in the fort at Mumrills, about 60 kilometres (37 miles) from Edinburgh (it is quoted at the start of this chapter).

Retiring Batavian auxillaries offered their weapons and armour at the temple of Hercules Magusanus in thanks for a safe return to their homes. It is rare to find weapons or armour as Roman votive offerings because soldiers usually had to hand in their kit at the end of their period of service. It is uncertain whether Batavians serving with the army were given an exemption for religious reasons or if they had

Gold coin of the Batavian emperor Postumus, who was the most famous of the worshippers of the god Hercules Magusanus.

special offertory gear made in lieu of the real thing – as is known to have happened elsewhere in the region.

One particularly fine offering retrieved from Empel is a helmet. It has a hole, which must have been fatally inconvenient for the original wearer, but thereafter that hole served nicely to hang the thing from the temple wall.

During the crisis of the third century, when the Roman empire started to come apart due to the stresses of plague, civil war and barbarian incursions, Gaul broke away to form an autonomous empire that included Britain and parts of Spain. The first 'Gallic emperor' was Postumus (r. AD 260–69), who featured Hercules Magusanus on his coinage, possibly because Postumus was himself a Batavian.

## Until today

This may explain why the temple at Empel was burned down at around the time that the Romans reclaimed Gaul in AD 274. It seems that religious rites were still performed at the sacred grove until the end of the Roman era, at which time the stone blocks of the temple foundation were urgently needed for the walls of a stone fort that was being hastily assembled nearby.

Thereafter the grove was indeed lost and forgotten until the 1980s, when a local archaeologist first rediscovered traces of the site. Some of the artefacts from the temple are now in the Noordbrabants Museum. Those wishing to pay their respects to Hercules Magusanus in person can find the remains of his temple by following the signs on the footpath from the village of Empel to the archaeological site, where information boards explain the history of the place in some detail.

# *c.* AD 550 to March 2001
# **The Buddhas of Bamiyan**
## Greco-Buddhist Monument

*The traveller surveying...the vast and mysterious idols...will scarcely fail to be absorbed in deep reflection and wonder...*

Charles Masson, *Narrative of Various Journeys in Balochistan, Afghanistan, and the Panjab*, Vol. II, 1842, pp. 392–93

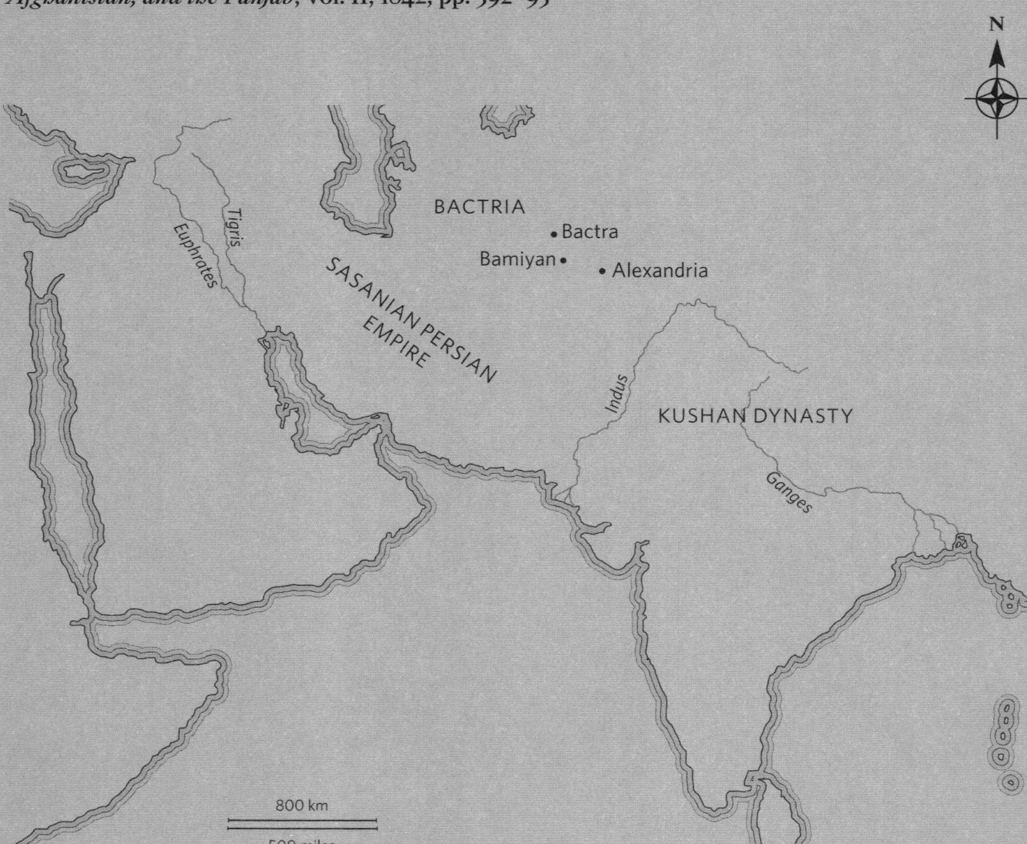

The lands around the Hindu Kush, a massive mountain range on the border between modern Pakistan and Afghanistan, are seldom thought of today as a centre of Greek culture. Yet in the ancient world the Greeks of Central Asia were a thriving community and the mark they left on the region is discernible even today. The Buddhas of Bamiyan were – until the start of the present century – among the greatest of their monuments.

## Greeks in Central Asia

Most Greeks in Central Asia ended up there because Alexander the Great conquered the region in 330 BC. He intended to hold down the lands of his diverse empire by founding cities – many of them called Alexandria – and stocking them with Greek colonists who could supply soldiers for future armies. However, some Greeks may have arrived in the region even earlier than that. The Greek cities of Anatolia were conquered by the Persian armies of Cyrus the Great around 547 BC and they were not happy with their new overlords.

After putting down a major rebellion known as the Ionian Revolt, the Persians shipped many of the more recalcitrant Greek communities off into exile in Central Asia. These banished communities were rediscovered when the army of Alexander penetrated that far east. However, this reunification was short-lived. Alexander's empire fell apart soon after his death in 323 BC, and the rebellion of the Parthian peoples cut off the Greeks of Central Asia from the Mediterranean world. However, Greek kingdoms such as Bactria continued to thrive. This was partly because they controlled the mountain passes through which goods travelled on the so-called Silk Road between Europe and the Far East.

Two sides of a Bactrian coin featuring King Menander I (left) and Athena advancing, holding a shield and wearing her aegis (right).

## A succession of rulers

*Previous pages*
*Left* A print of the larger Buddha appeared in the *Illustrated News of London* in the late nineteenth century.
*Right* The same Buddha before it was destroyed by the Taliban.

The politics of the region were never stable and empires such as that of Menander I (r. *c.* 165–130 BC) tended to have short lifetimes. Menander was a Greek, born near the Central Asian city of Alexandria (present-day Bagram in Afghanistan) and went on to conquer an empire larger than Charlemagne's, yet his name is not widely remembered today.

After the Indo-Greeks came the Parthians, then the Scythians and finally, in the first century AD, the Kushan dynasty (hence the Hindu 'Kush' mountains) who occupied a huge area including northern India, Bactria and parts of Afghanistan.

Even under foreign rule the Greeks retained a strong cultural presence. Artefacts from the Greek world dating as late as the third century AD have turned up in the remains of fortified cities along the Silk Road. Greek traditions gradually merged with local culture, a phenomenon which can be traced today in the art produced in the region over the centuries. This cultural fusion of Greek and Indian styles is known today as 'Gandhara art' – Gandhara being the name of a region in present-day northeast Afghanistan and northwest Pakistan. Two of the best, and certainly the largest, of these artworks were the Buddhas of Bamiyan.

A fine example of Gandharan art showing a standing Buddha in Greek dress, first to second century AD.

## The Buddhas

Buddhism was introduced to the region some time in the third century BC. Menander I, for example, seems to have been a Greco-Buddhist, following a form of worship which syncretized Hellenistic religion and Buddhism.

Around the time of the fall of the western Roman empire in the fifth century AD the Kushan state was conquered by a people called the Hephthalites, or 'White Huns'. Though these people did not immediately convert to Buddhism, under their rule the people of Bamiyan started work on their two Buddhas. These were massive monumental figures, one 38 metres (125 feet) and the other 55 metres (over 180 feet) in height. They are usually referred to as statues, but because the fronts of the bodies were carved from the sandstone cliff face but the backs remained joined to it, they were not, properly speaking, statues but gigantic reliefs.

The two colossal Buddhas had strong Greco-Roman characteristics, and one of the minor figures at the base even sported a Corinthian helmet. Though carved in the Gandhara style, the statues had the dress and appearance of the region's new Hephthalite masters, with clean-shaven faces above the distinctive belted tunics of the

Hephthalite people. The faces appeared somewhat crude because (it is believed) the figures originally had gigantic but finely carved wooden masks. In the same way, fine detail on the figures was added with clay and the plaster held in place with a system of pegs and rope which endured for centuries. Each statue was then painted over, both to show fine detail and to create a uniform appearance of earth and stone.

## The post-Classical era

In later years the caves in the cliff at Bamiyan were further decorated with sacred art, dating mostly from the sixth and seventh centuries. Although the Roman empire was by then a memory and trade on the Silk Road much diminished, these artworks still displayed Greek influences from the Byzantine empire. Portraiture in these paintings came to an end with the Muslim conquest of the region. While the Quran does not specifically forbid the depiction of living forms, most artists preferred abstract designs.

At the end of the twelfth century the Bamiyan region was devastated by the armies of the Mongol warlord Genghis Khan, but he respected the sanctity of the statues and left them alone. With the region now non-Buddhist, the statues remained a local monument, not carefully maintained but also not severely vandalized, until 2001. In that year the Taliban, having taken control of Afghanistan, destroyed the statues with explosives.

A Taliban spokesman, Mullah Omar, explained to the *Guardian* newspaper, 'Why preserve false idols? And if they have no religious character, why get so upset? It is just a question of breaking stones' (quoted in *Guardian Unlimited*, 3 March 2001). The cave paintings and murals were, likewise, to be obliterated.

The Taliban leaders certainly recognized the sacred nature of the site, for they explicitly claimed that one reason for its destruction was so that no one could worship there in the future. The demolition of these ancient monuments created international outrage, including from some Muslim countries. Apologists have countered that the destruction of sacred sites by competing religions is far from new, and point to the dismantling of the Serapeum and temple of Artemis in Ephesus as examples. Many, though, see the wrecking of the statues as barbaric and believe that the fanaticism that inspired it has no place in an enlightened modern world.

*Following pages* Site of the smaller Buddha after its destruction by the Taliban. Small caves were carved into the surrounding cliffs by Buddhist monks during antiquity.

## *c.* 300 BC – AD 391

# The Serapeum of Alexandria

## Magnificent Temple to a New God

*The Serapaeum, which is diminished when one describes it with mere words, adorned with far-reaching columned halls and with statues that seem almost alive....*

Ammianus Marcellinus, *History*, 22.16.12

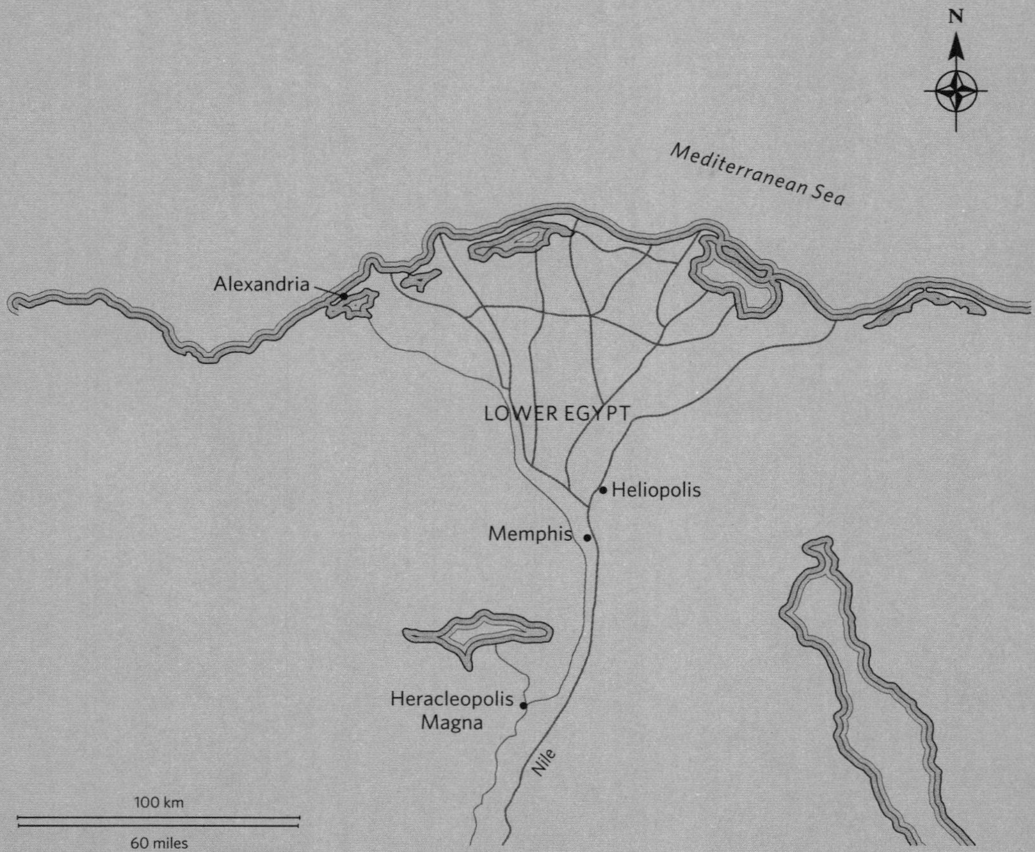

As the fourth-century historian Ammianus Marcellinus points out, few buildings in the ancient world were as magnificent and imposing as the temple in Alexandria dedicated to the mysterious god Serapis. Indeed so splendid was this place of worship that those entering might be excused for wondering if the god was compensating for something by the magnificence of his dwelling.

This was true in a way, for Serapis was discovered somewhat late in Classical history – indeed an unkind cynic might claim that the god was invented for purely political reasons. The politician in question was Ptolemy I, pharaoh of Egypt from 305 to 282 BC. Ptolemy's problem was that although he was ruler of Egypt, he himself was a Macedonian who had taken over the ancient kingdom after the conquests of Alexander the Great.

Ptolemy was eager to integrate his new kingdom with the wider Mediterranean world. His highly conservative and insular subjects were much less so inclined. What was needed was a way to spread Egyptian influence abroad while simultaneously assuaging the Egyptian distrust of foreigners – a category which included Ptolemy himself.

## Making a god

The answer came to him in a dream. The Roman historian Tacitus (*Histories* 4.83) tells the story that the sleeping Ptolemy envisioned a young man of amazing beauty who told him to find a certain statue and bring it to Egypt, because the city which possessed the statue would become great and glorious. Thereafter the messenger ascended to the heavens in a blaze of light.

It turned out that the statue in question was in the city of Sinope, which lay on the Black Sea in present-day Turkey. The people of that city were reluctant to part with the effigy, so the god simply moved himself aboard the Egyptian ship, which promptly raised anchor and hastened to Alexandria. There the statue was revealed to be the god Serapis, a minor aspect of the sacred bull of Osiris/Apis, venerated throughout Egyptian history. So minor an aspect, in fact, that few had previously heard of him.

This was to change. Ptolemy began vigorously promoting the worship of Serapis, not only in Egypt but across the Greco-Roman world, ignoring charges that he had literally dreamed up a god and sent his minions to steal an appropriate statue. It certainly helped with the promotion of Serapis abroad that, unlike the traditional animal-headed Egyptian gods, Serapis had the human form of a Classical Greco-Roman deity. It also helped that Ptolemaic Egypt

Bust of Serapis, the Greco-Egyptian god whose worship spread across the Mediterranean world. The *kalathos* on his head is a grain measure symbolizing his connection with fertility and the earth.

The Apis bull is shown to the people in a sacred procession. The god Serapis was originally a minor manifestation of Apis, who for centuries was a major deity in Egypt.

was extremely rich and its rulers were happy to subsidize the construction of Serapeums (temples to Serapis) wherever they felt Egyptian influence could be usefully extended. (The '-eum' suffix on a sacred building references the deity worshipped within. Thus Mithras had a Mithraeum and we have an Atheneum for Athena and a Museum for the Muses.)

## Location, location, location

Naturally the grandest of the Serapeums was in the Ptolemaic capital of Alexandria – the city which was (and is) a fusion of Mediterranean and Egyptian culture. Ptolemy III (r. 246–222 BC) decided that the already splendid building dedicated by his grandfather was not enough for the country's very own Egypto-Macedonian god. So he partly extended, partly demolished and partly built over the previous temple to construct the magnificent Serapeum which was to stand for the next six hundred years.

The imposing temple stood in an already impressive location. It dominated a small plateau in the west of the city with views over Alexandria and the sea. The body of the temple was limestone, enclosing an area of some 13,500 square metres (145,300 square feet), with massive 7-metre-tall (23-foot) granite columns lining the colonnades and galleries. As was the case with the Capitoline temple in Rome, a trinity of gods was worshipped within the Serapeum. The

Capitoline had Jupiter, Juno and Minerva; the Serapeum had Serapis, the goddess Isis and their child Harpocrates, the god of hope.

Dominating the interior was a statue to Serapis 'so large that the right hand brushed one wall and the left hand the other...the statue was furbished with gold and silver and fragments of sapphire, hematite, emerald and topaz....the interior walls, they say, were plated with gold, silver and bronze' (Clement, excerpts from his *Ecclesiastical History* 11.2 and *Exhortation to the Heathen* 4.3).

## Prayer and study

So extensive was the Serapeum that the spare rooms at the back were used as a depository for the pharaonic book collection (also known as the Great Library of Alexandria). By some estimates the Library ultimately had some 400,000 books in its possession, and some of the overflow – an estimated 35,000 books – were stored at the 'daughter library' in the Serapeum.

As with the Great Library, the Serapeum attracted not only the religious but also scholars, researchers and philosophers. It was

This sculpture of the Apis bull was one of the few survivors of the riots that destroyed the Serapeum. Now it has found sanctuary in the Greco-Roman Museum at Alexandria.

It is believed that at one time this tunnel beneath the Serapeum held thousands of papyrus scrolls salvaged from the Library of Alexandria. These scrolls were destroyed along with the building above.

visited by the emperor Vespasian while he was in the east in the first century AD. The cult of Serapis became more widespread during the centuries that followed, spread by an ever-growing stream of pilgrims. It helped that the Ptolemies had never quite explained exactly what kind of god Serapis was. He became, therefore, whatever his worshippers wanted to project on to him, be that a god of the underworld, a solar deity or a god of plenty and the harvest. Though best known for his biographies, the ancient writer Plutarch was also a priest and in his text *On Isis and Osiris* (28, 29) he explains that 'Serapis is a god of all peoples in common...[it is] the name of he who sets the universe in order'.

The Serapeum was badly damaged in riots in Alexandria in AD 116 and the building was so extensively restored by the emperor Hadrian that modern archaeologists still debate which features of the building are Hadrianic and which were part of the original Ptolemaic design.

## A violent end

In late antiquity the very fame of the Serapeum made it a target for the more militant type of Christian. In AD 391 the Roman emperor Theodosius I issued an edict forbidding 'pagan worship', which led Alexandrian Christians to believe that the Serapeum could be dispensed with altogether. There followed a tense confrontation between those determined to see 'The temple, its priests and the wicked sinners vanquished and relegated to the flames of hell and the vain superstition and the ancient demon Serapis finally destroyed' (Rufinus, *Historia ecclesiastica* 2.2) and those who were clinging stubbornly to their ancient beliefs and were well prepared to fight for them.

It helped the Christian side that there were a goodly number of soldiers in the crowd and these were at the forefront of the assault that finally captured the building, which was thereafter demolished column by column. The head of the broken statue of Serapis was triumphantly carried into the city and there burned on a triumphal pyre.

So completely was the Serapeum first plundered and then destroyed that everything that is known of the building comes from extensive archaeological digs on the below-ground foundations. However, despite the lack of standing ruins the site is still a magnet for tourists today, both because of the commanding view from the plateau and because the area is rich in other ancient sites of interest. Of the temple to Serapis one column – now called the 'column of Pompey' – still stands as a lonely reminder of what was once one of the greatest temples of the ancient world.

# AD 43 – *c.* 600
# **Aquae Sulis**
# Bathing and Worship

*Lucius Marcius Memor, haruspex, gave this gift to the goddess Sulis.*

A Roman soothsayer records his votive offering, *Roman Inscriptions of Britain* 3, 3049

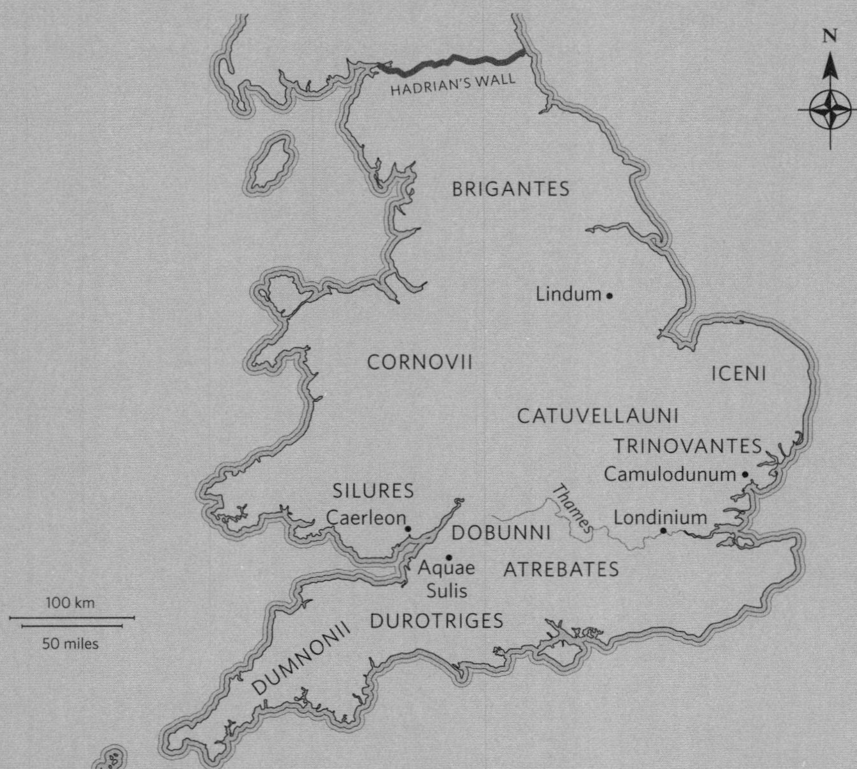

When rain falls on the Mendip Hills in Somerset, England, the water slowly percolates downward through cracks and fissures in the limestone rock – and keeps going, eventually reaching depths of over 4 kilometres (2½ miles) beneath the earth. At this depth the natural heat from the Earth's core raises the temperature of the water close to boiling point and it comes bubbling back to the surface, losing some, but by no means all, of that heat along the way.

## The coming of Rome

When the Romans arrived in the area around AD 43 the legions were in the process of conquering Britain. Their first interest in the site of the sacred spring was purely strategic, because this location controlled a useful crossing point of the river Avon. (The Romans called it the Abona, from the Celtic for 'river', so even today this waterway has the rather silly name of 'River River'.) Once they had

The head of Sulis Minerva discovered in Bath. The gilt bronze head is estimated to be around 1,800 years old.

established themselves at the crossing, and so taken control of the Avon valley and gained access to the Severn crossing, the Romans turned their attention to the hot springs.

These were rather hard to ignore, as most of the underground water came steaming out of three fissures at the rate of over a million litres (220,000 gallons) per day. For the Romans, who had made large, heated public baths an integral part of their culture, these hot springs must have seemed almost a gift from the gods: more particularly, from a particular goddess. It turned out that the springs were sacred to Sulis, who had been worshipped there by the local Dobunni tribe for centuries before the Romans arrived.

## The divine Sulis

Sulis was very much a local deity – outside Aquae Sulis only one ancient inscription has been found (in Germany) that refers to her. The Indo-European roots of her name suggest that Sulis was a solar divinity, given the connection with words like 'sun' and 'solar', and also because heat links both the sun and the sacred spring.

The Romans promptly set up a large public baths at Aquae Sulis. The town is unique in that, despite a few scattered buildings, no Roman domestic, commercial or industrial areas have been found. Aquae Sulis seems to have been almost entirely given over to the overlapping purposes of bathing and worship. Judging from relics and inscriptions found by later archaeologists, many of those who came to pay their respects to Sulis were Roman soldiers, especially those from two particular legions: II Augusta at Carleon and and VI Victrix, the latter dedicating at least three altars in the town.

## The temple

The Romans were in the habit of considering local gods from various parts of their empire as manifestations of aspects of the major gods in their own pantheon. Therefore, having decided that Sulis was an aspect of their goddess Minerva, they built a temple to Sulis Minerva at the site of the sacred spring. This was one of the few temples in Roman Britain constructed along strictly Classical lines – the other being the temple of Claudius in Colchester. As with all Roman-style temples this building stood on a tall pediment, in this case around 2 metres (6½ feet) above ground level. There were four Corinthian columns across the front and above that an enigmatic frieze.

Today the central figure in this frieze is often called 'The Gorgon' and this is probably wrong, because the mythological Gorgons were

A head, believed to be that of a Gorgon, which adorned the pediment of the temple of Sulis Minerva at Aquae Sulis. A reconstruction can be seen in the Roman museum in modern-day Bath.

female and this apparition sports a long, flowing beard. From the modern remains of the frieze it can be seen that this bearded man is flanked by two images of the goddess of victory – unmistakable because their iconography is the same as that of clearly labelled images of her found elsewhere.

Other constructions around the temple were added over the next three centuries. There was a small workshop beside the temple which made pewter urns (several of which were dropped into the spring, where they remained for over a millennium). It is believed that those seeking to benefit from the healing powers of Sulis Minerva would dip an urn into the sacred spring and then pour the water over themselves as a way of communing with the goddess.

## The spring

This spring rose within the area enclosed by the temple courtyard, where Roman engineers built upon the earthen embankment already made by earlier generations of Celtic worshippers. They added a stone retaining wall, lined with non-corrosive lead, after

The baths today. The injunction for modern visitors is 'look but don't swim', but the waters remain capable of performing their ancient function.

first driving wooden piles into the ground below to support the structure – a design so effective that it is still doing its job almost two thousand years later.

As humans seem wont to do with fountains and springs everywhere, visitors to the sacred spring at Aquae Sulis were in the habit of tossing in coins or other offerings. After they had done this for three hundred years, from the first to the fourth century AD, the spring accumulated a small fortune in loose change, with over twelve thousand coins having been retrieved so far by modern archaeologists. Other votive offerings at the spring range from jewelry and ceramics to crude figurines in wood and leather. The inscription on a nearby altar shows the sentiments of those who sacrificed treasured belongings here: 'To the goddess Sulis Minerva. Sulinus, son of Maturus, has willingly and suitably done as he promised' (*Roman Inscriptions of Britain* 150).

Also found in some abundance at the spring are curse tablets. They were often deposited by those who, having sacrificed, went for a relaxing dip in the hot baths and returned to find their clothing stolen. The tablets call down the goddess's vengeance on the perpetrator:

*To the goddess Sulis Minerva*

*I Solinus surrender to your divine majesty my bathing tunic and my cloak. Grant no sleep or health to that person who has wronged me, whether be a this man or a woman, slave or free, unless that person confesses and brings these items to your temple.*
(*Roman Inscriptions of Britain*, Tab. Sulis 32)

## A head start in archaeology

One of the most spectacular finds at Aquae Sulis came in the early modern era when workmen in 1727 found a gilt bronze head, which probably came from a cult statue in the former temple courtyard. This is one of the few bronze items of statuary found in Roman Britain, and a good example of the 'lost wax' casting technique favoured by ancient sculptors. It is reasonably certain that this head, which even today gleams with its layer of gold, depicts Sulis Minerva, as there is a break at the top of the head that is almost certainly where Minerva's distinctive (but now lost) helmet was attached.

The discovery of the head sparked a contemporary interest in Roman Bath and modern researchers are still trying to undo some of the damage done by those enthusiastic but very unskilled eighteenth-century antiquarians. Scientific work by modern archaeologists has shown that the baths and especially the temple suffered neglect after the legions left Britain in the early fifth century. Repairs were crude and ineffective and poor maintenance of the drains meant that much of the temple sank into the now marshy ground. Ironically, this helped to preserve much of it, as it seems there was an attempt to demolish the above-ground portions in the sixth century.

Archaeological efforts have also been hindered by the fact that the thriving city of modern Bath has been built directly atop the Roman remains. Although bathing in the Roman pools is no longer allowed, the city remains as popular with tourists as it was back in the Classical era.

1st to 4th century AD
# The Temple at Garni
## The Easternmost Classical Temple

*Obeying his lord who wears the crown,*
*Menneas the stone-cutter made this for*
*the mighty and revered god*

**First-century AD Greek inscription, now in front of the temple in Garni**

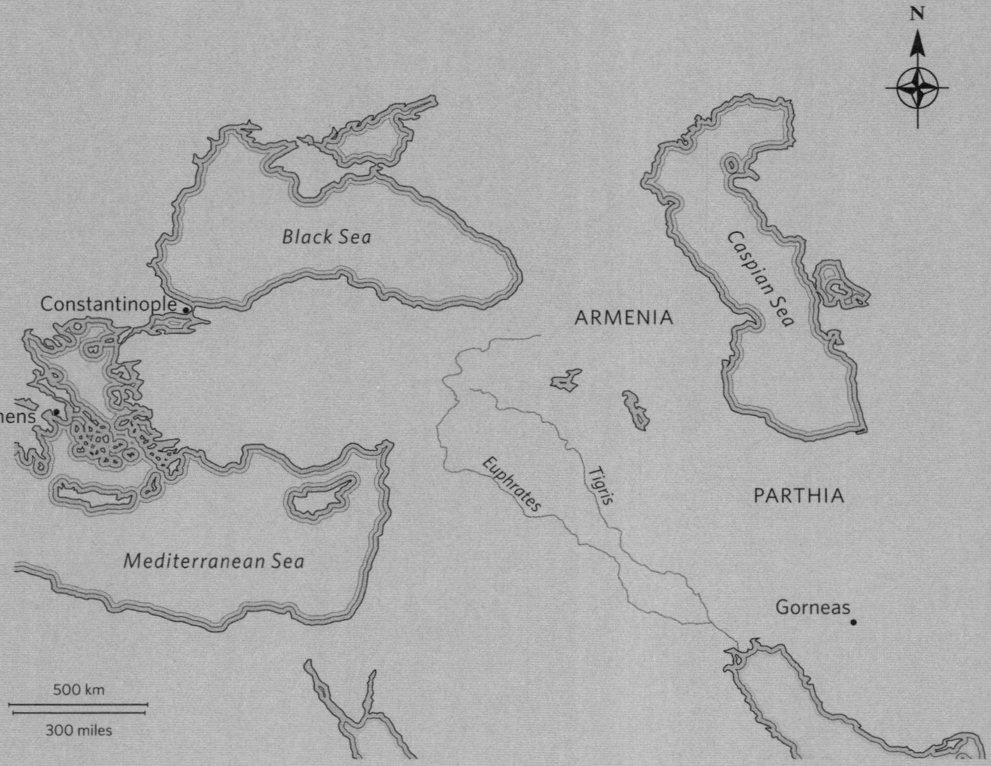

Garni is a village set amid spectacular scenery in central Armenia, in a region troubled by both political and tectonic instability. Armenia's political problems go back to the Classical era, when the nation found itself situated precariously between the Roman empire in the west and the Parthians in the east. While Armenia tried desperately to remain neutral, both superpowers had a keen interest in dominating the strategically positioned state.

In AD 58 the Parthian king decided to take charge of matters directly and forcibly installed his brother on the Armenian throne. The Romans took strong exception to this and a short but brutal war followed. No one seems to have consulted the Armenians, whose land was devastated by the warring armies. In AD 63 an agreement was reached (again without consulting the Armenians). The Parthian king could remain on the throne – but on condition that he was crowned by the Roman emperor Nero. After the coronation, performed with lavish ceremony in Rome, the Roman government contributed craftsmen and provided 50 million drachmas to repair some of the damage caused by the war.

## Birth of a temple

These circumstances and Roman money seem to have resulted in the building of a small but beautiful temple in the grounds of an ancient fortress in Gorneas (present-day Garni). Inscriptions by Greek workmen suggest that the temple was built in the eleventh year of the reign of Helios Tiridates, who was the king crowned by Nero. It certainly seems that the temple dates from this period, as

Mithra, guardian of the cosmic order, protector of the light as he appears on this Roman bas-relief laden with symbolism. Note the Phrygian caps, the herald's staff on the bottom right and the snake altar.

it uses the contemporary method of holding the stone blocks in place with iron clamps, which were sheathed in lead to prevent them rusting.

The temple was dedicated to the sun god Mithra (possibly an earlier form of the later Roman god Mithras), but its form was that of a Classical temple of the Ionian order, which any Greek or Roman would immediately recognize. The statue that once stood in the central *cella* (inner sanctuary) is now gone, but the space still retains a sacred feel through its high ceiling and echoing acoustics.

In the fourth century AD admirers of the temple had to work fast to save the building from fanatics determined to erase any trace of 'paganism' from newly Christianized Armenia. Exactly how this building survived is the topic of some academic debate, but it seems likely that the temple underwent the pagan equivalent of deconsecration and was defended from demolition on the grounds that it was now simply a decorative building within the fortress grounds – and possibly also the designated prestigious tomb for a high-ranking and well-connected aristocrat.

## Ruin

Sadly, the status of the building as a mere scenic embellishment to the fortress meant that the iron and lead clamps holding it together were deemed inessential, and reused when defenders needed iron for weapons and lead for ammunition. Nevertheless, the soundness of the original construction meant that the little temple remained intact until 1679. That was when a major earthquake hit Garni, and the weakened temple and much of the village were levelled to the ground.

For the next 250 years or so the temple remained as a crumbling ruin, of interest only to passing Westerners who looted the more attractive fragments for their national museums. (Bits of the Garni temple are spread around Europe, from the Hermitage in Leningrad to the British Museum in London.)

Yet most of the parts of the temple remained where they had fallen. In the 1960s this led to the thought that it would not be impossible to put them back together again. At this time the Soviet government of Armenia was working on restoring interest in pre-Christian Armenia in ways that did not involve arousing separatist national sentiment. A rebuilt temple seemed to suit this purpose admirably. (As indeed it has over the subsequent decades.)

## Rebirth

There is an established protocol for putting parts of ancient buildings together again. Suitably enough the word for this process comes from ancient Greek – *anastylosis,* which translates roughly as 'building again'. At the same time that Soviet architects were considering rebuilding the temple at Garni, an international convention in Venice was deciding how this should best be done for all ancient buildings that might be suitable for at least partial reconstruction. Few buildings of antiquity could be rebuilt as comprehensively as the temple at Garni, but its construction nevertheless adheres closely to the Venice Protocol of 1964.

Among other things this protocol states that imaginative restoration of missing parts is not allowed and any new parts added to the building must be immediately distinguishable from the original pieces. Even by this strict measure the Garni temple is an

The temple as it stands today. The somewhat piebald appearance is a deliberate modern artefact showing where modern materials were combined with the ancient stones for the reconstruction.

ideal subject for *anastylosis*. The original foundations remain and have proven solid enough to support a renewed building. Some 80 per cent of the decorative elements, such as column heads and friezes, were either lying around, or even better, safely preserved from damage by being buried in the soil around the site.

Many of the building blocks were too shattered for restoration, but fortunately the quarry whence they had come could be reopened for business. In the end, this added around two-thirds of the stonework to complement the undamaged original third. Only two columns could be fully reconstituted, but these served as a model for the reconstruction of the missing drums of the remainder. The stone was shipped to the site where it was cut into shape, though the rebuilders had no inhibitions about using power tools for the job rather than replicating the efforts of Classical Greek craftsmen.

In any case the new components make no pretence of being original. They are of plain undecorated stone, all the better to distinguish them from the original temple. This does mean that the temple will, for some time, have a somewhat piebald appearance until the new stone weathers into place, but the use of modern building techniques meant that by 1975, after three centuries as a ruin, the temple was reborn.

## The temple today

The rebuilt temple is not painted as the ancient version would have been, but the plain stone is given additional grandeur by the magnificent scenery of the Garni gorge above which it stands.

Almost immediately after its reconstruction the temple became a magnet for tourists as a magnificent survivor from the thousands of temples which once were spread across the ancient world, a wonderful example of Hellenistic architectural elegance emphasized by its dramatic clifftop location above the Azat river. The clean lines and balanced proportions carry a sense of harmony that reflects Pythagorean and Platonic principles of sacred geometry. This temple is the easternmost Classical temple yet found, and its grey basalt walls distinguish it from the pale marble of Mediterranean temples.

Garni is once again a sacred site. It serves as the focal point of worship for Armenian Neo-Pagans who follow a religion related to that of the Zoroastrians who worshipped here centuries before the coming of Rome. The temple also makes a spectacular backdrop for concerts and theatrical events.

The painstakingly reconstructed temple ceiling continues to please modern tourists as it did visitors to the temple in ancient times.

# Before 400 BC – *c.* AD 320
# **Sanctuary of Hecate at Lagina**
# The Witch-Goddess

*Hecate whom Zeus the son of Cronos honoured above all.*

Hesiod, *Hymn to Hecate* 1.1

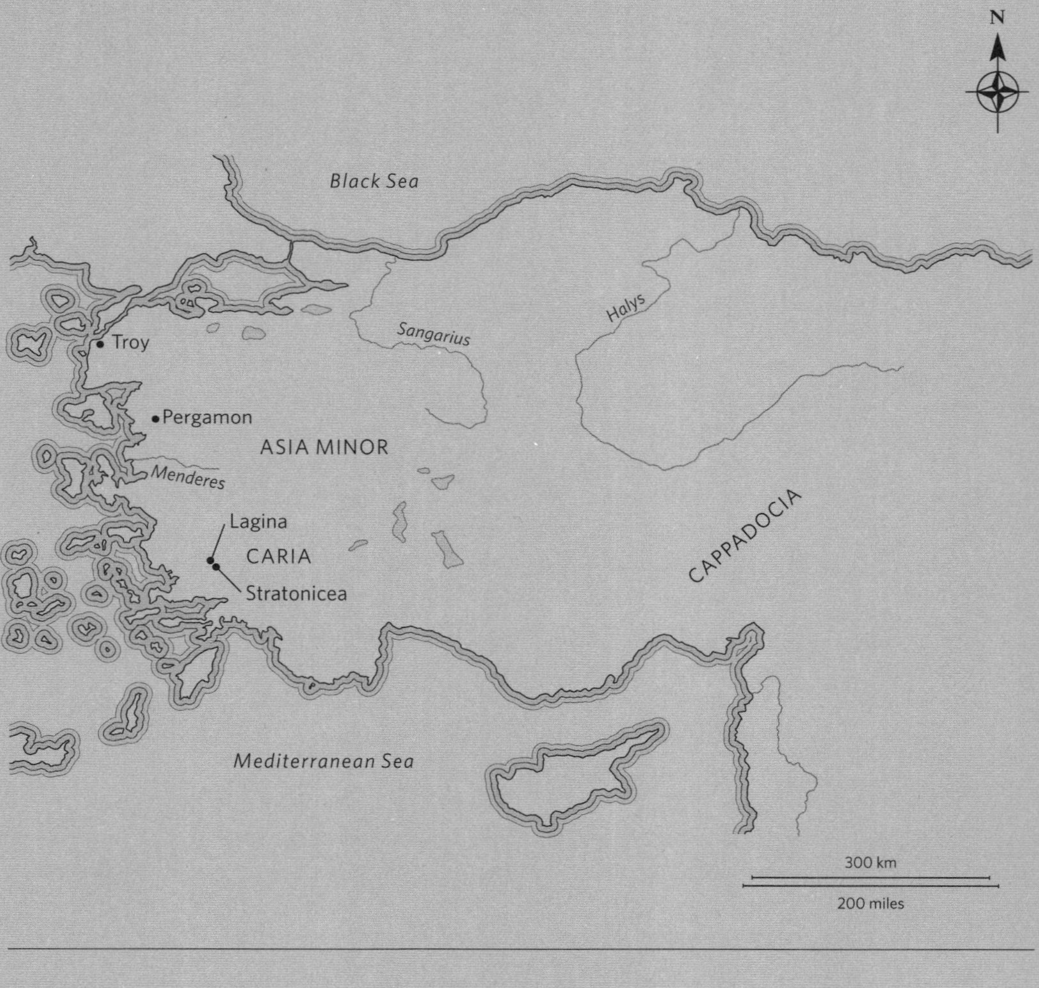

Hecate is the witch-goddess, the dreaded queen of the night who meets with the witches in Shakespeare's *Macbeth* as 'the close contriver of all harms'. To the Romans she was the goddess of the crossroads, one of the great gods of the Underworld and associated with demons, ghosts and dark magic. Her origins are variously described by the Classical authors as being in Thrace (the traditional home of the best and nastiest witches) or in Caria, a wild mountainous region on the south coast of Anatolia.

Modern researchers tend to believe that the ancient home from which the worship of the goddess spread westwards was indeed Caria, and that the deity worshipped there bore little resemblance to the monstrous creature she became in later mythology. Some of the strongest evidence for this earlier form of Hecate comes from the sanctuary to the goddess at Lagina.

Hecate, goddess of the crossroads. Her triple body is often shown facing in three directions – as a Classical 'crossroads' was what today we call a T-junction – hence the goddess's Latin name of 'Tri-via'.

## Hecate at home

While the worship of Hecate in Asia Minor went back for centuries before that, there is little evidence that Hecate's great sanctuary at Lagina is more than three thousand years old. The sanctuary is built on a hillside above the plain of the Harpasus river and consists of a complex of several buildings spread over an area of some 1,000 square metres (10,700 square feet).

A road lined with columns, called the Sacred Road, joins the sanctuary to the Greco-Roman city of Stratonicea, which is 4 kilometres (2½ miles) away. Strabo, the Roman geographer, informs us that: 'There are two temples in the country of the Stratoniceians, of which the most famous, that of Hecate, is at Lagina, and every year it draws great assemblies to her festival' (*Geography* 14.2.25). The festival emphasized a different aspect of the goddess. As well as being a triple-bodied denizen of Hades and mistress of snakes and ghosts, accompanied by baying hounds, in Caria she was the goddess of entrances and doorways. The procession to Lagina along the Sacred Road was led by a maiden designated as the 'Key Carrier' who ceremonially opened the gates to start the festival.

## Hecate abroad

For the people of Anatolia, Hecate was a maiden goddess who oversaw child-bearing, justice and protection from malign spirits. As goddess of justice she was particularly popular with the poor, over whom the rich and well-connected often ran roughshod. If nothing else would work, perhaps a well-crafted prayer to the dread goddess might balance the scales somewhat. Being poor and oppressed was not a condition unique to Asia Minor, so it was hardly surprising that Hecate's worship spread irresistibly west. The Greeks and Romans were not sure what to make of this goddess of the underdog, who did not fit well into their Classical pantheons. They tried to associate her with their more orthodox gods, such as Artemis, who was also a maiden. Thus the Roman historian Tacitus refers to Stratonicea as 'maintaining the worship of Diana of the crossroads'. Another association was with the Anatolian mother-goddess Cybele, who like Hecate at Lagina was served by eunuch priests.

In western sculpture Hecate is generally depicted with torches, which she used to guide the corn-goddess Demeter into the Underworld to search for her daughter, and also to slay the giant Klytios. No torches have been found as decorations at the sanctuary, nor yet dogs or weasels, both totemic animals of the goddess. (Dogs because Hecate transformed Hecuba, queen of Troy, into a black dog to save her from getting killed, and weasels because Hecate adopted into her entourage a woman who was transformed into a weasel because she had angered Hera, queen of the gods.)

## The sanctuary

However, Hecate is no one but herself in the sanctuary at Lagina, where rather than being an outsider-goddess she is very much at

Bas-relief from Lagina (the significance of the items depicted is uncertain), the ancient home of Hecate where the goddess took a more conventional form than her monstrous role abroad.

Titled *Hecate: Procession of the Witches*, this seventeenth-century oil painting shows how Hecate became a symbol of evil as she was literally demonized by the medieval Church.

home. One interesting feature of her sanctuary is that in all the buildings, with their rich frescoes and bas-reliefs, nothing is to be found of the attributes associated with her in religious worship farther west. Instead one sees gatherings of the gods, their battles and other scenes featuring Amazons and events from the mythology of Hecate.

Visitors to the sanctuary entered through a gate in the *peribolus*, the wall which in the ancient world divided sacred ground from the profane. Interestingly this gate carries an inscription thanking the Roman emperor Augustus for his support for the goddess. On the western side of the sanctuary was a covered stoa, a sort of porch from where spectators at festivals of the goddess could watch events. Archaeological finds of hundreds of coins and vessels of glass and terracotta, as well as offerings of gold, bone and ivory, show that such festivals were well attended. Because the Romans believed that Hecate's sanctuary was a particularly potent place for magic, those looking for that special incantation to suit their purposes also made their way there at other times of the year. It helped that the attendants at the shrine are believed to have been skilled with herbs, potions and incantations.

Not unexpectedly, the main feature of the sanctuary at Lagina was a large temple of Hecate. The ruins visible today are of the

The ruins of the sanctuary at Lagina are becoming a sacred site once more as a growing number of Neo-Pagans visit to experience a spiritual connection to the ancient gods.

splendid temple built in the Roman era, though beneath this are the remains of an older temple which probably dates back to the fourth century BC. As was traditional with Roman temples, that to Hecate stood on a large raised platform and was approached by a wide staircase.

## Honoured by the 'deathless gods'

Nearby was a nymphaeum. This shrine to the nymphs was probably dedicated to a particular breed of the species, namely the Lampades. As with the pack of sacred hounds who accompanied Hecate on her nocturnal travels, the Lampades ('torch-bearers') were part of the retinue of the goddess. Allegedly they were given to her by Zeus himself out of gratitude for her help in his battles to hold on to his throne on Olympus. The Greek poet Hesiod says:

*Zeus gave her splendid gifts and allowed her a share of the earth and the barren sea. She receives honour also in the star-covered heavens, and is greatly honoured by the deathless gods. Even today, when any man on earth offers rich sacrifices and prays for divine favour, by custom, he calls first upon Hecate.*

(*Theogony* 412)

Sadly, one god who did not honour divine Hecate was 'earth-shaking' Poseidon. One can infer this from an earthquake that devastated the site and split the altar in front of the temple. Thereafter the stoa was replaced with a large basilica, which remained in use until the sixth century AD.

Worship of Hecate endured for centuries after Christianity had seen off other 'pagan' deities. This may be one reason why the goddess was depicted by churchmen in medieval times as a being dedicated totally to evil. Nevertheless, a goddess who supported the cause of the underdog would remain popular for so long as there were underdogs; and the Church also had to issue special sanctions against women who continued to bring their infants to the crossroads to ask for Hecate's blessing.

## Today

As a result, though the sanctuary of Hecate was allowed to fall into ruin it was never forgotten, and excavations there began in the nineteenth century. Today many of the fallen columns of the temple have been restored and present-day Neo-Pagans visit the underground chambers where they believe the secret rituals of the goddess took place.

AD 43 – 60

# The Temple of the Divine Claudius

## Emperor and God

*The temple built for the deified Claudius was always visible, looming as the symbol of an enduring tyranny.*

**Tacitus, *Annals* 14.31**

From the time of Julius Caesar the Romans were in the habit of making their rulers into gods after their deaths, a process called *apotheosis*. Not all Roman rulers took this process completely seriously. On his deathbed, the emperor Vespasian remarked to those around him 'I fear I may be turning into a god'. However, apotheosis was not merely political theatre. Classical religion did not draw a hard line between human and divine and it was possible – just – for some humans to ascend to the heavens and attain divinity through sheer merit and ability (though having some divine blood in the first place also helped).

Across their empire, the Romans found it easier to keep control if subject peoples thought their imperial ruler was divine or at least a demi-god. The Egyptians had long afforded semi-divine status to their pharaohs, and in the Hellenistic east it had not been unusual for some kings to proclaim themselves as gods; the Romans built upon such traditions where they could. The emperor Claudius (r. AD 41–54) may have felt that he had a reasonable claim to be considered a god, since his very ancient family claimed descent from the goddess Venus. And since Claudius had brought to fruition the long-held Roman ambition of conquering Britain (or at least much of it), what better place to start his campaign for godhood than on the very island he had just subjugated?

Bronze sculpture of the emperor Claudius retrieved from the river Alde in 1907. Its mistreatment demonstrates how strongly the Britons felt about their conqueror.

## A symbol of power

The first step was to build a temple to the Divine Claudius so that the Britons could give due reverence to their conqueror. Camulodunum (modern Colchester) was the chosen site for this temple, for two reasons. Firstly, before the Roman conquest it had once been the centre of the powerful tribe of the Catuvellauni. Secondly, after the conquest many discharged Roman legionaries had settled there and it was evident from the start that a certain degree of coercion was going to be required if the Britons were to accept their new god.

The temple was built on a massive scale, the purpose being partly to make a deep impression on the natives. The base of the temple was 25 metres (82 feet) across and 31.5 metres (103 feet) long. The entire foundation was raised 3 metres (10 feet) from ground level even before the building atop it began. (It appears that the builders had difficulty obtaining enough suitable stone for this, because they skimped on the interior part of the foundation, leaving four large voids in the stonework which they filled with sand. People of later ages were to find these spaces very useful.)

Going by the standard design of Greco-Roman temples, such a foundation would have supported a building with eight columns across the front, each around a metre (3 feet) wide and 10 metres (33 feet) tall. This was an imposing edifice indeed, though the Romans of Rome were less impressed. After Claudius died (with the help of a dish of poisonous mushrooms) the writer and philosopher Seneca the Younger described Jupiter, king of the gods, as inquiring scornfully, 'So he thinks he should become a god, does he? Shouldn't he be content with a temple in Britain where barbarians can worship him and pray to find mercy from a fool?' (Seneca, *Apocolocyntosis* 8.3).

## Religion and oppression

In fact the Britons were finding Claudius far from a benevolent deity. The Roman settlers in Camulodunum acted as though they had complete sovereignty over the area. Families that had farmed their lands for generations were driven out by ex-legionaries who took the land just because they could, knowing that Roman courts would refuse to listen to the claims of the outraged natives.

The Romans also seized on a way of weakening any British leaders about whom they felt resistance might coalesce. They appointed such men as priests of Claudius – an 'honour' which meant that these men had to exhaust their personal fortunes in paying for sacrifices and lavish festivals for their imperial god.

The temple of Claudius as it might have appeared just before its destruction. This picture is of a model now in the museum in Colchester Castle.

'Under the pretext of religion the priests, forced into service, were compelled to pour out their fortunes like water' says Tacitus (*Annals*, 14.31).

The Romans did not confine their excesses to Camulodunum. In the lands in the east of Britannia the pent-up fury against Rome finally erupted in AD 60/61. Boudicca, queen of the Iceni, raised the standard of rebellion after Romans sacked her palace, gave her a whipping and raped her daughters. This, not unnaturally, convinced the queen that the only good Roman was a dead Roman and she and her rapidly growing army of followers set about putting this principle into practice. Camulodunum was a natural target for their fury, and a convenient one also, because while they had spent a fortune on building their massive temple to Claudius, the city's governors had neglected some basic essentials, such as city walls.

## Destruction

In fact, just about the only defensible building in the city was that very temple of Claudius, with its single entrance and solid stone walls. A fifth column of Britons within Camulodunum sabotaged the

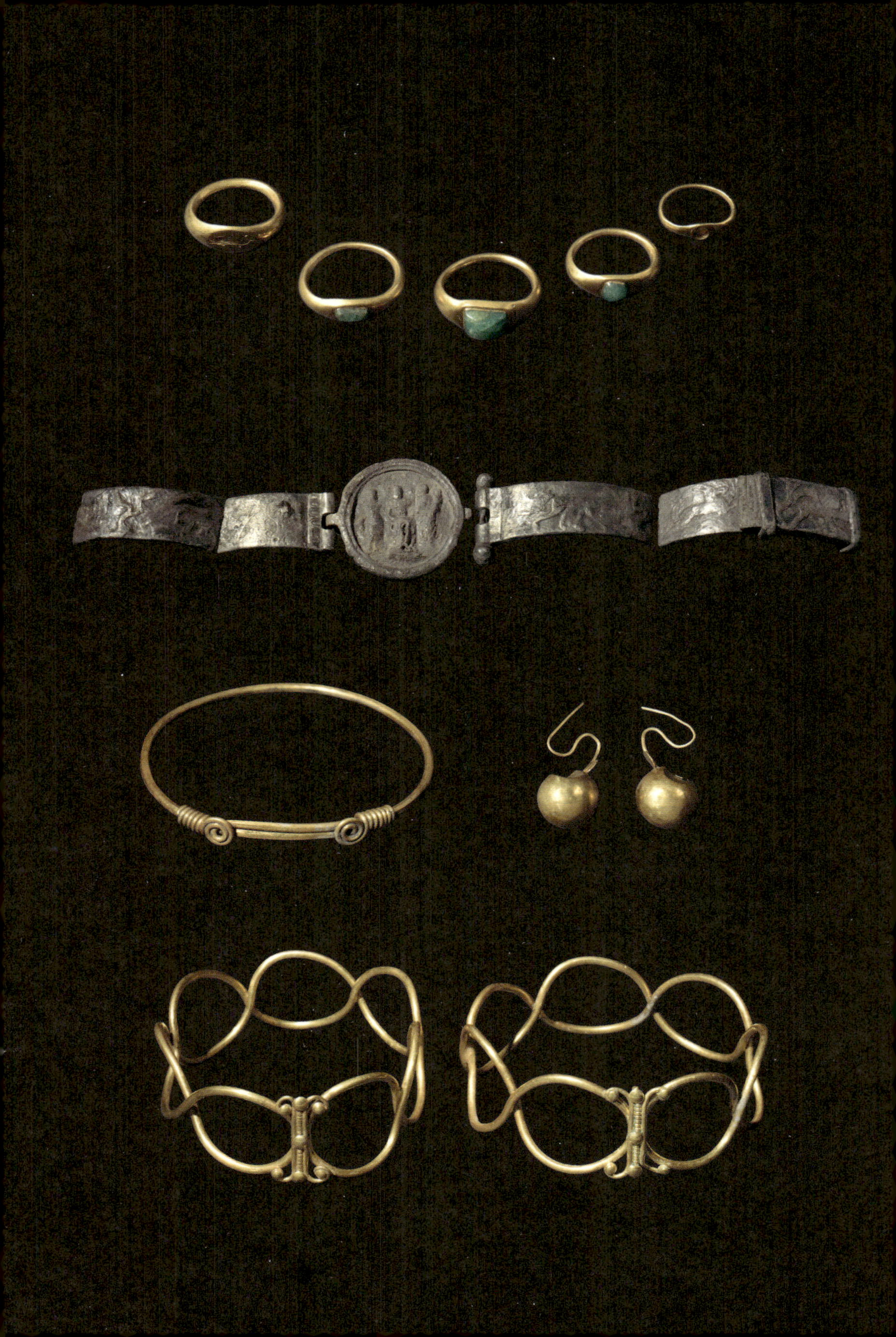

When Boudicca and her rebels descended on Colchester many buried their wealth and fled. This hoard, never retrieved by its owner, was discovered in 2014.

hasty Roman attempts to construct other defences and revealed the Roman defensive strategy to the rebels. In the end all the veterans could do was to make a stand in the temple while any who failed to find shelter there were killed as Boudicca's army plundered the rest of the town. Certainly the alleged sanctity of Claudius was no protection – rather, his unloved temple became the focus of the malign attention of the rebels.

As might be expected of Roman veterans the defenders did not succumb without a fight, but they must have known from the start that their situation was hopeless. After two days of bitter fighting the temple was taken and the defenders massacred. Thereafter the Britons set about dismantling the temple with an enthusiasm they had never demonstrated during its construction. So comprehensive was the looting and subsequent destruction that few artefacts remained for later archaeologists to unearth.

After the Roman reconquest of Britain, the new administration wisely decided not to rebuild the hated symbol of the previous tyranny. The remains of the temple – namely the huge stone foundation – stood neglected until the Norman conquest of Britain, when once again a conquering people decided that they needed a structure that would awe and subdue the natives. Finding a handy foundation already in place, they built a castle on the site – the largest of its kind outside London. The sand-filled gaps in the foundation they excavated to make a set of underground vaults.

## Museum and memorial

Colchester Castle still stands upon the temple foundations, though some parts were later demolished and the remainder of the building was used as a prison. After being purchased by the Borough of Colchester, the site was restored as a museum. Today guided tours take visitors through the building's past as a Roman temple, fortress and prison. The museum contains numerous displays and artefacts, including coins, pottery and religious offerings from elsewhere in Roman Colchester. Some exhibits explore how the military and divine cult intertwined, acknowledging the memory of those Roman veterans who fought to the death just metres above the vaults where the relics are now displayed.

AD 250 – *c.* 390

# The London Mithraeum

## Mysterious Mithras

*Ulpius Silvanus, veteran of the Legion II Augusta redeemed his vow. He was initiated* [into the cult of Mithras] *at Arausio.*

**Inscription from the London Mithraeum**

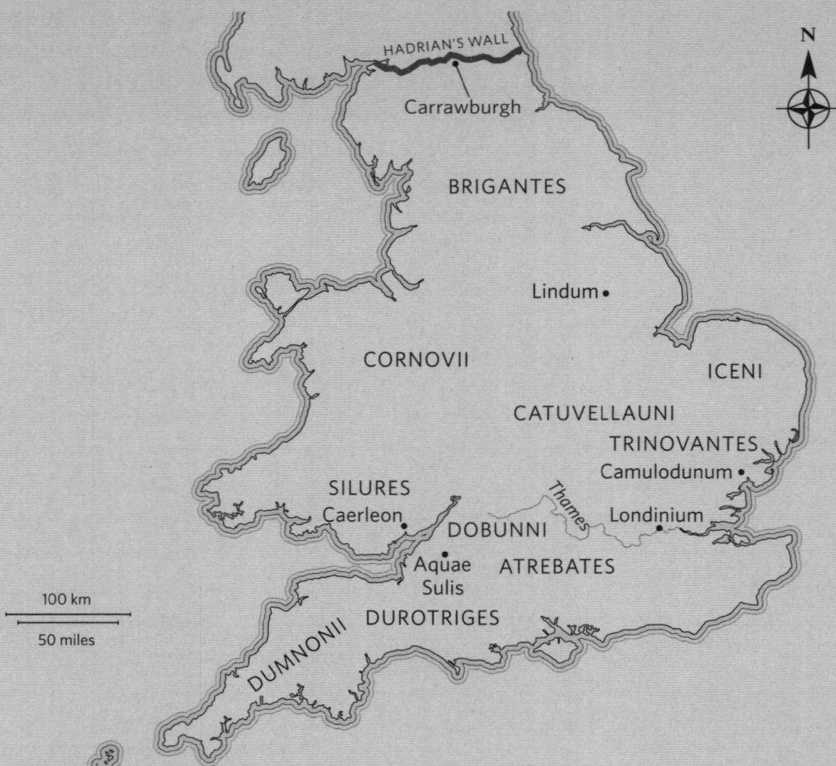

Few Roman deities are as mysterious as Mithras, the god worshipped across the later Roman empire, especially by members of the army. There was a very ancient god called Mithra who was worshipped in Asia Minor by the Hittites a thousand years before the Roman empire came into being, but modern researchers are uncertain how much the two gods may have had in common. They certainly shared a very similar name, and the worship of Mithras, like that of Mithra, seems to have begun in the Middle East. Followers of Mithras then carried their faith with them to other parts of the empire, but exactly what these men believed is virtually unknown.

The climactic event in the story of the god involves his slaying a bull. This event took place in a cave and it is speculated that the slaying symbolized the destruction of the powers of darkness and the bringing of light and order to the world. As a result, from the beginning – which seems to have been around the time of the emperor Trajan (r. AD 98–117) – places of worship of Mithras were built as cave-like structures, preferably underground or partly underground and, for reasons not now understood, near running water.

A modern imagining of secret rites within the Mithraeum. How accurate the painting may be is anyone's guess, as Mithraism fully deserves its name as a mystery cult.

Sculpture of Mithras and the bull. That Mithras appears to have slain this beast is one of the central tenets of Mithraism, though what the act signifies is now unknown.

## Mithras in London

The London Mithraeum was not the only or the first such temple constructed in Britain – for example, another has been found close to Carrawburgh, a Roman fort on Hadrian's Wall. However, the London Mithraeum was a somewhat larger and more costly construction, something which has intrigued modern archaeologists as the Roman army did not have a particularly large presence in third-century London. (The Roman empire was in a state of crisis at the time and the army was urgently needed elsewhere.) Therefore it is assumed today that this particular Mithraeum was attended by civil servants and merchants as well as soldiers. What is certain, though, is that these worshippers were all male – the mystery cult firmly excluded women from its rites.

In the present-day City of London, Walbrook is a ward containing such edifices as the Bank of England and St Paul's Cathedral. The origin of its name is a brook which, until the modern era, ran close to the city wall and into the river Thames. This brook provided the running water that followers of Mithras preferred to have adjacent to their place of worship (despite the challenges which damp unstable soil presented to those building partly underground). The temple was designed so that such light as shone into the 'cave' came from small windows set high in the walls – if indeed any light was admitted into the main room at all. As was the case with most Mithraea the temple was set on an east–west axis, perpendicular to the stream outside. As was most of Roman London, the Mithraeum was north of the Thames, in this case just to the west of the Forum Basilica.

## Worshippers and worshipped

Followers of Mithras valued courage, virtue and honour. Exactly how they did so was a mystery, not just to later researchers but also to the general public of Roman London and indeed to the majority of the followers of the cult. This was because initiation into its secrets happened in stages, with few progressing to the ultimate seventh stage. It is certain that a lot of male bonding happened at the Mithraeum, where members met regularly to share communal meals in their underground room. As with all temples of this god, the central figure in the London Mithraeum was a statue of Mithras slaying the bull. Around this various astronomical and astrological signs described the universe, which the god had created by his symbolic act.

The London Mithraeum also contained statues of other deities including Mercury (which is significant, as among his other aspects Mercury was the god of merchants), Minerva, goddess of wisdom, and Serapis. The latter is a somewhat surprising addition, as this Greco-Egyptian god was closely connected with Apis, the sacred Egyptian bull. There is also a mysterious figure usually considered to have been a water deity, perhaps embodying Oceanus or the river Thames. If it is the latter, then this statue must have been specially commissioned, as examination of the statues suggests that they were carved in Italy and imported for the temple.

These statues have survived because in the early fourth century the floor was raised to street level and the statues carefully buried beneath it. Votive offerings and cult symbols for the later period of the shrine's existence seem more suited to the god Bacchus than to the worship of Mithras. There is evidence that in the late third century the Mithraeum needed urgent repairs following the collapse of the southwest ceiling, so it is possible that those using the site decided that the god Mithras had signalled his displeasure with his present location. Therefore, the building was raised to a safer level

The interior of the London Mithraeum, beautifully and evocatively reconstructed today.

and the site rededicated to Bacchus – the god of wine, who also worked well in the context of male communal gatherings.

## Rediscovery and re-relocation

This is all necessarily speculation as the only evidence for what happened at the site is the testimony of the stones themselves – and they have had a somewhat disturbed history since their rediscovery in the twentieth century.

In 1952 London was in the midst of a building spree to erase the damage from bombing in the Second World War. Workers preparing the foundations for a new office building came upon the remains of the Mithraeum some 7 metres (23 feet) below the modern street level. This was not an entirely unexpected development, as the new building was in an area that had been inhabited for thousands of years. After an archaeological excavation, the question arose as to how the remains of this ancient temple should be handled.

Eventually the stones of the Mithraeum were laid out on the grounds of nearby Temple Court, but this was generally considered an unsatisfactory solution.

In 2010 the original site of the Mithraeum was purchased by the Bloomberg Group as part of their proposed European headquarters. The group's proposal to restore the Mithraeum as part of the basement was enthusiastically taken up, and today the restored building contains much of the ambience which must have been felt by worshippers nineteen hundred years ago. The location is not exactly where it was before, as some newly discovered parts of the original structure are too fragile to serve as part of the publicly accessible site that the temple has now become.

Today visitors are allowed into the temple in small supervised groups. They are treated to an audio-visual display which explains the original function and history, the highlight of which is the reveal by a spotlight of the temple's original centrepiece, the white marble statue of Mithras slaying his bull – complete with the inscription by Ulpius Silvanus who centuries ago dedicated the statue in fulfilment of his vow. Those who have taken the tour report that the effect is both haunting and dramatic – a truly evocative display which brings to life religion in London as it was in the Roman era.

# EPILOGUE

## A New World: Divinity Reimagined

> *There was a grove and temple... dedicated to the foul demon known by the name of Venus....Our august emperor* [Constantine]...*decreeing that such a temple should not exist beneath the light of heaven, gave orders that the building and votive offerings within should be totally destroyed.*
>
> **Eusebius,** *Life of Constantine* 3.55

For most of the Classical era religion was transactional – communities provided their gods with sacrifice and worship, and in return the gods provided their people with divine protection. The third century AD saw this arrangement break down. Amid barbarian invasions, devastating plagues and continual civil war it was clear that the gods were not holding up their part of the bargain. Therefore (to make a broad generalization) the people of the empire turned to a different faith – Christianity. Christians argued that the world was collapsing because the 'end times' were near, and their God offered salvation not in this world but in the next. It was an attractive vision, which was ever more widely adopted. Yet this transformation was neither smooth nor universal. Previous beliefs did not vanish overnight. Instead, they lingered, adapted and, in some places, fiercely resisted the tide. Sacred pagan spaces – temples, groves and altars – became battlegrounds of cultural memory and spiritual resistance.

### The persistence of traditional practice

In much of the empire early Christianity was largely an urban phenomenon. In rural areas 'pagan' rituals were closely intertwined with the agrarian cycles of the community. Things like harvest festivals and solstice ceremonies were a way of life embodied in traditions which could not be simply wiped away by an imperial decree.

Sacred places were focal points of communal identity. From the architectural marvels of the Serapeum in Alexandria and temple of Artemis in Ephesus to countless roadside shrines, these were spaces where rituals connected worshippers to divine power and where mythic histories intimately connected with the local environment.

Some of these places were now abandoned, left to the elements and the slow erosion of time. In other cases the authorities hastened the process. 'The entrances of the temples in several cities had the doors removed by imperial decree. Others had their tiles removed and the roofs destroyed leaving them exposed to the weather', reports the Church Father Eusebius (*Life of Constantine* 3.54), with great satisfaction. Some sacred sites were repurposed. Temples became converted into churches, idols became saints reimagined with Christian symbols. Yet even in their transformed state these places retained a whisper of their original purpose, both disturbing and inspiring the new worshippers within. Another blow to the ancient sacred sites was the loss of statues and other dedications that had accumulated over the centuries. Many of these dedications were of gold or silver, which had given rise to an issue called 'treasurization'. Bullion stored in temples was removed from the money supply and, while this was not the primary cause of the inflation that bedevilled third-century Rome, it certainly did not help. The emperor Constantine the Great (*c.* AD 272–337) resolved the issue at a stroke. Between AD 331 and 336 he issued decrees stripping the temples and altars of gold, silver and bronze to create a new currency – one which remained stable for centuries thereafter.

## Reshaping the divine

The late Roman religious landscape was filled with conflict and compromise. Some pagan festivals were shifted into a Christian context – most famously the winter solstice celebrations, which have been repurposed to celebrate Christmas. (Something worth recalling by those pastors who urge their commercially minded flock 'to remember the original meaning of Christmas'.) Holy wells remained sites of pilgrimage long after their pagan significance was forgotten, while some forest groves associated with divine mystery were cut down. Yet many others remained untouched, quietly visited by those who remembered the old ways – even as they attended church on Sundays. The ancient sacred geography resonated in the imagination, memory and emotional landscape of ordinary people with meaning deeper than official dogma.

## Legacy

Thus the sacred places of paganism were not suddenly wiped out. Rather they went through a slow twilight interspersed with sparks of resistance and moments of accommodation. Even after the fall of Rome and the – literal – demonization of the ancient gods, their worship was still practised by a few as a secret act of rebellion against established authority. Today, modern Neo-Pagans again openly celebrate their (largely invented) rituals at the ancient sites. For others these ruins continue to provoke reflection, not only on lost architectural splendour but on the deep spiritual ties that exist between people and place. The Western world may have pivoted toward monotheism, but the memory of older gods lingers still, with reminders carved in stone, whispered in winds through broken columns and as a haunting presence in wild forests and mountains.

*What leaf-fring'd legend haunts about*
*thy shape*
*Of deities or mortals, or of both,*
*In Tempe or the dales of Arcady?*
....
*Who are these coming to the sacrifice?*
*To what green altar, O mysterious priest,*
*Lead'st thou that heifer lowing at*
*the skies,*
*And all her silken flanks with*
*garlands drest?*
*What little town by river or sea shore,*
*Or mountain-built with peaceful citadel,*
*Is emptied of this folk, this pious morn?*
*And, little town, thy streets for evermore*
*Will silent be; and not a soul to tell*
*Why thou art desolate, can e'er return.*

**John Keats, 'Ode on a Grecian Urn', 1819**

# Further Reading


PART ONE: Sacred Places of Prehistory

**Göbekli Tepe**

Clare, L., 'Göbekli Tepe, Turkey. A Brief Summary of Research at a New World Heritage Site (2015–2019)', *e-Forschungs Berichte des DAI* (2020), pp. 1–13.

Najafova, A., 'Decoding Gobeklitepe: Insights into Prehistoric Rituals and Society', *Acta Globalis Humanitatis et Linguarum* 2(2) (February 2025), pp. 29–37.

Schmidt, K., *Göbekli tepe* (Istanbul, 2007).

**The Great Ziggurat of Ur**

Beaulieu P., 'The City of Ur and the Neo-Babylonian Empire. Ur in the Twenty-First Century CE', *Proceedings of the 62nd Rencontre Assyriologique Internationale at Philadelphia* (January 2021), p. 153.

McMahon, A., 'Reframing the Ziggurat: Looking at (and from) Ancient Mesopotamian Temple Towers', in *Elements of Architecture* (London, 2016), pp. 321–39.

Woolley, C. Leonard, 'The Excavations at Ur, 1923–1924', *The Antiquaries Journal* 5(1) (1925), pp. 1–20.

**The Giant's Bed**

Bakker, J. A., *The Dutch Hunebedden: Megalithic Tombs of the Funnel Beaker Culture* (New York, 1992).

Bakker, J. A., *Megalithic Research in the Netherlands, 1547–1911: From 'Giant's Beds' and 'Pillars of Hercules' to Accurate Investigations* (Leiden, 2010).

Lubach, D., 'On the Hunebedden, or Cromlechs, in the Province of Drenthe, in Holland', *The Journal of the Anthropological Institute of Great Britain and Ireland* 6 (1877), pp. 158–67.

**Lerna**

Caskey, J., 'Excavations at Lerna: 1956', *Hesperia: The Journal of the American School of Classical Studies at Athens* 26(2) (1957), pp. 142–62.

Caskey, J. and Blackburn, E. T., *Lerna in the Argolid: A Short Guide* (Athens, 1997).

Salowey, C., 'Labor II: The Lernean Hydra', in D. Ogden (ed.), *The Oxford Handbook of Heracles* (Oxford, 2021), pp. 45–61.

**Su Tempiesu**

Ialongo, N., 'Sanctuaries and the Emergence of Elites in Nuragic Sardinia during the Early Iron Age (ca. 950–720 BC): The Actualization of a "Ritual Strategy"', *Journal of Mediterranean Archaeology*, 26(2) (2013), pp. 231–53.

Lilliu, G., *La Civiltà dei Sardi dal Neolitico all'età dei Nuraghi* (Turin, 1988).

Tanda, G., *La Religione dei Sardi Nuragici* (Cagliari, 1995).

**The Colossi of Memnon**

Bowersock, G., 'The Miracle of Memnon', *The Bulletin of the American Society of Papyrologists* 21(1/4) (1984), pp. 21–32.

Łukaszewicz, A., 'Memnon, his Ancient Visitors and Some Related Problems', in *Tradition and Transformation: Egypt under Roman Rule: Proceedings of the International Conference, Hildesheim, 2008* (Leiden and Boston, 2010), p. 255.

Rosenmeyer, P., *The Language of Ruins: Greek and Latin Inscriptions on the Memnon Colossus* (Oxford, 2018).

**The Tophet of Carthage**

Bonnet, C., 'On Gods and Earth: The Tophet and the Construction of a New Identity in Punic Carthage', in E. S. Gruen, *Cultural Identity in the Ancient Mediterranean* (Los Angeles, 2011), pp. 373–87.

Stager, L. and Wolff, S., 'Child Sacrifice at Carthage – Religious Rite or Population Control', *Biblical Archaeology Review* 10(1) (1984), pp. 30–51.

Xella, P., 'The Levantine Roots of the Tophet Sanctuary', *Journal of Ancient History* 11(2) (2023), pp. 291–303.

**Stonehenge**

Bender, B., 'Theorising Landscapes, and the Prehistoric Landscapes of Stonehenge', *Man* (1992), pp. 735–55.

Pearson, M. P., *Stonehenge – A New Understanding: Solving the Mysteries of the Greatest Stone Age Monument* (New York, 2014).

Richards, J. (ed.), *The Stonehenge Environs Project* (Liverpool, 2014).

**Croghan Bog and Hill**

Giles, M., 'Iron Age Bog Bodies of North-western Europe. Representing the Dead', *Archaeological Dialogues* 16(1) (2009), pp. 75–101.

Kelly, E., 'The Bog Body from Cashel Bog, Co. Laois', *Ossory, Laois and Leinster* 5 (2012), pp. 1–18.

Kilfeather, A., 'Legend and Wetland Landscape in Ireland', *Journal of Wetland Archaeology* 3(1) (2003), pp. 37–50.

**The Mystery of the Sphinx**

Lehner, M., 'Reconstructing the Sphinx', *Cambridge Archaeological Journal* 2(1) (1992), pp. 3–26.

Schoch, R., 'A Modern Riddle of the Sphinx', *Omni* 14(11) (1992), pp. 46–51.

Zivie-Coche, C., *Sphinx: History of a Monument* (Ithaca and London, 2004).

**The Hal Saflieni Hypogeum**

Magli, G., 'The Island of the Goddess', in G. Magli, *Mysteries and Discoveries of Archaeoastronomy: From Giza to Easter Island* (New York and London, 2009), pp. 47–67.

Mifsud, A. and Mifsud, S., 'The Subterranean Sanctuary at Ħal Saflieni', in *Prehistoric Society of Malta* (Malta, 1999), pp. 149–68.

Skeates, R., 'Religious Experience in the Prehistoric Maltese Underworld', in D. A. Barrowclough and C. Malone, *Cult in Context: Reconsidering Ritual in Archaeology* (Oxford, 2007), pp. 90–96.

PART TWO: The Early Classical Era: Rationality and Belief

**Mount Helicon**

Langdon, M., 'Mountains in Greek Religion', *The Classical World* 93(5) (2000), pp. 461–70.

Mojsik, T., 'Muses in a Landscape – Helicon in Ancient Culture', *The Classical Review* 72(1) (2022), pp. 30–32.

Robinson, B., 'Mount Helikon and the Valley of the Muses: The Production of a Sacred Space', *Journal of Roman Archaeology* 25 (2012), pp. 227–58.

**The Oracle at Dodona**

Frank, K., *Oracular Inquiries and Daily Life. The Oracle of Dodona in the Classical and Hellenistic Period* (PhD dissertation, University College London, 2021).

Parke, H. et al., 'Dodona', in *Oxford Classical Dictionary* (Oxford, 2015), oxfordre.com.

Parker, R., 'Seeking Advice from Zeus at Dodona', *Greece & Rome* 63(1) (2016), pp. 69–90.

**The Telesterion at Eleusis**

Clinton, K., 'Eleusis', in *Oxford Classical Dictionary* (Oxford, 2012), oxfordre.com.

Clinton, K., 'The Sanctuary of Demeter and Kore at Eleusis', in N. Marinatos and R. Hägg (eds), *Greek Sanctuaries* (London, 2002), pp. 101–11.

Evans, N., 'Sanctuaries, Sacrifices, and the Eleusinian Mysteries', *Numen* 49(3) (2002), pp. 227–54.

**The Tomb of Achilles**

Anghelina, C., 'Achilles' Funeral in Early Greek Epic', *Eranos* 107 (2012), pp. 1–14.

Burgess, J., *The Death and Afterlife of Achilles* (Baltimore, 2009).

Hedreen, G., 'The Cult of Achilles in the Euxine', *Hesperia: The Journal of the American School of Classical Studies at Athens* 60(3) (1991), pp. 313–30.

**The Altis at Olympia**

Barringer, J., 'The Temple of Zeus at Olympia, Heroes, and Athletes', *Hesperia: The Journal of the American School of Classical Studies at Athens* 74(2) (2005), pp. 211–41.

Morgan, C. et al., 'Olympia', *Oxford Classical Dictionary* (Oxford, 2012), oxfordre.com.

Price, M., 'The Statue of Zeus at Olympia', in P. A. Clayton and M. Price, *The Seven Wonders of the Ancient World* (London, 2013), pp. 59–77.

**The Temple of Artemis at Ephesus**

Frayer-Griggs, D., 'The Beasts at Ephesus and the Cult of Artemis', *Harvard Theological Review* 106(4) (2013), pp. 459–77.

Hooker, M., 'Artemis of Ephesus', *The Journal of Theological Studies* 64(1) (2013), pp. 37–46.

Trell, B., '4 The Temple of Artemis at Ephesos', in P. A. Clayton and M. Price, |*The Seven Wonders of the Ancient World* (London, 2013), pp. 78–99.

**The Sanatorium at Epidaurus**

Elderkin, G., 'Tholos and Abaton at Epidaurus', *American Journal of Archaeology* 15(21) (1911), pp. 61–167.

Rousselle, R., 'Healing Cults in Antiquity: The Dream Cures of Asclepius of Epidaurus', *The Journal of Psychohistory* 12(3) (1985), p. 339.

Tomlinson, Richard Allan, 'Epidaurus', *Oxford Classical Dictionary* (Oxford, 2015), oxfordre.com.

**The Oracle at Delphi**

Lloyd-Jones, H., 'The Delphic Oracle', *Greece & Rome* 23(1) (1976), pp. 60–73.

Manolis A. and de Jongh, B. (trans.), *Delphi* (Athens, 1995).

Maurizio, L., 'Delphic Oracles as Oral Performances: Authenticity and Historical Evidence', *Classical Antiquity* 16(2) (1997), pp. 308–34.

**The Menelaion of Sparta**

De Armond, T., *The Menelaion: A Local Manifestation of a Pan-Hellenic Phenomenon* (Thesis, Wesleyan University, Connecticut, 2009).

Wace, A. et al., 'Excavations at Sparta, 1909: 6. – The Menelaion', *Annual of the British School at Athens* 15 (1909), pp. 108–57.

Whitley, J., 'Menelaion', in *Oxford Classical Dictionary* (Oxford, 2016), oxfordre.com.

**The Temple of Poseidon at Sunion**

Ainian, A., 'Early Greek Temples', in M. M. Miles, *A Companion to Greek Architecture* (Chichester and Malden, 2016), pp. 15–30.

Paga, J. and Miles, M., 'The Archaic Temple of Poseidon at Sounion', *Hesperia: The Journal of the American School of Classical Studies at Athens* 85(4) (2016), pp. 657–710.

Theodoropoulou Polychroniadis, Z., 'Terracotta Offerings from the Sanctuaries of Poseidon and of Athena at Sounion', *Les Carnets de l'ACoSt (Association for Coroplastic Studies)* 11 (2014).

**Sacred Sites at Paestum**

Hodge, A., 'Notes on Three Western Greek Temples', *American Journal of Archaeology* 68(2) (1964), pp. 179–84.

Johannowsky, W., Pedley, J. G. and Torelli, M., 'Excavations at Paestum 1982', *American Journal of Archaeology* 87(3) (1983), pp. 293–303.

Symeonoglou, S., 'The Doric Temples of Paestum', *Journal of Aesthetic Education* 19(1) (1985), pp. 49–66.

**Grove of Academus**

Chroust, A., 'Plato's Academy: The First Organized School of Political Science in Antiquity', *The Review of Politics* 29(1) (1967), pp. 25–40.

Kalligas, P., Balla, C., Basiotopolou-Valavani, E. and Karasmanis, V. (eds), *Plato's Academy: Its Workings and its History* (Cambridge, 2020).

Nails, D., 'The Life of Plato of Athens', in H. Benson (ed.), *A Companion to Plato* (Malden and Oxford, 2006), pp. 1–12.

**The Cecropia**

Beard, M., *The Parthenon*, Wonders of the World (Cambridge, MA, 2010).

Schlaifer, R., 'The Cult of Athena Pallenis', *Harvard Studies in Classical Philology* 54 (1943), pp. 35–67.

Stuttard, D., *The Parthenon: Power and Politics on the Acropolis* (London, 2013).

PART THREE: The Coming of Rome

**The Ara Pacis**

Holliday, P., 'Time, History, and Ritual on the Ara Pacis Augustae', *The Art Bulletin* 72(4) (1990), pp. 542–57.

Kellum, B. A., 'What We See and What We Don't See: Narrative Structure and the Ara Pacis Augustae', *Art History* 17(1) (1994), p. 26.

Ryberg, I., 'The Procession of the Ara Pacis', *Memoirs of the American Academy in Rome* 19 (1949), pp. 77–101.

**Grove of Egeria**

Ballentine, Floyd G., 'Some Phases of the Cult of the Nymphs', *Harvard Studies in Classical Philology* 15 (1904), pp. 77–119.

Larmour, D., 'Nights of Egeria: Juvenal's De Memoria Deorum', *Memory and Urban Religion in the Ancient World* 2 (2012), p. 149.

Menconero, S., 'Piranesi at the Nymphaeum of Egeria: Perspective Expedients', in *Congreso Internacional de Expresión Gráfica Arquitectónica* (Cham, 2020).

**The Curia**

Bond, S., 'Curial Communiqué: Memory, Propaganda, and the Roman Senate House', in L. L. Brice and D. Slootjes (eds), *Aspects of Ancient Institutions and Geography. Studies in Honor of Richard J. A. Talbert* (Leiden and Boston, 2015), pp. 84–102.

Mason, G. G., 'Senacula and Meeting Places of the Roman Senate', *The Classical Journal* 83(1) (1987), pp. 39–50.

Pohlsander, H., 'Victory: The Story of a Statue', *Historia: Zeitschrift für Alte Geschichte* H. 5 (1969), pp. 588–97.

**Sacred Places at Hadrian's Villa**

Clark, E., 'Hadrian's Villa', *The Kenyon Review* 12(3) (1950), pp. 377–432.

De Franceschini, M. and Veneziano, G., 'Architecture and Archaeoastronomy in Hadrian's Villa near Tivoli, Rome', *Nexus Network Journal* 15(3) (2013), pp. 457–85.

Mari, Z. and Sgalambro, S., 'The Antinoeion of Hadrian's Villa: Interpretation and

Architectural Reconstruction', *American Journal of Archaeology* 111(1) (2007), pp. 83–104.

**The Capitoline Temple**

Moralee, J., *Rome's Holy Mountain: The Capitoline Hill in Late Antiquity* (Oxford, 2018).

Perry, E., 'The Same, But Different: The Temple of Jupiter Optimus Maximus Through Time', in B. D. Westcoat and R. G. Ousterhout, *Architecture of the Sacred: Space, Ritual, and Experience from Classical Greece to Byzantium* (Cambridge and New York, 2012), pp. 175–200.

Ridley, R., 'Unbridgeable Gaps: The Capitoline Temple at Rome', *Bullettino della commissione archeologica comunale di Roma: CVI, 2005* (2005), pp. 83–104.

**The Pantheon**

Joost-Gaugier, L., 'The Iconography of Sacred Space: A Suggested Reading of the Meaning of the Roman Pantheon', *Artibus et Historiae* (1998), pp. 21–42.

La Rocca, Eugenio, 'Agrippa's Pantheon and its Origin', in T. A. Marder and M. Wilson Jones (eds), *The Pantheon: From Antiquity to the Present* (Cambridge and New York, 2015), pp. 49–78.

MacDonald, W. L., *The Pantheon: Design, Meaning, and Progeny* (Cambridge, MA, 2002).

PART FOUR: On the Edge of the Empire

**The Tomb of Cyrus**

Kuhrt, A., 'Cyrus the Great of Persia: Images and Realities', in M. Heinz and M. H. Fedman (eds), *Representations of Political Power: Case Histories from Times of Change and Dissolving Order in the Ancient Near East* (Winona Lake, 2007), pp. 169–91.

Mowlaiey Kordshooli, H., Zare Kordshooli, F. and Karami, H., 'Memorials and Petroglyphs of Cyrus the Great's Tomb', *Parseh Journal of Archaeological Studies* 5(17) (2021), pp. 111–32.

Strabo, *Geography, Volume I: Books 1–2,* trans. H. Jones, Loeb Classical Library 49 (Cambridge, MA, 1917).

**The Ploutonion of Hierapolis**

Cantisani, E. et al., 'The Ploutonion of the Archaeological Site of Hierapolis (Turkey): A Gate for the Underworld and the Knowledge', *Open Access Journal of Archaeology and Anthropology* 1(3) (2019), pp. 1–8.

Mazzorin, J. D. G. and Minniti, C., 'Bird and Other Animal Sacrifice in the Ploutonion of Hierapolis, Phrygia (Turkey): Some Results from Two Votive Deposits', *Kolloquien Zur Vor-Und Frühgeschichte* 26(1) (2018), p. 39.

Semeraro, G., 'Archaeology of the Cult in the Sanctuary of Apollo in Hierapolis', *Scienze dell'Antichità* 20(2) (2014), pp. 11–29.

**Grove of Hercules Magusanus**

Roymans, N., 'Hercules and the Construction of a Batavian Identity', *Ethnic Constructs in Antiquity: The Role of Power and Tradition* 13 (2009), p. 219.

Roymans, N., Janković, M. A., Mihajlović, V. D. and Babić, S., 'The Batavians between Germania and Rome: The Emergence of a Soldiering People', in *The Edges of the Roman World* (Newcastle upon Tyne, 2014), pp. 232–51.

Saddington, D., 'Roman Soldiers, Local Gods and *interpretatio Romana* in Roman Germany', *Acta Classica: Proceedings of the Classical Association of South Africa* 42(1) (1999), pp. 155–69.

**The Buddhas of Bamiyan**

Higuchi, T. and Barnes, G., 'Bamiyan: Buddhist Cave Temples in Afghanistan', *World Archaeology* 27(2) (1995), pp. 282–302.

Morgan, L., *The Buddhas of Bamiyan* (Cambridge, MA, 2012).
Ottone, R., 'Commemorating 20 Years Since the Destruction of Two Buddhas of Bamiyan, Afghanistan', *UNESCO News* (21 March 2021), https://whc.unesco.org/en/news/2253.

**The Serapeum of Alexandria**

Dawson, D., 'A Cult of Fusion', *Vulcan Historical Review* 18 (2014), pp. 142–50.
Hanrahan, M., 'Paganism and Christianity at Alexandria', *University Review* (1962), pp. 38–66.
McKenzie, J. S., Gibson, S., Reyes, A. T. and Grimm, G., 'Reconstructing the Serapeum in Alexandria from the Archaeological Evidence', *The Journal of Roman Studies* 94 (2004), pp. 73–121.

**Aquae Sulis**

Davenport, P., *Roman Bath: A New History and Archaeology of Aquae Sulis* (Cheltenham, 2021).
Forbes, S., 'Aquæ Sulis', *Journal of the British Archaeological Association* 22(1) (1916), pp. 26–32.
McBurney, J., *The Cult of Sulis-Minerva at Bath: The Religious Ritual of the Patron Goddess at Bath* (PhD dissertation, Open Access Te Herenga Waka-Victoria University of Wellington, 2016).

**The Temple at Garni**

Antonyan, Y., '"Reconstituting" Religion: Neo-Paganism in Armenia', *Laboratorium* 2(1) (2010), pp. 103–28.
Boghosian, S. E., *Beyond Romanization: Design and Practice at the Ionic Building at Garni (Armenia)* (PhD dissertation, University of British Columbia, 2023).
Giambruno, M. and Pistidda, S., 'A Journey Through Armenian Heritage', in *Heritage for a Sustainable Development: The World Heritage Sites and Their Impacts on Cultural Territories: Case Studies from Armenia* (Cham, 2022), pp. 27–53.

**Sanctuary of Hecate at Lagina**

Berg, W., 'Hecate: Greek or "Anatolian"?', *Numen* (1974), pp. 128–40.
Şahin, N., 'The Cult of Hecate in Lydia: Evidence from the Manisa Museum', *Gephyra* 13 (2016), pp. 1–48.
Williamson, C., 'City and Sanctuary in Hellenistic Asia Minor', *Constructing Civic Identity in the Sacred Landscapes of Mylasa and Stratonikeia in Karia* (PhD thesis, University of Groningen, 2012).

**The Temple of the Divine Claudius**

Drury, P. J., 'The Temple of Claudius at Colchester Reconsidered', *Britannia* 15 (1984), pp. 7–50.
Fishwick, D., 'The Temple of Divus Claudius at Camulodunum', *Britannia* 26 (1995), pp. 11–27.
Fishwick, D., 'Templum divo Claudio constitutum', *Britannia* 3 (1972), pp. 164–81.

**The London Mithraeum**

Beck, R., 'The Mysteries of Mithras', in *Voluntary Associations in the Graeco-Roman World* (London, 2002), pp. 176–85.
Bowden, Hugh, 'When Things Don't Fit: Looking at the London Mithraeum', *Journal of Classics Teaching* 19(38) (2018), pp. 1–3.
Gordon, R., 'The Story of the Walbrook Mithraeum, London', in J. D. Shepherd, *The Temple of Mithras: Excavations by W. F. Grimes and A. Williams at the Walbrook*, English Heritage Archaeological Report no. 12 (London, 1998), pp. 736–42.

# Sources of Illustrations

Images are listed by page number
a = above, b = below, c = centre, l = left, r = right

**2** muART/Alamy Stock Photo; **6–7** Stefanos Kyriazis/Shutterstock; **8** World History Archive/Alamy Stock Photo; **12** PRISMA ARCHIVO/Alamy Stock Photo; **17** Courtesy Amin Hadjaran; **19** German Archaeological Institute, Göbeklitepe Archive, Erhan Küçük, 2011; **20** Ayse/AdobeStock; **23** akg-images/Balage Balogh/archaeologyillustrated.com; **25** The Trustees of the British Museum; **26** PRISMA ARCHIVO/Alamy Stock Photo; **29** Rudmer Zwerver/Alamy Stock Photo; **30, 31** piemags/rmn/Alamy Stock Photo; **32** Chris Howes/Wild Places Photography/Alamy Stock Photo; **35** Mary Harrsch; **36** Mead Art Museum/Gift of Thomas A. Fox/Bridgeman Images; **37** GrandPalaisRmn (musée du Louvre)/Hervé Lewandowski; **38** Art Institute Chicago. Gift of Mrs. Eugene A. Davidson; **41** alex.pin/Adobe Stock; **43** Raimund Franken/ullstein bild via Getty Images; **44al** Ashmolean Museum/Heritage Images/Getty Images; **44ar** A. De Gregorio/© NPL - DeA Picture Library/Bridgeman Images; **44c** PRISMA ARCHIVO/Alamy Stock Photo; **44bl** DeAgostini/Getty Images; **44br** Dmitriy Moroz/Alamy Stock Photo; **47** The Metropolitan Museum of Art, New York. Rogers Fund, 1956; **48** The Metropolitan Museum of Art, New York. Purchase, Edward S. Harkness Gift, 1926; **49** Salzburg Museum, Austria; **50** Art Directors & TRIP/Alamy Stock Photo; **51** acceptphoto/Shutterstock; **53** akg-images/Erich Lessing; **54** Classic Image/Alamy Stock Image; **56** Peter Horree/Alamy Stock Photo; **57** The Print Collector/Alamy Stock Photo; **59** British Library archive/Bridgeman Images; **60** Skyscan Photolibrary/Alamy Stock Photo; **63** Penelope Barritt/Alamy Photo Stock; **65** Silverback/Alamy Photo Stock; **66a** Art Images/Getty Images; **66b** Werner Forman/Universal Images Group via Getty Images; **68** PA Images/Alamy Photo Stock; **71** EmmePi Travel/Alamy Photo Stock; **73** DeAgostini/Getty Images; **74** haoliang/Getty Images; **77** imageBROKER.com/Alamy Photo Stock; **79** DEA/A. DAGLI ORTI/De Agostini via Getty Images; **81** Paul Almasy/Corbis/VCG via Getty Images; **82** The Metropolitan Museum of Art, New York. Rogers Fund, 1914; **87** Museum of Fine Arts, Boston; **89** Ruslan Gilmanshin/Alamy Photo Stock; **90** AIFA Visuals/Alamy Photo Stock; **91** Viktor Posnov/Alamy Photo Stock; **93** DEA PICTURE LIBRARY/De Agostini via Getty Images; **94** Hum Images/Alamy Photo Stock; **95, 96** The Print Collector/Alamy Stock Photo; **99** Pictures Now/Alamy Stock Photo; **100** Brigham Young University Museum of Art; **102** Luisa Ricciarini/Bridgeman Images; **105** Images & Stories/Alamy Stock Photo; **106** Reproduced by permission of Chatsworth Settlement Trustees/Bridgeman Images; **107** Images & Stories/Alamy Stock Photo; **108** Mike P Shepherd/Alamy Stock Photo; **111** The Metropolitan Museum of Art, New York. Fletcher Fund, 1926; **113** NPL - DeA Picture Library/Bridgeman Images; **114–15** Amazing Aerial/Alamy Stock Photo; **116** PA Images/Alamy Stock Photo; **119** Gokhan Dogan/Shutterstock; **120** EvrenKalinbacak/Shutterstock; **121** The Metropolitan Museum of Art, New York. Gift of George A. Hearn, 1910; **122** blickwinkel/Alamy Stock Photo; **125** Wellcome Collection, London; **127** Peter Horree/Alamy Stock Photo; **128** Wellcome Collection, London; **131** Lefteris Papaulakis/

Shutterstock; **132–3** Beaux-Arts de Paris, Dist. GrandPalaisRmn/image Beaux-arts de Paris; **134** Andronos Haris/Shutterstock; **135** University of Michigan, Museum of Art; **136** Bill Anastasiou/ Shutterstock; **139** Abaca Press/Alamy Stock Photos; **141** The Metropolitan Museum of Art, New York. Gift of A. J. B. Wace, 1924; **143** Archivio J. Lange/© NPL - DeA Picture Library/Bridgeman Images; **145** Petr Svarc/Alamy Stock Photos; **146** Habib M'henni; **147** Adam Eastland/Alamy Stock Photos; **148** Tate, London; **151** Sirio Carnevalino/Shutterstock; **152** Pushkin Museum of Fine Arts, Moscow; **153** Peter van Evert/Alamy Stock Photos; **154** DeAgostini/Getty Images; **157** Adam Eastland/Alamy Stock Photo; **159** Viacheslav Lopatin/Shutterstock; **160** jozef sedmak/ Alamy Stock Photo; **163** Staatliche Museen zu Berlin, Antikensammlung/Johannes Laurentius; **164** Respiro/Shutterstock; **167** DRONEQUESTGR/Shutterstock; **168** Stefano Tammaro/Shutterstock; **173** INTERFOTO/Alamy Stock Photo; **174–5** Museo Nacional del Prado, Madrid; **176** Cortyn/ Shutterstock; **179** piemags/SMKM/Alamy Stock Photo; **181** Museo e Real Bosco di Capodimonte, Napoli; **182** Dmitriy Moroz/Alamy Stock Photo; **185** Vito Arcomano/Alamy Stock Photo; **187** Walters Art Museum, Baltimore; **188** Wojciech Stróżyk/Alamy Stock Photo; **191** ANDREAS SOLARO/AFP via Getty Images; **192** Stefano Tammaro/Shutterstock; **193** Kamira/Shutterstock; **194** Dmitriy Moroz/Alamy Stock Photo; **197** Royal Academy of Arts, London; **198** Peter Horree/ Alamy Stock Photo; **200** The Trustees of the British Museum; **203** clemMTravel/Alamy Stock Photo; **204** The Metropolitan Museum of Art, New York. Rogers Fund, 1918; **205** volkova natalia/ Shutterstock; **206** National Gallery of Art, Washington, DC. Samuel H. Kress Collection; **208** iLongLoveKing/Shutterstock; **213** Art Institute Chicago. Purchased with funds provided by Mrs. Harold T. Martin; **215** Leonid Serebrennikov/Alamy Stock Photo; **216** Mohammad Domiri; **219** Russian Museum, St. Petersburg; **221** Guillaume Angleraud/Alamy Stock Photo; **222** Azoor Photo/ Alamy Stock Photo; **225** Mikko Kriek/Heritage department s-Hertogenbosch; **227** Penta Springs Limited/Alamy Stock Photo; **228** piemags/Alamy Stock Photo; **231** The Trustees of the British Museum; **232** duncan1890/Getty Images; **233** De Agostini/Getty Images; **234** CPA Media Pte Ltd/ Alamy Stock Photo; **236–7** robertharding/Alamy Stock Image; **239** DEA/G. DAGLI ORTI/De Agostini via Getty Images; **240** Private Collection; **241** AMIR MAKAR/AFP via Getty Images; **242** EVREN KALINBACAK/Alamy Stock Image; **245** imageBROKER.com/Alamy Stock Image; **247** Guy Bell/Alamy Stock Image; **248** Oscarhill/istockphoto; **251** DEA/G. DAGLI ORTI/De Agostini via Getty Images; **253** tunart/Getty Images; **254** Ekaterina Kriminskaya/Alamy Stock Image; **257** funkyfood London - Paul Williams/Alamy Stock Image; **258** Murat Tegmen/Shutterstock; **259** Apsley House, London; **260** Emiralikokal/Dreamstime.com; **263** CM Dixon/Print Collector/Getty Images; **265** Susie Kearley/Alamy Stock Image; **266** Colchester and Ipswich Museums Service. Colchester Borough Council Collection; **269** Museum of London; **270** Ore Ste/Alamy Stock Image; **272** Nick Harrison/Alamy Stock Image.

# Index

Page references in *italics* refer to illustrations.

*Part opener captions:*

**Part One**
p. 12 Fragment of the Stele of Ur-Nammu, from the Third Dynasty of Ur. This scene possibly depicts the divine mandate given to the king to build the Great Ziggurat. Dated to 2097–2080 BC it is currently housed in the Penn Museum, Philadelphia.

**Part Two**
p. 82 Triptolemus, son of the king of Eleusis, stands between Demeter and Persephone. This Roman copy of a Greek original is in the Metropolitan Museum of Art, New York.

**Part Three**
p. 168 The baths at Hadrian's villa in Tivoli, Italy, 'Villa' understates the size and complexity of Hadrian's country retreat, which housed thousands of people at a time.

**Part Four**
p. 208 In modern Bath, the Roman building still looks ready for bathers 2000 years later.

**Endpapers**
haoliang/Getty Images.

First published in the United Kingdom in 2026 by Thames & Hudson Ltd, 6–24 Britannia Street, London WC1X 9JD

First published in the United States of America in 2026 by Thames & Hudson Inc., 500 Fifth Avenue, New York, New York 10110



Maps by Martin Lubikowski



EU Authorized Representative: Interart S.A.R.L.
19 rue Charles Auray, 93500 Pantin, Paris, France
productsafety@thameshudson.co.uk
interart.fr

A CIP catalogue record for this book is available from the British Library

Library of Congress Control Number 2026935852

ISBN 978-0-500-02974-9
01

Printed in China by RR Donnelley

MIX
Paper | Supporting responsible forestry
FSC® C144853